Art-Centered Learning Across the Curriculum

Art-Centered Learning Across the Curriculum

Integrating Contemporary Art in the Secondary School Classroom

Julia Marshall
David M. Donahue

with contributions by

Rick Ayers,
Ruth Cossey,
Steven D. Drouin,
Lawrence Horvath,
and Anne Thulson

foreword by

Lois Hetland

Teachers College,
Columbia University
New York and London

Published by Teachers College Press, 1234 Amsterdam Avenue, New York, NY 10027

Library of Congress Cataloging-in-Publication Data can be obtained at www.loc.gov

ISBN 978-0-8077-5581-5 (paperback)
ISBN 978-0-8077-5582-2 (hardcover)
ISBN 978-0-8077-7326-0 (eBook)

Printed on acid-free paper
Manufactured in the United States of America

21 20 19 18 17 16 15 14   8 7 6 5 4 3 2 1

David dedicates this book to his parents
for nurturing his love of art and lifelong learning.

Julia dedicates the book to her husband, Leonard Hunter,
for his boundless encouragement and support.

Contents

Foreword

I am so excited about this book! The visuals alone are enough to clue teachers in on ways that contemporary art can blow their curriculums open to become engaging, relevant vehicles for their students to ride across the 21st century. From the first scan, readers cannot help but see the power of contemporary art in transforming classrooms and learning.

My own journey into understanding how contemporary art transforms thinking hit the fast track when I joined the faculty of MassArt in 2005. Surrounded by contemporary makers, my ignorance caught me by surprise, and I was determined to take on this daunting field. I started with Art21 videos and books (http://www.pbs.org/art21/), was informed by Julia Marshall at an NAEA conference in Chicago, and was schooled in ongoing ways by my colleagues at MassArt, led by Steve Locke. California colleagues opened the window wider, and I was privileged to work with Art21 educators Jess Hamlin and Joe Fusaro, who designed a program to help educators of all stripes teach the contemporary. I'm hooked now, attending Biennales, constantly browsing the web and museum and gallery shows, and completely convinced: Contemporary art has *enormous* potential to enrich education across subject areas.

But what about classroom teachers without such good fortune, friends, and resources? This book is the invitation to an answer. First, it offers a cogent rationale for *why* art, contemporary art, and arts-integrated learning are such resources for education—because education relies on a system of disciplines that includes art; and art, by its nature, is a synthesizing and critical discipline. Julia Marshall and Dave Donahue, long-time colleagues in appreciating that understanding is a central aspiration of education, draw together strands from Harvard Project Zero's history of ideas to make a conceptually clear and compelling argument in the first chapters for how contemporary art supports understanding.

Second, the authors name and clarify the murky area of "arts integration," which has been amorphous for so long and too often left as a distracting ornament. Their phrase "art-centered integrated learning" is explicitly defined: "applying the thinking strategies of art to knowledge in other disciplines." With thinking and research identified at the center of the enterprise, we're well launched. And with their focus on how the disciplines with which art can be integrated, the project is not only launched, but grounded. We are led steadily to connect topics through essential disciplinary structures rather than surface features.

Howard Gardner once remarked that a good lecture, article, or book "meets you at kindergarten and takes you through graduate school." This book does just that. It guides us from why contemporary art "troubles," to how that troubling benefits inquiry-based learning. It unpacks the dimensions of the disciplines taught in schools, offers explicit categories and methods one can exploit in artistic research in art and when art is linked to other disciplines, and provides many rich and specific examples from a range of disciplinary contexts for how to go about that. It leads us on a path from bewildered not-knowing to confident exploration within the unknown, using art strategies and mental habits that benefit students across the academic disciplines.

As arts educators and educators in general, we *need* this book to deal with the vagaries and rapidly shifting complexities of our globalized world, because the education we offer must prepare students for that. Now we have this resource, as compass, gyroscope, and map. I can't wait to use it with my college students, who will run with it directly into schools, museums, and community centers.

Hallelujah and thank you Julia, Dave, and your coauthors! We owe you a mountainous debt of gratitude.

ERRATIC,
UNPEDICTABLE,
EXTRAVAGANT,
MANIFESTATION
ACTION, OR
NOTION

Lois Hetland
MASSACHUSETTS
COLLEGE OF ART

" THE ARTS NEED TO BE
VALUED FOR THEIR
OWN INTRINSIC REASONS.
LET'S FIGURE OUT WHAT
THE ARTS DO TEACH. "

STUDIO THINKING
- BENEFITS OF
VISUAL ART EDUCATION

Acknowledgments

This book owes its existence to the wisdom and support of many people. We thank our coauthors Rick Ayers, Ruth Cossey, Steven D. Drouin, Lawrence Horvath, and Anne Thulson for their collaboration on this project and for all they have contributed to our learning. We also thank Ben Garcia and Ira Jacknis of the Phoebe A. Hearst Museum of Anthropology at the University of California, Berkeley, for their invaluable assistance with Chapter 4. We are grateful to colleagues who push our thinking about how and why to teach art, add to our understanding about the value of art education and arts-integrated learning, advocate for the centrality of art in all children's education, and frame access to arts learning as an important equity issue in schools. In particular, we want to acknowledge Lois Hetland for her vision and our colleagues Tana Johnson, Kimberley D'Adamo, Ann Wettrich, Louise Music, Trena Noval, Todd Elkin, Jennifer Stuart, and all the members of the Integrated Learning Specialist Program team in Alameda County who are the "on the ground" innovators and leaders bringing learning through creative inquiry into the schools.

We appreciate the colleagues at our institutions who enrich our lives as scholars and teachers. First and foremost, we thank Derek Fenner, David's research assistant at Mills College, for his dogged work in tracking down images for this book, contacting artists, and securing permissions. We cannot imagine this book without his help.

David thanks Anna Richert in the Mills College School of Education, who has been a mentor since the start of his academic career and whose advice on many drafts improved this book immeasurably. He also thanks Michael Beller at the Mills College Library for his unstinting help in researching the latest information across a variety of subjects. David is also grateful for financial support for work on this project from the Mary Metz Endowed Chair for Creativity and Excellence in Teaching at Mills.

We are grateful to the staff at Teachers College Press, particularly Marie-Ellen Larcada, who has been a champion of publishing arts education scholarship and whose advice has made this a better book. She has made this project not only a joy but also a learning experience for us. Thanks to Aureliano Vazquez Jr. and his production team for the careful editing of the manuscript.

Art-Centered Integrated Learning
for Understanding

Is there a link between switchgrass in Nebraska and the stock exchange in New York? How can a foreign microorganism upset the natural balance in a pond? How are story quilts and comic books connected? These are the kinds of questions thinkers and researchers ask. They are the questions that emerge from our desire to find order in chaos, reasons for occurrences, and meaning in the world.

Artists raise these questions too in their search for meaning. Take Nina Katchadourian, for example. She raised a question and went right to the kernel of it; she went to popcorn. Popcorn, you ask. How could popcorn have anything to do with meaning? Actually, that could be the question Katchadourian asked when she put a microphone into a popcorn machine, poured in the kernels, turned on the machine, and recorded the random pops that filled the air (*Talking Popcorn*, 2001; see Figure 1.1). Do these pops have any rhyme or reason to them? Do they have meaning? If they do, can we decode the pops to find out what that meaning is? Katchadourian followed that train of thought and converted the pops into Morse code. She then used a computer to translate the Morse code message into English. From there, a computer-generated voice read aloud the messages. These messages were transcribed, and the transcriptions were displayed near the popcorn machine so viewers could read the "secret" messages—the hidden meaning behind random acts of popcorn (see Figure 1.2).

At first glance, this work may seem nutty, and perhaps it is. It is just that nuttiness, that gloss of nonsense, however, that takes us to deeper, more philosophical questions. Indeed, in a whimsical way, Katchadourian's work takes us as deep as it goes—into the workings of the mind.

So how does Katchadourian's artwork do this? Popcorn pops do not fit into language as we know it; they are random patterns of sound generated by a natural physical process. Popcorn pops really have nothing to say. That is why Katchadourian chose to decode them. In translating these pops into Morse code and English, Katchadourian puts words into the popcorn's mouth; she filters its noise through two symbolic systems to attach meaning to it—to make sense out of nonsense. By giving popcorn "voice," she points at the fundamental need of the human mind to make sense of the world by discovering the hidden connections among things. And she points at our ways of making sense by skewing phenomena

Figure 1.1. Nina Katchadourian,
Talking Popcorn, 2001.

Figure 1.2. Nina Katchadourian,
The Popcorn Journal, detail, 2001.

Courtesy of the artist and Catharine Clark
Gallery, San Francisco.

Image courtesy of the artist and Catharine
Clark Gallery, San Francisco.

through the lens of a system or imposing a system upon them. To Katchadourian, it appears this search for meaning or understanding can lead to misconceptions, especially when the system is ill suited to the phenomenon. Although it can lead us in the wrong direction, the desire for understanding is the impulse that has propelled us forward. It is, after all, the foundation of all our research and questionings, and the basis of all our academic disciplines, from the natural sciences, to the social sciences, to mathematics, and to language arts.

We begin our exploration of integrated learning through contemporary art with *Talking Popcorn* for a number of reasons, the first of which is Katchadourian's focus on systems and the hidden order and interconnections behind both the natural and social worlds. Another reason is Katchadourian's exploration of the human desire to understand those systems and to impose human-made systems to do so. Understanding systems and how things are connected is at the core of integration of all the disciplines, including art.

Still another reason for starting with this artwork is what it reveals about art; this simple aesthetic statement demonstrates how art can address significant concepts and prompt viewers to think about them, perhaps for the first time or more deeply than they have before. In prompting reflection, Katchadourian's art is up to "trouble." Indeed, much of contemporary art "troubles"; it disrupts our habits of mind; it problematizes conventional thinking. To do so, it must catch us off guard, and Katchadourian does that. In her mischievous way, she takes an eccentric perspective on concepts and she surprises us. This prompts us to wonder, How did she come up with that?

Curiosity

The answer is through *artistic thinking,* which is largely an amalgam of logical reasoning and associative thinking. Associative thinking involves making connections that are somewhat logical or defy conventional logic altogether. This kind of thinking differs from *logical reasoning*, identified with the sciences, common sense, and solving problems in everyday life. It characterizes art, fiction, creative inventions, and poetry. Associative thinking and logical reasoning are present in most everything we do. Indeed, we complement logic with associative thinking in everyday thought and actions; we take our analyses of things and make connections among them. In art, however, while we use logic to find and solve problems and make inferences, we highlight associative, even nonsensical, thinking in our interpretations of topics and ideas, often generating eccentric associations and perspectives.

Katchadourian's body of work is a classic example of how artistic thinking blends logic and associative thinking. She thinks logically in addressing her topic, in figuring out how to get her ideas across, and in making the physical object itself. Associative thinking comes into the mix when she conceives of the work and plays with ideas. In *Popping Popcorn*, we see how this sideways way of thinking complements logic; it allows thinking to be nimble, flexible, even balletic in its ability to tiptoe among profound ideas and concepts. We also see how in art logic can be jumbled with and by nonlogical associations until it is pushed to the absurd. In *Popcorn*, it appears Katchadourian's nonlogical associations—her associative thinking—played a trick on logic.

SYSTEMS THINKING AND ART-CENTERED INTEGRATED LEARNING

Katchadourian's *Popcorn* also encourages us think about how things fit together in systems and how such systems work. Anthropologist Robert Murphy (1989) describes a culture as a system much like systems in nature, as an organism in which all parts make sense in relationship to each other and together form a coherent and continuous plan for action. That is to say, in a culture, knowledge, practices, and ways of thinking are thoroughly interconnected and they have a purpose—first and foremost, to sustain the system and, second, to perform in concert some kind of action. When we take Murphy's definition of a cultural system and apply it to schooling, we perceive education as a dynamic web of entities and interactions with a purpose—to educate.

Understanding education as a system, we believe, has significant implications for our understanding of arts integration and the critical role it can play in schools. From a systems perspective, academic disciplines are components of a system of inquiry and knowledge in which all parts contribute to the workings and purpose of the system. Art, as a component of the system and as a mode of investigation and interpretation, can support the system and knit it closer together by promoting systemic, integrated learning. For that reason and also to highlight art integration as part of system of knowledge and inquiry, we cast art integration in this book as *integrated learning through art*, or as *art-centered integrated learning*.

WHY CONTEMPORARY ART?

While all forms of art can serve as means of learning in other disciplines, contemporary art, such as Katchadourian's, is rarely used for such purposes, possibly because teachers in content areas other than art focus on what they know best: looking at "canonical" works from art history and making what Efland (1976) calls "school art," a formulaic type of art that bears little resemblance to actual studio practice or thinking.

Perhaps teachers' aversion to making or interpreting contemporary art in their classrooms stems from contradictory beliefs about contemporary art; on the one hand, art is not taken seriously (anyone could paint that) and, on the other, it is seen as inscrutable (what is that about, anyway?).

Interestingly, these two beliefs are part of the reason why encountering or practicing contemporary art is especially appropriate for integrated learning across the disciplines. Why is this so? First, because contemporary art does not necessarily require technical expertise; learners can engage in making real art and real thinking whether they are proficient in traditional art skills or not. As Mayer (2008) reminds us, "Good art is always about something important; it is not solely the exercise of technical skills" (p. 78).

Second, because contemporary art raises fundamental questions about meaning, students can engage with others in construction of understanding that would be harder to accomplish with familiar artwork that only requires what Dewey (1934/2005) called "recognition" rather than "perception." By this, Dewey meant that when we are familiar with a work of art, we do not perceive it so much as recognize it. This recognition can be a kind of anesthesia, a hindrance to perception and the experience of the work. Contemporary art, on the other hand, is often unfamiliar and surprising and, therefore, not as cozy. Indeed, contemporary art can be "difficult," and it is this difficulty that compels a viewer to experience the work directly and, therefore, be susceptible to its provocation.

What makes contemporary art difficult and off-putting for many viewers, and the questions this art raises, are what make it ideal for authentic integrative inquiry. Our goal in this book is to demystify contemporary art enough so teachers see such difficulty not as a problem but as a spark for thinking that is "broad and adventurous" as well as "clear and deep" (Perkins, 1994) and also understand how difficulty connects beyond the world of contemporary art to investigation and learning across the disciplines.

No doubt when you think of Duchamp's *Fountain* (1917) or Rothko's *No. 14* (1960), you not only picture a particular work of art but you "fit it into a context that is defined by a chronology, by national identities, by materials, by subject matter, and by a whole complex of social relations" (Diepeveen & Van Laar, 2001, p. 95). This context provides a "set of instructions" about how to understand such works. As a result, you are not likely to be shocked or confused by these works. Although they sparked outrage and confusion when new, they are now part of the canon, accepted and understood as important in defining identifiable periods in Western art. You can probably do the same kind of interpretive thinking with works by Robert Mapplethorpe and Keith Haring even though they were censored and denounced by public officials only a few decades ago. Even these more recent works now come to us with instructions for meaning making from historians, curators, and critics.

By contrast, think back to *Talking Popcorn*, or imagine other recent works of contemporary art like Damian Ortega's *Cosmic Thing*, 2002 (see Figure 1.3), a disassembled 1989 Volkswagen Beetle, the pieces of which are suspended from the ceiling on barely visible wires, or Francis Alÿs's *Paradox of Praxis I* (1997), a video that captures the artist pushing a block of ice through the streets of Mexico City until it is reduced to nothing but a small puddle. Or consider Jon Rubin and Dawn Weleski's *Conflict Kitchen*, 2010–ongoing (see Figure 1.4), a pop-up takeout restaurant in Pittsburgh, Pennsylvania, that serves food from areas of the world, such as El Salvador, North Korea, and Iran, that are now or once were embroiled in conflicts with the United States.

Because recent works like these do not easily fit into historical contexts, they are difficult to understand, and not just for the general public. Art critic Leo Steinberg (1972) described "the shock of discomfort, or the bewilderment or the anger or the boredom which some people always feel, and all people sometimes feel, when confronted with an unfamiliar new style" (p. 5). These emotions are not the result of viewers' individual failings. Rather contemporary art is supposed to provoke such emotions when it is effective.

Effective contemporary art also raises questions for many viewers, including one that is particularly glaring: Is this art? As Lan Tuazon (2011) notes,

> With contemporary art especially, there is a built-in uncertainty about its status. Even though articles, essays, and books abound that prescribe analysis of contemporary art, such works do not yet have the necessary framing of experts and art historians to help deconstruct their meanings; not enough time has transpired to provide the critical distance required to accept them as verified truth. (pp. 28–29)

Ortega's, Alÿs's, Katchadourian's, and Rubin's works are all celebrated by different factions of the art establishment. Ortega is well known in museums and gallery circles for his play with common objects to expose the poetry of the mundane; Alÿs works within a 50-year-old avant-garde performance-art tradition of

Figure 1.3. Damian Ortega, *Cosmic Thing*, 2002.

Image courtesy of the artist and Kurimanzutto, Mexico City.

Figure 1.4. Jon Rubin and Dawn Weleski, *Conflict Kitchen*, 2010–present.

Image courtesy of Conflict Kitchen.

walking city streets to call attention to urban places (see Chapter 8, "Geography"); Katchadourian is a newly established presence in the gallery world; and Jon Rubin is one of many artists working within the "art as social practice" movement, a genre of art since the 1960s (see Chapter 4, "The Social Sciences"). The inclusion of their work in these art worlds should settle to some extent the question of whether this is art, but viewers are still left with unsettling and not easily answered questions like, Why should this be considered art? and Why is it so difficult to understand? These questions are troubling because humans are meaning-makers and artwork that is difficult to interpret stymies our desire to understand. This obstruction often lies at the *beginning* of difficult work. The piece throws us off balance (Diepeveen & Van Laar, 2001). The imbalance we feel, however, is valuable because it is generative; it prepares the way for work that can be meaningful and groundbreaking—for building understanding in new and creative ways.

Furthermore, difficulty transcends disciplinary boundaries. The inscrutability we find in new or unfamiliar art echoes the challenge of new or unfamiliar problems in the other disciplines. How do biologists determine the cause of a previously unknown disease? How do physicists determine the smallest particle that makes up matter? How do historians define the most recent period in history? How does a writer convey truth through fiction? Chances are that these researchers will be stymied in their inquiry, particularly at the beginning, as they pursue leads that go down blind alleys. These stumbles are likely to be as frustrating as they are necessary to understanding.

The challenges in academic disciplines, like the difficulty of understanding contemporary art, are not insurmountable. They just take work. Authentic disciplinary questions eventually become settled, or at least the terms of investigation become clearer and our capacity for understanding previously challenging questions increases. Possible causes of disease are ruled out. Historical events, with perspective, can be seen as watersheds. In a similar vein, students can figure out tricky new art and, in puzzling with art, they build the mental muscles needed to grapple with questions for which there are no set answers. This is in high contrast to answering "comprehension questions" posed in textbooks—questions that are already settled. This is why grappling with contemporary art can be more useful than conventional curriculum in developing the habits of mind that support inquiry in the academic disciplines.

Furthermore, contemporary art belongs in the classroom because it airs difficult questions. Artists want to engage the public in dialogue about those questions. It is ironic, therefore, that contemporary art is often cast in popular media as elitist and as speaking only to an "in group." The same misperceptions exist about biologists or historians who supposedly engage in studies divorced from "real life" with no desire to create greater public discourse. Teaching with contemporary art can challenge such misperceptions and promote the kinds of inquiry and dialogue intended by contemporary artists and researchers in other disciplines. In contrast to stereotype, we believe contemporary art is fundamentally democratic. As Jerry Saltz, art critic for *New York* magazine, writes, "The art world is now like Wikipedia: It is vast, multilingual, collaborative, inconsistent, and contradictory, and coming from everywhere. As with Wikipedia, anyone can participate" (as quoted in Taylor, 2008, p. 5).

Because contemporary art prompts dialogue and connects to diverse worlds outside the classroom, looking at and interpreting art makes an ideal vehicle for exploring questions across the disciplines. Moreover, making contemporary art to answer questions that matter to artists, biologists, and historians, as well as thinkers and researchers in every field who seek to expand our capacity to understand the new, the unfamiliar, and the difficult, draws on knowledge from a wide array of disciplines. We will explore how this works further in this book.

UNDERSTANDING: THE PURPOSE OF EDUCATION

Acquisition of knowledge, skills, and understanding is the principal goal of education (Perkins, 1998). Because knowledge and skills are most readily acquired and assessed, schools tend to focus on them. Understanding, however, is education's very purpose, a valued goal throughout its long history from the ancient Greeks to John Dewey and Jerome Bruner (Perrone, 1998). Moreover, understanding is the purpose behind each and every academic discipline, and the ultimate rationale behind art.

Understanding art entails connecting an artwork to its creator and his or her time, culture, and place and to the world outside art—seeing a work in context, or, as Perkins says, "in the web of associations that give it meaning" (1988, p. 114). Likewise, understanding art also means linking a work of art to one's own experience, engaging with the aesthetic experience of a work, and grasping the perspective the work embodies. Where understanding in art links up with notions of understanding in education and the academic disciplines is in its underlying purpose of making sense out human experience—of seeking to understand our selves and the world we inhabit.

In an education context and in the academic disciplines, understanding is also seen in terms of thinking and performance skills. Understanding denotes a learner's ability to take knowledge and use it in new contexts to solve authentic problems or answer real questions—to use knowledge and skills flexibly (Perkins, 1998). Perkins argues that understanding is constructed and demonstrated through doing—through performance. The *performance view of understanding* espoused by Perkins emphasizes putting what we know (knowledge) and can do (skills) to work and, in so doing, advancing our understanding. As both a process of coming to understand and as a way of demonstrating and assessing what is understood, a *performance of understanding* has three intertwining purposes: learning something, demonstrating what you are learning or have learned, and assessing how well you have learned it. These performances can be solving a problem, constructing an argument, or creating a product.

Art intersects most overtly with the performance view of understanding in the creation of art. Indeed, all three understanding performances are part and parcel of the art studio experience, and the model for performances of understanding espoused by Perkins is studio practice in the arts and crafts. Why is art making the prototype for performances of understanding? Creating a work of art is a way to engage with ideas and information actively and make them one's own—to absorb them, to find connections between them and one's personal life, and to apply them. We add to this other reasons for art practice's deep abiding relationship to understanding. For one, in art, application of knowledge can be imaginative; in making art we can play freely with ideas and take them to new places, even to the absurd. Katchadourian's *Talking Popcorn* is a case in point. For another, art taps into the emotions and feelings that often play a critical role in understanding.

For still another reason, art builds understanding through sensory and kinesthetic experience; it engages the body as well as the mind.

Also, creating art and making meaning from art *require* understanding, understanding that is complex. This is the kind of understanding needed for engaging in sophisticated scholarly work, preparing for demanding knowledge-based jobs, and working through the dilemmas of living in democratic societies. For these reasons, we see art as a powerful way to build understanding, and the studio—whether it is an art room, a general classroom, a hall, a playground, a street, or a child's bedroom—as the arena in which it happens.

INTEGRATED LEARNING AND DEEP KNOWLEDGE OF THE DISCIPLINES

Jerome Bruner famously postulated that any discipline could be taught in an intellectually honest way to persons of any age. He made clear he did not mean that 5-year-olds could learn calculus, but that they could explore the concept of limits, which underlies calculus. Similarly, we see art-centered integrated learning as providing opportunities for such intellectually meaningful learning, particularly by enabling learners to understand the structures and the purposes of the disciplines. In *The Process of Education*, Bruner (1960/1977) writes that "grasping the structure of a subject is understanding it in a way that permits many other things to be related to it meaningfully. To learn structure, in short, is to learn how things are related" (p. 7). A logical corollary to this is that when we teach curriculum that connects one discipline to another, learners' opportunities to learn the structure or ways of thinking of a discipline are greater. This is especially true in classrooms where art and another discipline are integrated for understanding and learner attention is drawn toward disciplinary structures, thinking, processes of inquiry, and knowledge construction.

Bruner also highlights disciplinary thinking. In *Towards a Theory of Instruction* (1966), he emphasizes the centrality of thinking to understanding the disciplines and the imperative to teach students such thinking, "the forms of connection, the attitudes, hopes, jokes, and frustrations that go with it. . . . At the very first breath, the young learner should, we think, be given the chance to solve problems, to conjecture, to quarrel, as these are done at the heart of the discipline" (p. 155). Bruner's conception of disciplinary thinking goes beyond memorizing the postulates of a discipline or the linear steps to thinking like a scientist or historian, as explained in some textbooks. Instead, he encourages teachers to engage students in the messiness of disciplinary work because such messiness—"conjecturing" and "quarreling"—are part and parcel of "doing" and understanding a discipline.

Engaging in messiness, however, does not mean the teacher neglects planning. Instead, it requires more thought than lessons "covering" disciplinary material because learners must engage with questions that are neither trivial nor too hard and teachers must anticipate where an inquiry into these questions will lead. Indeed, they must prepare to facilitate a process in which learners discover and construct significant disciplinary knowledge themselves. Teachers are also charged with the important task of creating opportunities for learners to develop "a sense of excitement about discovery—discovery of regularities of previously unrecognized relations and similarities between ideas, with a resulting sense of self-confidence in one's abilities" (Bruner, 1960/1977, p. 20). To assisting students in finding the relationships and similarities between ideas, we would add teachers' responsibility to help learners see the relationships and similarities among disciplines. Both understanding the structure of an academic discipline and grasping how the disciplines contrast, connect, and complement each other are critical to integrated learning.

Comparing and contrasting disciplines opens up questions about what we know and how we know it. When questions about ways of knowing are included in a curriculum integrating art and other disciplines, students learn not only about the knowledge in various disciplinary realms but also how artists, scientists, writers, and others create or construct knowledge in the disciplines. They also come to understand that the knowledge we have today in all disciplines was constructed over time by many researchers and scholars who built upon each other's work. In the present, knowledge is rarely created by individual scholars working in the isolation of an artist's studio, a scientist's laboratory, or a poet's corner. Rather, artists, scientists, writers, and other intellectual workers in various disciplines talk and work collaboratively to figure out problems or answer questions, a process that is called social constructivism because scholars and learners work with others in dialogic processes to build or "construct" their knowledge. In other words, they do not labor alone until ideas pop into their heads.

According to Vygotsky (1978), knowledge is constructed socially and then internalized by individuals. Disciplinary realms are one social context for constructing knowledge. Contemporary artists often talk and work with each other to develop understanding. Similarly, scientists talk and work with each other. In these contexts, principles embedded in the knowledge, purpose, methods, and forms of disciplines shape the understanding that individual artists and scientists claim as their own.

Classrooms are another context where knowledge can be created socially and internalized individually. Learners can talk and work with each other to solve problems and develop understanding. Teachers can scaffold learning so students can internalize it and use that understanding in new and authentic contexts outside the classroom (Fosnot, 2005). In a classroom that features art-centered integrated learning where students work together on art projects or interpret works of art together, teachers can connect social constructivist classroom learning processes to disciplinary learning processes, which share similar social constructivist characteristics such as collaboration, experimentation, dialogue, negotiation, and analysis. As a consequence of such constructivist connections between disciplinary realms and classrooms, students see that learning in the classroom is not separate from the "real world" but connected to it in terms of examining important problems and in terms of how and why learners are examining those problems.

At the same time, as learners think about how one comes to knowledge together and on one's own, teachers can help them develop metacognitive skills that foster their own learning about learning in the disciplines, and thus foster students' continued academic growth. Students can learn to think about how they know something, about what questions they have, and about why following questions to their answers matters.

SKILLS AND DISPOSITIONS LEARNED FROM
ART-CENTERED INTEGRATED LEARNING

While disciplinary knowledge has value in and of itself, that intrinsic value is of most concern to those who conduct research in the disciplines. In contrast, in education, the value of such knowledge resides more in how that knowledge contributes to the overall development of the learner. Dewey (1902/1976) wrote that teachers' primary concern should be "not with the subject matter as such, but with the subject matter as a related factor in the total and growing experience of the child" (pp. 285–286). Later, Bruner (1960/1977) wrote in a similar vein, "The first object of any act of learning, over and beyond the pleasure it may give, is that it should serve us in the future" (p. 17). Art-centered integrated learning, which involves applying the thinking strategies of art to knowledge in other disciplines, allows learners to develop habits of mind that not only are useful for learning across the curriculum but also will be critical to their development as learners and to their learning in the future.

Hetland, Winner, Veenema, and Sheridan (2013, p. 6) identified eight habits of mind that art practice entails. These habits include the following:

1. *Develop craft:* Technique: Learning to use tools (e.g., viewfinders, brushes) and materials (e.g., charcoal, paint); learning artistic conventions (e.g., perspective, color mixing). Studio Practice: Learning to care for tools, materials, and space.
2. *Engage and persist:* Learning to embrace problems of relevance within the art world and/or of personal importance, to develop focus and other mental states conducive to working and persevering at art tasks.
3. *Envision:* Learning to picture mentally what cannot be directly observed and imagine possible next steps in making a piece.
4. *Express:* Learning to create works that convey an idea, a feeling, or a personal meaning.
5. *Observe:* Learning to attend to visual contexts more closely than ordinary "looking" requires, and thereby see things that otherwise might not be seen.
6. *Reflect:* Question and explain: Learning to think and talk with others about an aspect of one's work or working process. Evaluate: Learning to

judge one's own work and working process and the work of others in
relation to standards of the field.
7. *Stretch and explore:* Learning to reach beyond one's capacities to explore
playfully without a preconceived plan, and to embrace the opportunity to
learn from mistakes and accidents.
8. *Understand the art world:* Domain: Learning about art history and
current practice. Communities: Learning to interact as an artist with
other artists (i.e., in classrooms, in local art organizations, and across the
art field) and within the broader society.

These habits not only speak to what most Americans value in education but
also align with the emphasis on conceptual and procedural skills highlighted in the
Common Core State Standards. They also have corollaries in other disciplines and,
therefore, could be a cornerstone of integrated learning. Moreover, developing
learners' awareness and abilities in these habits of mind enables them to draw on
valuable kinds of thinking when engaging in inquiry in and across all disciplines
and to see how these habits are inherent in all areas of inquiry. Such habits of
mind can, of course, be developed in separate classrooms without arts-integrated
learning, but the thoughtful integration of art with the goal of understanding how
inquiry works across disciplines showcases thinking and doing as much as it fosters learning of disciplinary content.

The art studio experience and, therefore, art-centered integrated learning,
also fosters dispositions toward learning and understanding that are critical to
research in the disciplines and to learning in the classroom. These dispositions include curiosity, flexibility, tolerance of ambiguity, and the willingness to look at an
idea, issue, or problem from many vantage points, even a nonsensical one. These
are the dispositions that can thrive in a studio environment where serious inquiry
involves creative play with knowledge, forms, and methods with the purpose of
understanding.

THIS BOOK

To realize the potential of integrated learning through contemporary art, we must
think deeply about art and all the disciplines—what thinkers and researchers in
the disciplines understand, how they understand it, how they came to understand
it, and how they express that understanding. We must also grasp how all the disciplines connect—what the underlying common concepts and ways of thinking
are. That is to say, we must go deeply into the structure of disciplines as Bruner
(1960/1977) recommends, while thinking expansively about the overall structure
or system in which the disciplines reside. With this goal in mind, we present in this
book a guide and resource for integrated art-centered learning that goes both deep
and broad and is substantive and multidimensional.

The approach we present here is substantive because it goes beyond the add-on strategies of illustrating book reports or making posters to convey an idea. Instead, it gets at the substance—the big ideas—of the disciplines and the ways these ideas are constructed and understood. It also compels learners to explore cross-disciplinary goals, ideas, and topics using inquiry methods and forms from the academic disciplines in their art-making process. To support this integration and give it substance, this book goes into some depth about the disciplines taught in schools—the natural sciences, social sciences, creative writing, and mathematics—and has a chapter or chapters dedicated to each one of them. All of the disciplines have *purposes, knowledge, methods,* and *forms*, which must be understood or used and practiced for an integration of these disciplines to be substantive. Consequently, descriptions of the academic disciplines in Chapters 3 through 7 are divided into these four components of a discipline. We adapt these categories from Mansilla and Gardner (1998), who propose them as *dimensions of understanding,* the aspects of a discipline one should incorporate into one's inquiry into disciplinary knowledge in order to fully understand it. Picking up on the term "dimension," we call our approach multidimensional.

The book also explains art, particularly contemporary art, as an area of inquiry and describes how that designation affects classroom practice. We do that in Chapter 2. Deep and expansive art-centered integrated inquiry gets its models and inspiration from art. Therefore, we include at the end of each chapter examples of contemporary art and explain how these works explore the fundamental concepts of an academic discipline, either through appropriating methods and forms from one discipline to shed light on ideas associated with another discipline, or by viewing a discipline's concepts through the idiosyncratic prism of art. We also identify the creative strategy or strategies artists use in their works to take ideas further, to interpret and transform them into art.

Finally, we end the book with a chapter on integrated, inquiry-based curriculum inspired by contemporary art. This chapter includes guidelines for developing substantive multidimensional integrated art projects and inquiries and offers models of projects teachers can adapt to their students' interests and needs.

Please consider this as a resource book for your own explorations of contemporary art and integrated learning through art and as a guide for developing curriculum that propels and conducts your learners down their own trails of learning. For those teachers who are not familiar with contemporary art, this book is intended to introduce you to its potential and to demystify it enough to enable you to use it; for those familiar with art, this book is meant to help you connect contemporary art more fully and profoundly with other disciplines and the system of knowledge in which they reside.

Robertson and McDaniel (2010) write that "the future will offer much that is unfamiliar. Learning to think about new art will provide tools for adapting to all manner of future events" (p. 4). It can also help us and our students navigate the present.

As Mayer (2008) writes,

Contemporary art is about *now!* It's about figuring out who we are, who we are becoming, and how to live, know, and act. Just as our learners are looking at the worlds around them and wondering what their role might be, what events mean, or what difference they can make, today's artists are pondering the same questions through their art. When we teach with contemporary art, the potential is present for learning that is centered not in the classroom, but in all the worlds beyond it and in learners' efforts to negotiate their relationships to those worlds. (p. 77)

We all want our youth to engage fully with their learning and their lives; we hope they will discover the excitement of "now" and pleasure that comes with living in it and understanding it. To this end, we present this book for teachers who care about the meaningfulness of their learners' learning.

REFERENCES

Bruner, J. (1960/1977). *The process of education.* Cambridge, MA: Harvard University Press.

Bruner, J. (1966). *Towards a theory of instruction.* Cambridge, MA: Harvard University Press.

Dewey, J. (1976). The child and the curriculum. In J. Boydston (Ed.), *John Dewey: The middle works, 1899–1924: Vol. 2. 1902–1903* (pp. 273–291). Carbondale: Southern Illinois University Press. (Original work published 1902)

Dewey, J. (2005). *Art as experience.* New York, NY: Perigee. (Original work published 1934)

Diepeveen, L., & Van Laar, T. (2001). *Art with a difference: Looking at difficult and unfamiliar art.* Boston, MA: McGraw-Hill Higher Education.

Efland, A. (1976). The school art style: A functional analysis. *Studies in Art Education, 17*(2), 37–44.

Fosnot, C. (2005). *Constructivism: Theory, perspectives and practice.* New York, NY: Teachers College Press.

Hetland, L., Winner, E., Veenema, S., & Sheridan, K. (2013). *Studio thinking: The real benefits of visual arts education* (2nd ed.). New York, NY: Teachers College Press.

Mansilla, V., & Gardner, H. (1998). What are the qualities of understanding? In M. S. Wiske (Ed.), *Teaching for understanding: Linking research with practice* (pp. 161–183). San Francisco, CA: Jossey-Bass.

Mayer, M. (2008). Considerations for a contemporary art curriculum. *Art Education, 61*(2), 77–79.

Murphy, R. (1989). *Cultural and social anthropology: An overture.* Englewood Cliffs, NJ: Prentice Hall.

Perkins, D. (1988). Art as understanding. In H. Gardner & D. N. Perkins (Eds.), *Art, mind and education: Research from Project Zero* (pp. 111–131). Chicago: University of Illinois Press.

Perkins, D. (1994). *The intelligent eye: Learning to think by looking at art.* Los Angeles, CA: Getty Trust.

Perkins, D. (1998). What is understanding? In M. S. Wiske (Ed.), *Teaching for understanding: Linking research to practice* (pp. 39–57). San Francisco, CA: Jossey-Bass.

Perrone, V. (1998). Why do we need a pedagogy of understanding? In M. S. Wiske (Ed.), *Teaching for understanding: Linking research to practice* (pp. 13–38). San Francisco, CA: Jossey-Bass.

Robertson, J., & McDaniel, C. (2010). *Themes of contemporary art: Visual art after 1980*. New York, NY: Oxford University Press.

Steinberg, L. (1972). *Other criteria: Confrontations with 20th century art*. New York, NY: Oxford University Press.

Taylor, P. (2008). Editorial. *Art Education, 61*(2), 5.

Tuazon, L. (2011). What's in it for me? Radical common sense in art and education. In E. Joo & J. Keehn II (Eds.), *Rethinking contemporary art and multicultural education* (pp. 27–35). New York, NY: Routledge.

Vygotsky, L. (1978). *Mind in society: The development of higher psychological processes*. Cambridge, MA: Harvard University Press.

2

Art-Centered Research and Integrated Learning

There are many ways to go about art integration. Drawing, painting, or sculpting a subject from science or social studies, such as a seed, a planet, a historical figure, or even a map of a place, is one way to go about it. Learners could also explore a concept from an academic discipline and translate their ideas about it into visual imagery. This second, more conceptual approach to art integration promotes abstract thinking and connects disciplinary concepts to students' lives (Parsons, 2004; The Ohio State TETAC Mentors, 2002; Taylor, Carpenter, Ballengee-Morris, & Sessions, 2006). Contemporary art, with its focus on ideas, is particularly suited to concept-based integration such as this.

Laudable as these approaches to art integration are, we propose going a step further and expanding on these methodologies in ways that make art integration more meaningful. One key to meaningful integration, we believe, is taking concepts and topics investigated in art integration further—digging deeply into them, expanding out to explore a wide array of connections, and extending from there to take ideas further or to realize their implications. For this, we take our clues from contemporary art, from artists' ways of doing and thinking, and from their proclivity to "push the envelope."

Another key to meaningful art integration is to think of art making as creative inquiry and to focus on the integrated nature of the learning that takes place when learners engage in it. Our focus on creative inquiry, and the integrated learning that takes place within it, is the reason we prefer to use the term *art-centered integrated learning* instead of art integration.

SUBSTANTIVE MULTIDIMENSIONAL
ART-CENTERED INTEGRATED LEARNING

We propose a version of art integration that incorporates illustration of topics and concepts while going deeper into why and how we study these things. This approach links depiction of academic topics and concepts to making conceptual and procedural connections across the curriculum to engender deeper more comprehensive understandings of content and ideas. We call our approach *substantive* and *multidimensional*. By substantive, we mean integration that builds on

16

the understanding of disciplinary structures that Bruner (1960/1977) argues is the foundation for meaningful learning. Art-integrated learning built on that groundwork can go beyond topics and themes to investigate the fundamental and critical concepts all disciplines address, the reasons why they address these concepts, and the ways they address them. We get to this substantive level through art-centered integrated learning that is multidimensional. By multidimensional, we mean integrated learning that engages all four dimensions of a discipline described by Mansilla and Gardner (1998) as *dimensions of understanding*. These dimensions are *purpose, knowledge, methods*, and *forms*.

Multidimensional art-centered integrated learning begins with the fundamental notion that the *purpose* of all inquiry is understanding the subject at hand. To get to that understanding, a learner begins with a research question, one that prompts investigation into the *knowledge* of a discipline on a deep conceptual level. This investigation is carried out through inquiry using the *methods* and kinds of thinking from art and the academic disciplines, and often uses their *forms* as tools for conceptualizing ideas and for conveying ideas. When augmented with ongoing reflection, which prompts the learner to become acutely aware of his or her inquiry and how all disciplines (including art) contribute to our understandings of phenomena, art-centered integrated learning becomes metacognitive. That is, learners become aware of how the systems work—their own system of learning and the ways the disciplines work and fit together systemically. We will go further into our vision of art-centered integrated learning later in the chapter, but first we take a look at its core principle: Art is a form of research, and artists are researchers.

ART AS RESEARCH: THE FOUNDATION

We don't often equate art and research. Research is something scientists do in laboratories or out in the field. Artists, on the other hand, make things. Attitudes about art are changing, however. The word research is creeping into the vocabulary of the visual arts, and "artist–researcher" is now a label the art world and artists themselves give to many contemporary artists. Take, for example, Roger Malina, the executive editor of Leonardo Publications, who refers to artists who bridge art, science, and technology as artist–researchers and researcher–artists. Malina tells us such research-oriented artists have been around for generations (Malina, 2013). It seems the art/research connection is not new after all. Perhaps the idea of "making things" is not so far removed from research in general. In fact, making things often is a part of a research process in all disciplines. For example, scientists make drawings and diagrams; social scientists make graphs, charts, and exhibits; geographers make maps. Indeed, making these forms is a critical part of any research because forms render ideas visible and, therefore, available to be understood and communicated. Moreover, the forms researchers construct allow research to go to new places—to new understandings.

It should also be noted that not all artists, especially contemporary artists, make things. Artists these days often "do" things. A case in point is Francis Alÿs, who walks urban landscapes and leaves trails of evidence behind him (see Chapter 1). Art actions such as Alÿs's are indicative of the "research turn" in contemporary art because they focus on ideas, in this case the nature of experience, and engender new perspectives on ideas. Alÿs's works also feel a lot like experiments; he seems to be trying things out, making trails to see what happens and how people along the trail react. Furthermore, in removing the seductive aesthetic art object from the equation, Alÿs makes the connection to research more direct and clear.

As Malina and many other art theorists attest, research is a critical component of art making for many contemporary artists, even those who make aesthetic objects. Artists often inquire deeply into a topic they explore in their artwork. Although research precedes the making of a work, it also permeates the entire process, the making and/or the doing of it. Also, artists often research complex themes and follow those themes in different ways through multiple artworks or projects. Often artists keep notebooks or, in the parlance of research, research books or field study books that thread separate works together as a string of related explorations. These books mix information, ideas, and plans for artwork. Often they are records of the progress of an idea as it goes through many phases of investigation and interpretation.

One exemplary contemporary artist–researcher is Mark Dion. Dion epitomizes the artist–researcher because he not only does copious research but he also investigates and interprets how and why others do research, particularly in the natural sciences, archeology, and anthropology. Indeed, Dion is an artist–anthropologist–archeologist who explores how scientists find, construct, understand, and tell their stories. He is interested not so much in nature itself but in how Western culture interprets nature (Dion, 2007). That is to say, Dion's *purpose* is to understand how scientists understand. To grasp this understanding, Dion explores the *knowledge* of science using the *methods* of scientists; he sets up labs in museums and investigates natural phenomena (*The Great Munich Bug Hunt*, 1993) (see Figure 2.1), he digs up artifacts and makes archeological displays (*Tate Thames— Dig Team on the Shore*, 1999) (see Figure 2.2), and he constructs museum displays that mimic and comment on natural history museum exhibits (*The Marvelous Museum Project*, 2010). In these works, Dion uses the *forms* of the various disciplines whose territory he invades. Certainly, Dion's work is multidimensional; it touches on all four dimensions of the disciplines he explores.

Dion also keeps detailed illustrated notes of his findings, his ideas, and his prospective projects in sketchbooks or research workbooks. These books reveal how metacognitive Dion's process is: He knows what he is doing, and he makes it visible (see Figures 2.3 and 2.4).

Dion also interprets his "findings" in imaginative ways, using creative strategies such as reformatting, metaphor, and juxtaposition. His imagery often startles or amuses viewers and then causes them to wonder, puzzle, and think. We see this

Figure 2.1. Mark Dion, *The Great Munich Bug Hunt,* **1993.**

Tree, collecting cabinet, specimens, lab equipment, dimensions variable. Images courtesy of the artist and Tanya Bonakdar Gallery, New York.

Figure 2.2. Mark Dion, *Tate Thames—Dig Team on the Shore,* **1999.**

Mixed media, dimensions variable. Image courtesy of the artist and Tanya Bonakdar Gallery, New York.

in Dion's *Survival of the Cutest (Who Gets on the Ark)* (1990), in which a wheelbarrow substitutes for Noah's ark and stuffed animals replace real animals. Here we have an artist's statement—a metaphorical image that suggests that the artificial and cuddly will outlive the natural (see Figure 2.5).

The art research of Mark Dion suggests that art begins with noticing, thinking about, and learning about a topic, an idea, or an issue. The research, however, does not stop there; it continues when the artist transforms the preparatory learning into new understanding—a new perspective on the subject—by casting the topic in a novel way. This is an example of how art making is a learning process in which artists come to understand their topic through investigation and through transforming ideas imaginatively. The learning, however, does not stop there; viewers, in interpreting the work, are also learning, and their process is a form of inquiry. Art, therefore, is a tool for learning both through making/doing and through viewing/interpreting.

CREATIVE CONCEPTUAL STRATEGIES

Below is a list of creative strategies artists such as Alÿs and Dion use in their art research. This list is not exhaustive or prescriptive. We realize that there are many more strategies. We encourage teachers and students alike to use them and also to look for them in their and others' creative inquiry and artwork.

Transformative strategies:
1. *Change scale:* Make an object or image larger or smaller.
2. *Reinterpret:* Change the style in which an image is rendered.
3. *Construct in an unusual medium:* Construct an object out of surprising materials.
4. *Translate:* Transform something into a different mode, code, or language.

Combinatory strategies:
1. *Hybridize:* Mix and replace parts of two or more entities.
2. *Synthesize:* Combine multiple things.

Juxtaposition strategies:
1. *Recontextualize:* Change the context of an object, image, or idea.
2. *Collage/juxtapose:* Juxtapose imagery to develop or reveal a concept that unites them.
3. *Assemble:* Place objects adjacent to each other to develop and reveal a concept that unites them.
4. *Layer:* Superimpose an image onto another image or form.
5. *Appropriate:* Use an existing image or style to draw upon its inherent meaning.

Figure 2.3. Mark Dion, *Book Stall—Sea Life/A Life at Sea,* **2010.**

Figure 2.4. Mark Dion, *Apostles,* **2010.**

Colored pencil on paper; 6 X 6 inches, 15.2 X 15.2 cm (unframed); 10 3/8 X 10 1/4 inches, 26.4 X 26 cm (framed). Signed, titled, and dated lower recto. Image courtesy the artist and Tanya Bonakdar Gallery.

Colored pencil on paper; 6 x 6 inches, 15.2 x 15.2 cm (unframed); 10 3/8 x 10 3/8 inches, 26.4 x 26.4 cm (framed). Signed, titled, and dated lower recto. Image courtesy the artist and Tanya Bonakdar Gallery, New York.

Figure 2.5. Mark Dion, *Survival of the Cutest (Who Gets on the Ark),* **From "Wheelbarrows of Progress" with William Schefferine, 1990.**

Toy stuffed animals, enamel on steel, wood and rubber wheelbarrow. Wheelbarrow, 63.5 x 68.5 x 141 cm. Image courtesy of the artist and Tanya Bonakdar Gallery, New York.

6. *Format:* Present an idea, movement, or relationship in a graphic format.
7. *Reformat:* Present an idea in a format from a nonart discipline to draw on the format's inherent meaning.
8. *Mimic:* Use the methods of a nonart discipline.
9. *Enact:* Take on the persona of a practitioner in another discipline.

Extension strategies:
1. *Extend:* Take images and ideas to logical or absurd conclusions or into fiction and fantasy.
2. *Amplify/magnify:* Exaggerate a phenomenon; make it larger than life, and call attention to it.
3. *Elaborate:* Take an idea or image further, add on to it, spin it, or take it to the absurd.
4. *Project:* Imagine, speculate, or envision what could come next.

Distillation strategies:
1. *Make use of metonymy:* Use a part of something to stand for the whole.
2. *Map:* Organize ideas and imagery graphically.
3. *Edit:* Remove extraneous things.
4. *Abstract:* Make visible the simple form within a complex one; pare a form down to its essentials; pare down information to the underlying concepts or relationships.

Associative strategies:
1. *Use visual analogy:* Compare one thing to another.
2. *Use metaphor:* Cast one thing as another.
3. *Use metaphor of materials:* Construct an object or image out of materials that have meaning in themselves.
4. *Recategorize:* Place something in a new category or in multiple categories.
5. *Substitute:* Replace something with something similar or very different.

These creative strategies are some ways artist–researchers develop, transform, and communicate understanding much as researchers in other fields have strategies for developing, transforming, and conveying their understandings. Indeed, creative strategies such as these are used in all disciplines. Researchers across a variety of disciplines distill, edit, recategorize, juxtapose, and synthesize information and concepts, and they use a variety of creative strategies such as formatting, analogy, and metaphor to interpret and communicate ideas. For example, historians distill and synthesize information from many sources to understand an era while social scientists observe, synthesize, categorize, and juxtapose (compare and contrast) ways people comport themselves to develop theories of social behavior. These researcher–practitioners often employ metaphors to explain their findings. Social scientists may couch human behavior in terms of theater (social roles and scripts), and historians may cast eras such as the Renaissance as "an awakening" and medieval times in Europe as "the Dark Ages." Perhaps the greatest use of metaphor is in the natural sciences where metaphorical comparisons are critical to understanding concepts and relationships. An example is Charles Darwin's use of the tree metaphor to describe relationships among species (Eldredge, 2005).

ART RESEARCH AND ART-CENTERED INTEGRATED LEARNING

Where does integrated learning through art inquiry fit into this art research paradigm? As discussed above, art and other disciplines are all areas of inquiry; every one of them does research and constructs knowledge and understanding through that research. Furthermore, they all use creative strategies. This means art shares *purposes* with the other disciplines and uses similar *methods*.

What is the inquiry process like? The process of research in all disciplines can be likened to a trail—a trail that is linear yet nonlinear, directed yet open-ended. Most often this trail-like process is cumulative and it progresses; it adds up and goes somewhere. The trail also can have multiple branches and paths that diverge and converge. A resourceful researcher explores many avenues in his or her pursuit of understanding; he or she is attentive to related phenomena, looks at a problem from many vantage points in multiple contexts, and experiments with diverse ideas. This, we believe, is a great model for art-centered integrated learning. That is, we see integrated learning occurring naturally in the process of following a research trail.

In this research-based model of art-centered learning, the learner pursues a topic, concept, or theme (a bit of *knowledge*), progresses along the research trail, and expands his or her research, crossing disciplinary lines as the learner follows his or her leads. Picture a path that meanders across disciplinary borders along which a learner connects the subject of his or her inquiry with ideas and subjects associated with different disciplines. As this organic integration expands, it becomes more and more conceptual and *substantive* as ideas about the topic are gathered and how we think about that topic in many different ways is revealed. This substantive, concept-based integration promotes integrated learning and thinking because it demonstrates how a subject is treated in multiple disciplines, allows students to construct their own meanings along the way, and corresponds with the natural way people learn.

Integrative learning and thinking are keys to this accrual of understanding because they construct connections that transcend disciplinary boundaries and place ideas or topics in broad cross-disciplinary "webs of associations" (Perkins, 1988). As we discussed in Chapter 1, Perkins maintains that understanding is perceiving an entity suspended in its web of associations that give it meaning. Integrative learning and thinking, because they weave webs, are particularly suited to building understanding—understanding that is expansive as well as profound.

In summary, art research is a foundation for substantive multidimensional art-centered integrated learning for the following reasons. First, research is a common denominator of all disciplines. Second, when learners do art-centered research on a theme, issue, or idea, they naturally cross over disciplinary boundaries to make conceptual connections. This leads to deeper thinking about significant ideas. Third, art-centered research encourages integrative thinking, which builds broad understandings of both the topic of the research and how the disciplines complement each other. Fourth, organic integration such as this emerges from researcher interest and creativity that is natural and not imposed from the outside.

MODELS

This section describes two models of arts-centered integrated learning through inquiry: independent research, which is based on the art inquiry model discussed above, and teacher-directed projects or lessons that serve as individual art-centered investigations that can be linked together along an inquiry trail.

Independent Research

Investigation. The following is a hypothetical example of independent research. An artist–researcher (a learner), who happens to have a pet rabbit, chooses to investigate rabbits. To begin, she reflects on how she feels about her rabbit. She then follows her rabbit closely and chronicles what her rabbit does all day. To get the inside story, she interviews her rabbit to see what her rabbit thinks about. Our learner then expands out to explore where rabbits fit in culturally (addressing the *knowledge* of social studies and literature)—how rabbits are anthropomorphized in the popular imagination, what kind of personality traits people associate with them, what rabbits symbolize in various cultures, and how people's fantasies about rabbits come alive in stories. She then explores how her peers feel about rabbits.

From there, the research expands further; the learning artist–researcher connects the rabbit to the scientific discipline with which it is most commonly associated: zoology. Delving into zoology and its umbrella science, biology, she investigates how rabbits are categorized in natural history taxonomies and how rabbits are often used in laboratory experiments. Here the artist–researcher begins her investigation of the disciplinary concepts and principles underlying the discipline of biology (*knowledge* of natural sciences) by exploring how animals in general serve in humanity's search for understanding of natural systems and organisms. She then looks at how visual imagery (*knowledge* of art and science) fit into this quest for knowledge—particularly how the artist/illustrators who created natural history illustrations rendered exact likenesses of animals, which advanced our knowledge of nature.

Our learner then looks at how the knowledge we gather from science shapes our interactions with animals—specifically, how rabbits are bred to create new species of rabbits for show and for food (*knowledge* of genetics). Rabbit breeding directs our researcher to consider how rabbits have become the symbol of fecundity. This, in turn, leads her into the realm of mathematics where she sees how rabbits multiply exponentially (*knowledge* of mathematics—the Fibonacci sequence).

The learning artist–researcher then begins to home in on a conceptual thread underlying all of her research: human power over animals. She grapples with the difference between laboratory animals and pets, pets and food. She is now ready to synthesize what she has encountered on her rabbit trail and formulate her creative response: her artwork. This is where creative strategies such as imaginative projection come in. Our artist–researcher "projects" into the psyche of a rabbit. Empathizing with rabbits, she comes up with a solution to their problem: She writes and illustrates a manual for rabbits on how to avoid becoming laboratory animals or food and, instead, become heroes of literature or popular culture. For models for her manual, she looks at guidelines for job interviews and instruction manuals. Going a bit further, she thinks about clothes for rabbits, answering the burning question, What would an ambitious rabbit wear to an interview? Raising this question leads her to survey various fashion magazines and add an addendum to her manual stipulating proper rabbit attire. Her foray into fashions for rabbits inspires the artist–researcher to sew clothes for newly minted rabbit heroes. Her empathy for rabbits (and interest in clothes) leads her to the artwork of Bill Burns, who makes protective gear for small animals (see Figure 2.6).

Figure 2.6. Bill Burns, *Safety Gear for Small Animals*, 1994–2006.

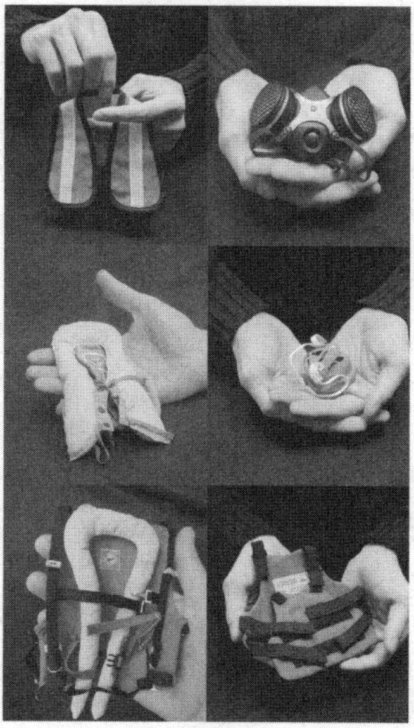

Image courtesy of the artist.

Exploring Meanings and Concepts in Visual Imagery. Art research not only involves making imagery but also includes decoding imagery to unearth meaning. Since visual images embody concepts, deciphering them is a major part of art research. In our rabbit research example, this visual decoding could include looking at how rabbits are portrayed in art from the extremely realistic depiction in *A Young Hare* by Albrecht Dürer, 1502, to Eduardo Kac's fluorescent *GFP Bunny*, 2000 (see Figure 2.7), in popular visual culture (Bugs Bunny, Crusader Rabbit, Jessica Rabbit, and Dunnys), and in literature (Peter Rabbit—see Figure 2.8—and the White Rabbit from *Alice's Adventures in Wonderland*—see Figure 2.9).

Figure 2.7. Eduardo Kac, *GFP Bunny*, 2000.

Figure 2.8. Beatrix Potter, Peter Rabbit, 1901.

Transgenic artwork. Alba, the fluorescent
rabbit. Image courtesy of the artist.

Figure 2.9. John Tenniel, White Rabbit from
***Alice's Adventures in Wonderland*, 1865.**

Research could also include examining imagery from the academic disciplines, such as illustrations, charts, and graphs, to glean meaning and how it is conveyed. Decoding imagery sets the stage for juxtaposing imagery. Juxtaposing contrasting images from different disciplines is a particularly effective way to reveal discipline-specific concepts. Imagine placing an anatomical drawing of a rabbit (see Figure 2.10) next to Beatrix Potter's portrait of Peter Rabbit, or juxtaposing Dürer's *Hare* with Tara McPherson's *Bubble Yucky Dunny* (see Figure 2.11). In analyzing these juxtapositions, a learner not only views rabbits from many vantage points but he or she can also access in these images the worldviews of the different disciplines and how they differ or overlap. This the learner can do through comparing their contrasting styles and visual tropes. For example, anatomical drawings are clear, simple, and laced with explanatory texts while Beatrix Potter's illustrations are impressionistic in style, featuring soft fuzzy textures and cheerful colors. What does this disparity say about science versus literature? Similarly, Dürer's *Hare* is hyperrealistic and Tara McPherson's *Bubble Yucky Dunny* is cartoony and ironically cute. How do these images reflect such different times?

Figure 2.10. Scientific Illustration of Rabbit Anatomy.

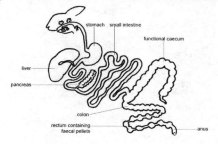

Figure 2.11. Tara McPherson, *Bubble Yucky Dunny,* **2007.**

"DUNNY" is a registered trademark and copyright of
Kidrobot, Inc. Image courtesy of the artist and Kidrobot.

Along with analyzing imagery from various disciplines, an artist–researcher also uses this imagery in his or her research workbook or as models and inspirations for artwork. Remember our researcher chose to write and illustrate a handbook for rabbits that choose to avoid laboratories or the dining table and instead become characters in stories. In her handbook, she could include directions for rabbits based stylistically on informational images she finds in instruction manuals. She could also appropriate imagery from cookbooks or images of dead rabbits from 17th-century Dutch still lifes. Appropriating visual imagery pulled from different disciplines brings home a very important point: Visual images are powerful media for generating and communicating meaning. Consequently, artists can tap into the meanings such images already embody and use them in their artwork to make new meanings. An example of juxtaposing imagery within an artwork is Jason Freeny's *Visible Vinyl* (n.d.), a "dunny" with his interior illustrated in the mode of an anatomical illustration (see Figure 2.12).

Figure 2.12. Jason Freeny, *Visible Vinyl Dunny*, undated.

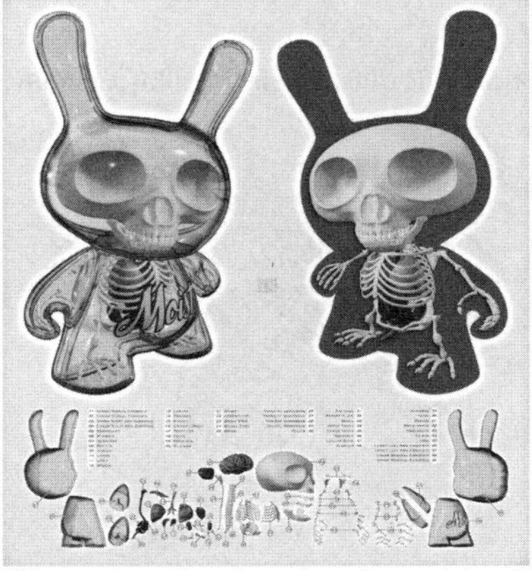

"DUNNY" is a registered trademark and copyright of Kidrobot, Inc. Image courtesy of the artist and Kidrobot.

The Method of Mimicry. *Mimicry*, using methods usually associated with disciplines outside of art, is a principal strategy in much art-centered research. To explore her rabbit, our artist–researcher mimics; she combines conventional art making with *methods* from the natural sciences, the social sciences, and the language arts. She begins her research with a method from journalism, psychology, and creative writing when she interviews her rabbit. To understand the cultural aspects of rabbits, she employs the methods of anthropology or sociology in using surveys and questionnaires to examine her peers' attitudes toward rabbits and various rabbit characters. In analyzing the images of rabbits in art and visual culture over time and connecting them to their cultural contexts, she acts as a cultural historian. In developing her manual, she practices expository writing methods of technical writers. Playacting in this way—as a technical writer, an anthropologist, a historian, a journalist, or any other researcher—permits learners, such as our artist–researcher, to inhabit the world of a discipline and, therefore, to understand what researchers in that discipline do, how they think and learn, and what their research or field is all about.

Reflection. All along the way, the artist–researcher reflects or thinks deeply about the ideas she encounters and the connections she makes. Reflection is central to constructing the understandings that emerge in an inquiry and cementing them in the mind. This is reflection about knowledge, particularly concepts. Deep reflection can also concentrate on the research trail as a process of learning, thinking, and invention. This is reflection about process. Reflection about both knowledge and process can help learning artist–researchers develop metacognition. Metacognition is the understanding of how one learns and the ability to guide and regulate one's learning (Pesut, 1990). Metacognition is essential to growing as a learner (Bransford, Brown, & Cocking, 2000), and it is also critical to sustaining a creative practice (Pesut, 1990). Harking back to our trail and street metaphor for art-centered research, reflection occurs when the artist–researcher takes an aerial view of the trails she has taken and the disciplinary "places" she has visited. Getting to that reflective perch often requires teacher support. Keeping a research workbook is also helpful.

Research Workbook. The art research process manifests itself in "products" many times along the trail. These products can range from sketches, diagrams, maps, collages, and notes to fully realized and crafted images and objects. They can be "art" or steps along the way to "art." Collecting these research milestones and seeing them as part of a procedural flow are critical to an art-centered research process and to the reflective deliberations necessary for building substantive understandings. For that reason, artist–researchers keep a *research workbook* in which they experiment, record, and reflect on their inquiry each step of the way.

The research workbook with its sequential series of imagery, commentary, explanations, and plans is the backbone of the research and the chronicle of the process. It gives structure to process and also acts as the spinal cord of the inquiry—an extended nerve center or conduit along which ideas flow, link up, and ignite. As a result, research workbooks are sites where ideas are hatched and worked out, understandings are built and visualized, and the research procedure, with its variety of thinking and creative strategies, becomes visible and concrete.

For most novice artist–researchers, creating a successful research workbook requires teacher guidance. We suggest that teachers set up structures or guidelines based on the following principles. First, art research should combine visual imagery with verbal "critique" (Sullivan, 2010). This is important because each modality has a distinct contribution to make. Visual images evoke or symbolize ideas and subjects; verbal description and explanation make ideas and subjects clearer and more concrete. The research workbook, therefore, should be filled with images and verbal explanations of the imagery that build on each other. Here is an example from a research workbook created by 12th-grader Acacia Masri at Berkeley High School in Berkeley, California (see Figure 2.13).

Second, art research benefits from mapping (see Figure 2.14). We suggest that students map conceptual connections at all stages of the research. These maps

Figure 2.13. Acacia Masri, *Awaicu Project Plan,* **2012.**

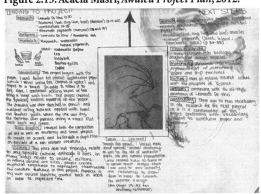

Image courtesy of the artist.

Figure 2.14. Julia Marshall, *Map of the Rabbit Trail, 2013*

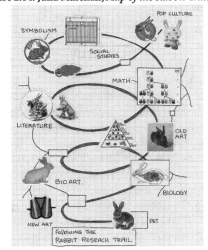

Image courtesy of the artist.

should be peppered throughout the research workbooks because they make the conceptual threads of the research visible. It is also advisable to create an ongoing, ever-evolving map of the research process. In doing this, learning artist–researchers can see how their research and ideas progress and can ascertain their next steps.

Third, the research workbook is a work of visual design. This means that it should be as visually engaging as it is conceptually compelling. It also should show progression of thinking and understanding. In other words, a research workbook is not a chaotic compilation of random, throwaway doodles and sketches. Thought should be given to what is put into the research workbook and where it is placed.

Fourth, the research workbook borders on art but is different from art. It does not share with art the critical art element of ambiguity; it is essentially literal and clear in its description of ideas and process. Teachers should make clear the distinction between art and the research workbook.

Structure, Guidance, and Support. Because the art-centered research discussed above is essentially independent inquiry, it may look at first glance like there is no role for the teacher, but that is far from the case. Teachers need to be as fully engaged in a learner's independent research as they are in teacher-initiated art lessons because art-centered research requires an immense amount of support and guidance. This guidance and support can vary; it can consist of scaffolding activities that all students partake in to jumpstart independent research, and it can be more personalized assignments tailored to individual students as they go along in their research.

We advise teachers to start with all-class activities that make the concept of art-centered research clear and concrete. One way to start is to delineate a basic structure of art-centered research. This calls for breaking down the process into components and steps. For example, we have divided art research into two primary segments: *investigation* and *interpretation*. Making the distinction between the two parts sets the stage for *investigation performances* and *interpretation performances*, prompts learners to think in those terms, and helps them see how the two functions are different, are complementary, and overlap. For example, in the rabbit research, our learner performed an investigative performance when she interviewed her rabbit. A corresponding interpretive performance was answering her interview questions for her rabbit. Gathering rabbit imagery was another investigative performance on the rabbit trail. The corresponding interpretive performance was juxtaposing those rabbit images to reveal a concept.

For a preparatory investigative activity, we recommend assigning a research project for the entire class that combines methods and formats from the sciences or social sciences with art making. For subsequent interpretive performance, we suggest students use creative strategies to interpret what they found in their investigation. This could mean interpreting their "findings" metaphorically, placing their findings in a different context, or projecting ahead or into the mind of someone else, as in the rabbit example.

To launch long-term independent inquiries, a teacher must prepare students by describing how, in art-centered research, investigation and interpretation are interwoven and build upon each other. In other words, a teacher should recount how artists and other researchers investigate, interpret their findings, probe some more based on their interpretations, and interpret further from there. It would also be wise to explain how this two-pronged process can be directional but is never strictly linear; it works in cycles, can slide or leap laterally among ideas and topics, and is primarily expansive. That means, if it goes unchecked, art research can just keep going in a circle and/or branching out.

Its proclivity to expand is one of art research's greatest assets. When a learning artist–researcher sees the webs of connections grow exponentially in his or her research like a living organism, he or she realizes the interconnectedness of things. This is an important lesson. However, research must also lead somewhere, and directing it calls for discipline and editing. While teachers can promote expansion by suggesting ideas or allowing students to wander freely, they should also direct expansion. For promoting and directing expansion, we suggest multiple ongoing all-class conversations and writing assignments that pose probing generative questions that trigger the creation of conceptual connections. These questions should be supplemented with individual one-on-one discussions between the teacher and each artist–researcher or with peer critiques and discussions. We cannot stress enough the importance of asking probing and generative questions to guide individual research and shape peer dialogue. The success and richness of this model rests on it.

Teacher-Directed Projects

The process described above is one way to engage learners in substantive multidimensional art-centered integrated learning. We began with the independent research curriculum format to show the reader how rich and multifaceted art and inquiry-based integrated learning can be. Teachers, however, can choose alternative ways of working and adapt this model in any way they see fit. Many of the kinds of learning that take place in the long-term independent model can occur in teacher-directed models designed for an entire class, and many learners may perform better in that environment. In a teacher-directed model, a curriculum could be composed of a string of guided inquiry-based lessons or projects in which learners explore a concept or related concepts in different ways. In this approach, each learner can keep a research workbook for chronicling topics, ideas, and thoughts explored in each project. As the learner compiles his or her workbook, he or she notes how ideas are explored in multiple ways in the projects and records the conceptual thread and inquiry processes that link them.

To build understanding and highlight connections, we suggest developing scaffolding strategies, formats, and language that are repeated in every project and that learners can use in their workbooks. One scaffolding strategy is to begin each project with a research question and follow that up with related generative questions to guide the student's thinking and inquiry. When each project begins, a learner records the introductory questions in his or her book. He or she then answers those questions in the workbook as the project progresses. Another scaffolding strategy is to provide consistent questions for reflection on the separate projects so that each student can record these questions and his or her answers to them in the student's research workbook. After an accumulation of questions, including research questions, generative questions, and reflection questions, habits of thinking and connection making will develop, and the learner, as well as the teacher, will have tangible proof of this. Another suggestion is to prompt students to collect imagery (images they are using in their projects, pictures of themselves working, and pictures of their artworks as they evolve during the process) and ideas they generate and accumulate as they follow the sequence of projects and lessons. This will give the workbooks a visual presence and help learners see the conceptual thread that winds through the individual lessons.

It must be noted that a full-on research workbook is not mandatory. For elementary grades, a less structured, shorter research book for sketches, ideas, and artist statements in grade-level vocabulary will do. In fact, teachers can opt not to assign research workbooks and simply enrich their existing curriculum using the principles and processes of substantive multidimensional art-centered integrated learning. Guidelines for developing inquiry-based integrated curriculum and ideas for projects are explored in Chapter 9 of this book.

Whatever model or combinations of models you decide to use, the keys to meaningful art-centered integrated learning are pursuing a topic or idea that is rich with potential that can take you and your students to new and deeper understandings, exploring that subject deeply and expanding outward to see it from multiple points of view, transforming knowledge and ideas through creative interpretation and invention, and drawing attention to the inquiry process. When you do this and allow for the unexpected, you and your students will discover an important thing: Enormous meaning and potential for meaning-making reside in almost everything, even a rabbit.

REFERENCES

Bransford, J., Brown, A., & Cocking, R. (Eds.). (2000). *How people learn: Brain, mind, experience and school.* Washington, DC: Commission on Behavioral and Social Studies and Education, National Research Council, National Academy.

Bruner, J. (1977). *The process of education.* Cambridge, MA: Harvard University Press. (Original work published 1960)

Dion, M. (2007). Interview. *Ecology, Season 4.* Art 21 PBS. Retrieved from www.pbs.org/art21/artists/mark-dion

Eldredge, M. (2005). *Darwin: Discovering the tree of life.* New York, NY: Norton.

Malina, R. (2013). Series foreword. In K. O'Rourke, *Walking as mapping: Artists as cartographers* (pp. xi–xii). Cambridge, MA: MIT Press.

Mansilla, V., & Gardner, H. (1998). What are the qualities of understanding? In M. S. Wiske (Ed.), *Teaching for understanding: Linking research with practice* (pp. 161–183). San Francisco, CA: Jossey-Bass.

Ohio State TETAC Mentors. (2002). Integrated curriculum: Possibilities for the arts. *Art Education, 55*(3), 12–22.

Parsons, M. (2004). Art and integrated curriculum. In E. Eisner & M. Day (Eds.), *Handbook of research and policy in art education* (pp. 775–794). Mahwah, NJ: Lawrence Erlbaum.

Perkins, D. (1988). Art as understanding. In D. Perkins & H. Gardner (Eds.), *Art, mind and education: Research from Project Zero* (pp. 111–131). Chicago: University of Illinois Press.

Pesut, D. (1990). Creative thinking as a self-regulatory metacognitive process: A model for education, training, and further research. *Journal of Creative Behavior, 24*(2), 105–110.

Sullivan, G. (2010). *Art practice as research: Inquiry in the visual arts* (2nd ed.). Los Angeles, CA: Sage.

Taylor, P., Carpenter, S., Ballengee-Morris, C., & Sessions, B. (2006). *Interdisciplinary approaches to teaching art in high school.* Reston, VA: National Art Education Association.

3

The Natural Sciences
Understanding the Natural World

Lawrence Horvath and Julia Marshall

How often do we hear that something is either an art or a science? When it is an "art," a task involves imagination and free interpretation; it is inexact, and the outcome is unclear. On the other hand, designating a venture as a "science" implies exactitude, precision, and logic; the task does not require imagination, and the result is predictable. Sometimes a project is both an art *and* a science. Here, the endeavor requires two distinct ways of thinking and doing. The polarization of art and science has a long history in Western culture; for centuries, they have represented two opposing sides of the mind, two thought systems, and two ways of doing things. In this chapter, we explore the scientific way of doing and knowing. Along the way, however, we will discover that the science–art dichotomy is not as simple or clear-cut as we anticipated.

WHAT IS SCIENCE?

The American Association for the Advancement of Science defines science as "the art of interrogating nature with the commitment to understand the natural world" (Gauch, 2012, p. 26). We commonly think of such interrogation in terms of peering through a telescope at stars, inspecting tiny creatures under a microscope, watching a storm front move across a landscape, noticing a new species of plant, or piecing together the bones of a dinosaur. Science begins with experiences and explorations such as these, and it is fueled by the curiosity and wonder they ignite (Newton, 2012). But that's just the beginning. Scientists shape those initial experiences into understandings, into a structure of theories and laws, and ultimately into a coherent vision of nature (Baggot, 2012). What distinguishes science from other versions of reality is not its coherence, however. Religions provide coherent cosmologies as well (Derry, 1999). It is that the knowledge of the world science presents is an evidence-based vision of reality constructed through a logical and explicit chain of reasoning that can be replicated and generalized and that is always open to skepticism, scrutiny, and critique (Aicken, 1991; Derry, 1999; Ingram & Sikes, 2005). Science is, then, the happy intersection of our experiences and observations in the world, our ability to connect and think them through in a systematic way, and our willingness to change our minds.

Purpose of Science

"One of the aims of science is to explain what the world is made of and why it is the way it is. It seeks to do this by elucidating the fundamental constituents of matter and the laws of nature that govern its behavior (Baggott, 2012, p. 19). Indeed, the ultimate goal of science is to understand, to satisfy our sense of curiosity and wonder (Gauch, 2012). The plausibility of science reaching the goal of understanding nature rests on two primary assumptions: The universe has some order to it, and it is ultimately understandable to the human mind (Beveridge, 1950/2004; Gauch, 2012).

There is also another compelling rationale for doing science: the sheer love of doing it. According to physicist David Bohm (1998), a scientist is interested in learning something fundamentally new, in discovering new orders of lawfulness in the world he or she perceives. This lawfulness is appealing not only for its formal coherence or even for its utility in making predictions. Its appeal is also in the process of discovery, in the apprehension of "a certain oneness and totality or wholeness constituting a kind of harmony that is felt to be beautiful" (Bohm, 1998, p. xvi). That is to say, for many scientists, the urge to understand the universe has an aesthetic motivation (Newton, 2012). Yes, scientists get a thrill—aesthetic and intellectual pleasure—out of learning something truly new or constructing an elegant theory (Dyson, 2006). The process of learning and discovery, of coming to understand how things fit together, and of building new models of reality is, therefore, inherently satisfying (Newton, 2012).

Knowledge of Science

Disciplines of Science. The sciences divide into disciplines organized into three general categories. These categories are similar in their reliance on evidence, in their use of hypotheses and theories, and in the kinds of logic they employ, but they are distinct in what aspect of nature they study, their store of knowledge, and their methods and tools (Gauch, 2012). Technology is often added as the fourth area of study in schools (Next Generation Science Standards, 2013). However, many scientists do not include technology in the list of sciences; to them, technology is not a science but an application of science (Hazen & Trefil, 2009).

The three general categories of science are the *physical sciences*, which are concerned with the nature and properties of matter and energy; the *Earth and space sciences*, which focus on the forms and properties of the Earth and the forces that shape it; and the *life sciences*, the study of living organisms. Each of these fields has many genres such as microbiology, quantum physics, and astronomy, and there are hybrid sciences like paleontology and ecology that combine knowledge and practices from different branches of science.

The genres of science reside on a continuum from the most exact, concrete, and law-abiding sciences that are most amenable to prediction (the "hard" sciences) to the most complex, inexact, and unpredictable ones (the "softer" sciences). Generally speaking, physics lies at the "hard" end of the spectrum, and the life sciences reside at the opposite, "softer" end (Beveridge, 1950/2004). Meteorology, a branch of physics, however, proves to be an exception; it joins psychology as one of the most inexact of sciences because the many variables it entertains make it most resistant to predictions (Aicken, 1991).

Information and Concepts. The knowledge of the natural sciences divides into two principal categories: *information* and *concepts*. Science is notable in that it is directly and perpetually tied to information. Information is obtained through observation and/or measurement of phenomena that can be tested empirically; it is evidence (Beveridge, 1950/2004; Derry, 1999). When we cannot directly observe a phenomenon, we detect evidence through the use of instruments and mathematical modeling. In such cases, we rely on indirect observations, measurements, mathematical relationships, technology, and simulations to discern information and extend our "factual" knowledge.

Information is not permanent; it can change. Observations can change, often due to new technologies. Thus, in the long run, information is not intrinsically true or stable. Rather, its viability is established through ongoing experiment and observation (Newton, 2012). For this reason, many scientists today prefer to use the word "information" rather than the word "fact" to describe the phenomena they observe and discover (H. Carmena-Young, March 2013, personal communication).

As important and grounding as information is in the natural sciences, a collection of bits of information is only meaningful if the scientist finds connections among the bits, connections that can explain the information and lead to understandings (Derry, 1999; Newton, 2012). These connections are called *concepts*. Scientists arrive at concepts through analysis, synthesis, and inference. This means they take information, evaluate it, connect it, and discern its implications.

According to the Next Generation Science Standards (2013), the core disciplinary concepts are as follows. In the physical sciences, matter, motion, and energy top the list. In the life sciences, the focus is on structures and processes of organisms and ecosystems and on the workings of heredity and evolution. The core ideas in the Earth and space sciences are Earth placement, Earth-based systems, and activities involving the Earth and humans.

Concepts that underlie all the sciences are called *crosscutting concepts*. They are patterns; cause and effect (mechanism and explanation); systems and systems models; scale, proportion, and quantity; energy and matter (flows, cycles, and conservation); structure and function; and stability and change (Next Generation Science Standards, 2013).

To enter into the knowledge of science, concepts, like information, must endure multiple tests and the scrutiny of the scientific community and must fit into the general scheme (laws and theories) of the time (Baggott, 2012). Although science works with agreed-upon and tested concepts, truth in science can never be proved; concepts are always provisional and open to revision as new discoveries and new ideas come along (Beveridge, 1950/2004; Newton, 2012).

Methods of Science

Not all scientists do the same thing (Aicken, 1991; Gauch, 2012). Some scientists perform experiments in laboratories; some scientists observe phenomena in the field; others construct hypotheses and theories using mathematical computations and abstract models; others seek out and categorize artifacts or species of animals and plants.

Stephen J. Gould categorized the natural sciences according to methods. Gould (1989) distinguished between sciences that are traditionally framed as "hard" sciences and those sciences that are called "soft" sciences, finding the "hard sciences" to be "rigorously experimental" and the soft sciences to be "merely descriptive" (p. 279). Furthermore, he identified the hard sciences as the experimental-predictive model ("Science A") and the soft sciences as the historical reconstructive model ("Science B").

Investigations in Science A involve observing phenomena, making hypotheses, and *experimenting* to test hypotheses and make generalizations or predictions based on conclusions. Experimenting is often done under controlled conditions in laboratories. Experimental-predictive sciences are predominately found in chemistry, physics, and biology.

This is not as cut-and-dried as it seems, however. The studies of biology (evolution), physics (astronomy), and the geosciences (plate tectonics) also entail the practices of Science B. "Science B's" are primarily those sciences that rely on inferences made without experimentation. Lacking the ability to experiment, they entail piecing existing evidence together to construct explanations and theories. The practice of Science B, therefore, amounts to logical, educated storytelling grounded in argumentation rigorously consistent with evidence. Biology falls under the rubric of Science B when experimentation on humans or animals is deemed unethical; physics becomes Science B when we explore the outer reaches of space; and geology becomes Science B in the study of plate tectonics, the history of the Earth's landmasses.

Many times the sciences use the methods in line with both Science A and Science B. Psychology, for instance, has practices consistent with Science A (Skinnerian experiments with animals and psychotropic drug trials) but often falls, due to moral issues, into the category of Science B (piecing together explanations of behavior based on past experiences, dreams, and present actions).

Generally speaking, however, all scientists do the following: ask questions; develop and use models; plan and carry out investigations; analyze and interpret data; use mathematics and computational thinking; construct explanations; engage in argument from evidence; and obtain, evaluate, and communicate information (Next Generation Science Standards, 2013). They also construct hypotheses and theories, test them, and make predictions (Gauch, 2012; Gimbel, 2011; Newton, 2012).

A hypothesis is primarily a hunch a scientist develops as he or she interprets his or her observations or data. A hypothesis can be the logical synthesis of an idea with observation, or it can appear fully formed from a scientist's mind (Aicken, 1991). The main function of a hypothesis is to suggest new experiments or new observations. To be sure, all research and experiments begin with a hypothesis. A vast majority of hypotheses are wrong, but if a hypothesis holds up to experimentation and scrutiny, it is elevated to the level of theory (Aicken, 1991; Beveridge, 1950/2004).

A theory can be framed as a hypothesis or as an integration of multiple hypotheses that survive testing and incorporate the modifications indicated by the tests (Aicken, 1991). When a hypothesis passes the test, the indication is that some truth has been established, and a theory is devised to explain that truth. A theory is not the whole truth, however; it is the current strongest explanation or model of phenomena and will continue to be modified and elaborated upon as new observations, experiments, and knowledge challenge or validate it. Derry (1999) maintains that theories are judged on four criteria. First, a theory must have explanatory power; a theory that explains more is better than a theory that explains less. Second, a theory must be simple; a simple, elegant theory with few assumptions will be valued over an elaborate, awkward theory although it explains a phenomenon equally well. Third, a theory must be productive; a theory should lead to new ideas, new applications, or new connections with extant theories; to refinements of itself; and ultimately to new theories. Fourth, a theory must have the potential to extend beyond its own predictions; it should lead to something unanticipated when the theory was first devised.

Hypotheses, experiments, and theories lead to prediction. Prediction, therefore, is the ultimate "performance of understanding" (Perkins, 1998) of science; it is where scientists take their understandings and project forward to apply them.

Scientific Process. Through their research, scientists strive to discover something, whether it is a new phenomenon, a new concept, or a new theory (Derry, 1999). Discovery most often occurs within the context of a historical theme. Scientists do not simply write theories out of the blue but work from knowledge and ideas developed by other scientists who have dealt with the theme before. Ideas evolve over time. Different scientists contribute separate pieces to the effort, new ideas are generated, good ideas are mixed with less useful ideas, observations are bettered, more new ideas are created, and good ideas are filtered out from ideas that don't work. Different combinations are tried, and eventually a consistent picture emerges. The development of a theory is, therefore, often a serial collaboration. Lately, we have seen this phenomenon in the long collaborative quest for and discovery of the Higgs boson particle (Baggott, 2012).

Newton (2012) maintains that there are many routes to scientific discovery. These routes can be quite logical and systematic, or they can entail nonrational, unconscious processing, intuition, or chance. In fact, many routes to discovery involve all these factors. This means that when uncontrollable events or involuntary processes contribute to the procedure, they must be followed up with methodical experimentation and analysis if they are to lead to a valid discovery.

Alexander Fleming's lucky discovery of penicillin is one fabled example. Fleming happened to notice the absence of bacteria surrounding a new mold growing in a petri dish in his laboratory. Because of his prior knowledge and his disposition to be searching for evidence (what the great microbiologist Louis Pasteur called "the prepared mind"), he realized that the mold could have antibacterial powers. While his sighting of the phenomenon was serendipitous, Fleming's recognition of the mold's implications was not, and his systematic follow-up with controlled experiments allowed his initial chance encounter to blossom into a discovery (Derry, 1999).

Scientists also report discoveries coming out of dreamlike visions. For example, chemist Friedrich August Kekulé, after much puzzling about the structure of the benzene molecule, dozed off and envisioned a snake curling around to bite its tail. This dream gave Kekulé the solution to his puzzle: the circular structure of the benzene molecule. Kekulé's story implies that the unconscious can generate the solution to a problem when the conscious mind has prepared the way and has run out of steam (Derry, 1999).

Kekulé's vision is closely related to intuition. Intuition is the sudden grasp of a situation, an illuminating idea that leaps into consciousness, which often arises when a scientist is thinking about something else (Beveridge, 1950/2004). Intuition is essentially passive; it happens to us. It is the consequence of an unconscious storehouse of knowledge, impressions, and ideas and is often connected to creative solutions and new trails of research. Scientists, such as physicist Albert Einstein, among many, have reported intuitive insights that propelled their thinking (Derry, 1999).

Not all ideas pop up so reflexively. Deliberately connecting knowledge and ideas also leads to discovery. For instance, scientists often intentionally apply knowledge from one area of science to unravel the secrets of something they are investigating in another area. An example of this is how physicist Felix Bloch, in attempting to understand how electrons move through metals, applied the newly invented theory of quantum mechanics and the recent discovery that ions in metals are organized according to regular lattice-like structures to the mystery of conductivity in metals. From these borrowed ideas, Bloch constructed a *conceptual model* of a metal through which electrons could pass freely. Subsequent variations and extensions of Bloch's model by other scientists eventually led to the discovery of superconductivity and semiconductors (Derry, 1999).

Discovery also arises from observation and dogged trial and error. Edward Jenner's discovery of the smallpox vaccine is one case in point (Aicken, 1991; Derry, 1999). Jenner heard the rumor that a person who was infected with cowpox had developed an immunity to smallpox, a much more lethal disease. After much systematic observation, trial and error, hypotheses, and analysis, Jenner finally hit on the answer and was able to create a viable smallpox vaccine. Jenner's method is an example of the *scientific method*, the classic process that is often touted as the foundation of scientific research (Derry, 1999).

Classic Scientific Method. First perfected by Isaac Newton, the scientific method is ideally a well-structured protocol consisting of four successive and distinct stages (Ben-Ari, 2005; Newton, 2012). The word "ideally" is key here as the scientific method, in reality, is highly variable and often counterintuitive (Gauch, 2012). The ideal "method" goes like this: The first stage is observation and recording of evidence. The second stage is induction, the examination of the evidence and the development of a generalization, hypothesis, or theory that can account for the evidence. Stage 3 is deduction, the use of logic to predict the consequences of the theory, and experimentation to see if the predictions pan out. Stage 4 is application of the theory to universal laws. This step-by-step process is also called the *hypothetico-deductive* method (Aicken, 1991; Ben-Ari, 2005; Derry, 1999).

Logic is central to the hypothetico-deductive process. Logic comes in two forms: inductive logic and deductive logic (Gimbel, 2011). Inductive logic entails observation and finding connections among specific occurrences to derive a hypothesis or arrive at a concept or generalization. In other words, inductive reasoning is discerning patterns in specific observed phenomena. As it begins with observation and experience, inductive reasoning is used to make sense of sensory data and is the process by which scientists discern *empirical* information—information based on observation, experience, and logic. It is, therefore, the logic of *empiricism*, the recognition that knowledge and understanding lie in connecting the rational mind to perception. Inductive logic is necessary. The problem with it is that it is unreliable; its inferences can never be proved (Beveridge 1950/2004; Gimbel, 2011).

Deductive reasoning, on the other hand, is more reliable. In deductive reasoning, one premise is directly connected to another, and this leads inevitably to a valid conclusion. The syllogism, which comes to us from ancient Greece, is the basic model of deductive reasoning (Gimbel, 2011). A syllogism goes like this: All dogs are carnivores; Fido is a dog; therefore, Fido is a carnivore. The validity of a syllogism is dependent on the first two premises' being true. Deductive logic is the foundation of *rationalism*—the belief that truth lies not in our unreliable perceptions but in reason. Taken to its extreme (decoupled from experience and inductive logic), deductive reasoning is a closed system and unproductive (Gimbel, 2011). When coupled with induction (conclusions and generalizations based on perception), however, deduction is productive; it validates an inductive hunch and generates reasonable, reliable predictions (Ben-Ari, 2005; Gimbel, 2011).

Although logic is important in scientific process and discovery, it is limited (Beveridge, 1950/2004; Newton, 2012). Many philosophers and practitioners of science such as mathematician Henri Poincaré and physicist Albert Einstein believed that reason has more to do with the extension of knowledge and less to do with the discovery or invention of it. Reason, therefore, is primarily employed for verification of knowledge (Derry, 1999; Newton, 2012).

Creativity in Scientific Process. As we have seen, the paths to discovery bear hallmarks of creativity (chance occurrences, sparks of intuition, and insights from the unconscious). The question arises, Is there a role for creativity in the scientific method itself? The answer is a definitive "yes" (Aicken, 1991; Ben-Ari, 2005; Beveridge, 1950/2004; Bohm, 1998; Derry, 1999; Dyson, 2006; Gauch, 2012; Newton, 2012). So, then, how does creativity fit in?

First, scientific discovery requires imagination (Aicken, 1991; Ben-Ari, 2005; Beveridge,1950/2004). Imagination is essentially the capacity to see what is not readily apparent (Ricoeur, 1991) or to picture in the mind how processes work (Beveridge, 1950/2004). In scientific inquiry, this means seeing the underlying patterns, connecting information, filling in gaps, and making inferences—essentially the strategies of inductive reasoning. Inductive logic, therefore, is inherently creative. Bohm (1998) recognized this and called inductive logic "imaginative fancy," describing it as the construction of associative links between newly noticed phenomena and existing scientific knowledge.

Imagination also stimulates lines of research in enabling us to see visions of possible consequences. It allows us to invent the hypothesis or theory and develop the questions that propel the research. Imagination has an equally active role in the invention of experiments and in the development of techniques and tools. As Beveridge (1950/2004) so aptly puts it, "Facts are dead in themselves and it is imagination that gives them life" (p. 58).

What are the specific creative thinking processes that constitute scientific creativity? For Jenner and his laborious route to the smallpox vaccine, creativity was manifested in his analysis of the problem, his divergent thinking or exploration of many possible answers, his inferences or interpretations, and the way he improvised and invented experiments. Furthermore, induction, a primary part of Jenner's process, involves fundamental creative thinking strategies such as recognizing similarities, forming associations, and seeing the abstract in the concrete. These are kinds of creative thinking described by Necka (1986).

In the case of Bloch and his successors, the imagination required for their eventual discovery of superconductivity involved all of the creative strategies associated with induction. Furthermore, these scientists incorporated associative or metaphorical thinking when they constructed analogies or models. Model construction entails making conceptual associations and recognizing similarities. These are both kinds of creative thinking described by Kirst and Dickmeyer (1973).

In constructing theories, scientists also use other creative strategies; they distill information to edit out the "noise" or the extraneous; they project from their findings and data to make predictions; and they break away from established ways of thinking to generate new ways of thinking. Cropley (1992) identifies these strategies as creative. Projection, in particular, is the tactic used in another creative act performed by scientists: problem finding.

Scientific method and research are also creative because they often lead to the unexpected. In the case of experimentation, scientists often anticipate outcomes. However, experiments do not always pan out as predicted, and thus scientists must be sensitive to the unexpected, open to changing their assumptions, and able to envision where this new information could lead. For this, scientists must be nimble and improvisational in their thinking (Beveridge, 1950/2004).

The elements of imagination, intuition, chance, and unexpected outcomes that characterize scientific process lead us to the conclusion that the scientific method, even in its most classical sense, is not a simple or linear lockstep process (Newton, 2012). In practice, scientific methodology can be circular, and scientists do not think linearly (Ben-Ari, 2005). Furthermore, scientific process is often iterative (it builds through successive repetition), emergent (it evolves through a natural progression, which determines the form it takes), and improvisational (Fleener, 2005).

Although creativity is a significant factor in scientific advancement, it is not boundless. Science is about real things happening in the world (Derry, 1999). It is, therefore, counterproductive for scientists to wander off on imaginative fantasies disconnected from nature or our understanding of it. Their facts must be copiously and appropriately generated and tested; their theories must be open to scrutiny and correspond to the scientific paradigm at hand. Above all, their conclusions and predictions must be evidence based and logically sound (Gauch, 2012; Newton, 2012; Paul & Elder, 2008).

Forms of Science

When we think of the tools of science, or for that matter of any discipline, we most often consider the devices a researcher uses to generate information. In the natural sciences, these are the technological tools scientists use to observe and experiment with evidence; they are how researchers come to know and make breakthroughs (Dyson, 2006). The capacities of these tools determine what scientists can know and what they can infer or imagine. For example, the microscope, the telescope, the computer, and the supercollider all allow scientists to observe invisible objects and events.

Observation, however, is just part of the process. Scientists also use conceptual tools to make sense of their observations and convey their understandings. These tools are the *forms* of science. The forms, or conceptual tools, of science are simplified idealized models, which are metaphorical in that they describe something in terms of something else. Derry (1999) describes conceptual or idealized models as imaginary simulations of a natural system a scientist is trying to understand. In other words, models are simplified versions of phenomena, with mathematical models being the most abstract and precise (Aicken, 1991). Models have always been important tools for achieving scientific understanding, and because of scientists' ability to use computers to generate and visualize models, models are increasingly crucial to scientific advancement.

The beauty of a model is that it allows a scientist to understand a phenomenon in light of a simplified analogy and then be able to test its implications. Models help us grasp phenomena that are extremely complex; they explain the dynamics of things like the flow of blood in the body, nuclear structures in all matter, human heredity, and (in the social sciences) social conflict. The knowledge of subatomic and theoretical physics, for instance, is represented as models, both pictorial and mathematical. A mathematical model is $E = mc^2$, Einstein's calculation of the relationship between energy and matter. An example of a pictorial model is Niels Bohr's concept in subatomic physics of an atom as a mini–solar system (Aicken, 1991).

Describing the atom as a solar system is one legendary example of how a model in science is metaphorical. And, although this metaphor proved to be less than perfect, it did lead to new understandings of subatomic structures (Baggott, 2012). Lightman (2006) argues that metaphors have been useful in explaining natural phenomena since the beginning of science. Metaphors in science attach abstract information and notions to something we can understand, something related to everyday experience. This anchoring gives information *form*. Today, in theoretical physics, such accessible form is more critical than ever since scientists are observing phenomena secondhand through complex technologies and constructing mathematical models and theories far outside our direct perception or experience (Lightman, 2006). Examples from contemporary physics are the characterization of the basic subatomic components of the universe as "strings" that stretch, vibrate, and break in string theory (Greene, 2003), and the Higgs boson particle as the "glue" that keeps the universe together (Baggot, 2012).

Often models are represented in illustrations. However, they are also articulated in charts, maps, graphs, and geometric shapes. These visual representations of conceptual models and metaphors enable scientists to think through their observations, invent new ideas, and build understandings. They are, therefore, in the parlance of education, performances of understanding (Perkins, 1998) in that they show understanding while generating new understanding. These are new understandings that propel us forward; coupled with advanced observational tools and modeling tools, such as computers, the forms of contemporary science lead us to understandings beyond our imaginations (Dyson, 2006).

POINTS OF INTEGRATION FOR ART AND SCIENCE

Why is understanding the scientific mind and enterprise so valuable for artists and teachers who aspire to think and teach in an integrative way? As mentioned above, the domains of science and art embody two basic ways of knowing the world. Contrasting scientific and artistic mentalities and approaches puts their commonalities and differences in high relief. Making these comparisons and contrasts, therefore, is critical to substantive art–science integration.

Why is this so? When artists contrast art with science in areas where they are different and correlate them where they are similar, they can come to see art more clearly. Similarly, for teachers, the comparisons of science and art reap a profound reward: a peek into the core of integrated thinking. This is because integrated thinking is a blend of both artistic and scientific ways of seeing and comprehending the world. Artistic and scientific ways of thinking are intrinsic to all domains— not just the natural sciences and the arts but also language arts, the humanities, and the social sciences. Understanding how scientific and artistic ways of thinking share common traits, intertwine, and complement each other allows us to see how they all play a part in learning.

Purpose

Do art and science have similar purposes? The purpose of science is to understand the physical world. Does art seek to understand the world? In many ways, it does. However, art seeks a different understanding than science—one that is dissimilar in kind, focus, and scope.

What kind of understanding does art pursue? Art historian Sian Ede (2005) and education theorist Graeme Sullivan (2010) both contend that art aims for understandings that are provisional, personal, and complex. They argue that these understandings are also often novel; they are new understandings of, or new perspectives on, phenomena. As Sullivan (2010) maintains, the purpose of art is not to develop new information but to put existing information into perspective. That perspective shapes the knowledge of art. In contrast, science discovers information and pursues understandings that are enduring, concrete, and grounded in evidence.

What is the focus of art? Generally speaking, while science attends to the physical world, art mines subjective human experience (Ede, 2005; Sullivan, 2010). Consequently, art that engages nature and science looks to find new understandings of human experience in relationship to nature and science. It is said that art layers the metaphysical map of the human mind onto the physical terrain of science. That is, art puts science and scientific knowledge into the context of human experience.

What is the scope of art? While science limits itself to the physical world and what we can know about it through scientific investigation and logic, art does not. Art wanders everywhere from the knowable and tangible aspects of physical reality covered by science to the ineffable, the metaphysical, and the spiritual.

Moreover, some people believe art does not aim to understand at all. Rather, art's job is to ask questions that instigate more questions and conversations and to complicate or bring complexity to our prior understandings. In fact, some art dedicates itself solely to disrupting prior or set understandings (Ede, 2005; Sullivan, 2010). We see this in the way many contemporary artists take aim at scientific assumptions and question whether we benefit from scientific discoveries and technological advances, without offering answers.

Art and science also diverge in the way science is strictly evidence based and art is not. Indeed, art, while it is inspired by experience, is not tethered to reality. What's more, science aims toward clarity in explanation and correctness in prediction while art plays with ambiguity and often leaves conclusions to the viewer (Ede, 2005). Art and science also diverge in their utility. Science most frequently strives to construct information and ideas that have utilitarian value; art, on the other hand, is often identified by its lack of practical application.

Lastly, Ede (2005) contends that artists and scientists are looking for different things. Scientists search for beauty and order. In contrast, artists, although they use aesthetic means to convey an idea, do not seek beauty in the world as much as they strive to reveal unattended-to realities. While they may call attention to the beautiful, they more often aim to unveil "ugly truths." In fact, artists are known to quarrel with the status quo. They go after the "establishment," whatever it may be. When the establishment is science, artists tend to critique and protest its ideas and practices, targeting four aspects of science in particular: how science explains human nature, the effects of new technologies on human life, the ethical controversies of scientific discoveries, and the way science tends to promote a universalist belief system that papers over cultural and personal differences.

In short, the answer to our question of whether art and science have similar purposes is an unequivocal "yes . . . and no." Science and art may share an underlying desire to understand the world, but they pursue different forms of understanding. Furthermore, art does not often pursue understanding in a direct way; it does not explain or predict so much as provoke thinking and questioning that could lead to complex and subjective understandings. And sometimes those understandings are about science.

Knowledge

The knowledge of the sciences is well defined; it is limited to the physical world. While the knowledge of art is not limited to the physical world, it does, however, have a historical and cultural theme or thread: the human experience in all its variety and complexity in different places, at different times, and over time. Where science and art overlap in knowledge is their understanding of nature and our relationship to it. Indeed, artists have long been inspired by nature, and artists work with some of the basic concepts of science: causality and chance (e.g., Matthew Ritchie, *Proposition Player*, 2003–2004; Ritchie, 2013), the finding and visualizing of patterns (e.g., Jer Thorp, Chapter 8), the interdependence of living systems (e.g., Amy Youngs, see Figures 3.2, 3.3, and 3.4), space and geometry, time (e.g., Christian Marclay, *The Clock*, 2010), and the dynamics of human–machine relationships (e.g., Ken Rinaldo, *Autopoiesis*, 2007).

Methods and Creative Process

Perhaps the greatest overlap of science and art is in the realm of process. Ede (2005) suggests that artists are especially agile in their thinking. However, she also attributes this flexibility to scientists who work at the edges of their fields.

As our discussion of creativity in science above suggests, doing science can entail intuition, serendipity, and associative thinking. It also involves many creative strategies in problem solving and problem finding. Artists also use these creative strategies, and they engage in basic processes found in science: asking questions, making inferences, making hunches (hypotheses), and developing theories (Sullivan, 2010).

Aicken (1991) suggests that the hypothesis stage, especially when a hunch spontaneously pops into one's head, is where the artist's process overlaps most overtly with that of the scientist. Artists also experiment with ideas and media to test their hypotheses and, while they may not make predictions in the scientific sense, they project beyond their initial investigations and ideas to make connections and meaning. Certainly, scientific process and artistic process share many attributes. They both combine intuition, imagination, logic, and rationality; they thrive on rigorous observation, making connections, distilling things down, and projecting beyond. Furthermore, artists use logic. They employ inductive reasoning; they are particularly empirical, and they link their experiences and interpretations inductively to see patterns and make connections. Artists also use deductive reasoning to solve technical problems or to develop an idea.

Both art and science also employ visual imagery (pictures, maps, and symbols) as conceptual tools to develop and convey ideas. Where science and art diverge is in the way contemporary science, with its reliance on technology and mathematical models, is increasingly removed from physical experience while art will always play in the realm of experience and the senses (Ede, 2005).

Forms

At first glance, the forms of art and science may seem to be quite different. Art has drawing, painting, sculpture, prints, installations, photographs, films, video, digital imagery, animation, and performances. Hmm . . . on second thought, the sciences do too. Their forms include everything from botanical illustration, to x-rays and CAT scans, to three-dimensional molecular models, to museum displays, to video documentation, to mimicry of the behavior of animals. Take, for instance, Jane Goodall's imitation of chimpanzees and Francis Crick and James Watson's building of a three-dimensional model of the DNA molecule. In both cases, forms similar to those in art were employed to construct and convey understanding. While these two examples did not tap into the aesthetics inherent in scientific forms that bring science closer to art, many forms in science are aesthetic, particularly scientific illustrations, microphotography, animation of fractal geometry, and museum installations. If in doubt about the aesthetics of scientific forms, visit the Hall of Biodiversity at the American Museum of Natural History in New York City and you will see a true—exquisitely beautiful and breathtaking—confluence of art and science.

Furthermore, art, like science, employs form to convey complex concepts and realities, and these are metaphorical "models." A couple of examples of metaphorical models in Western art are the style and perspective in Cubist paintings, which are visual representations of a world where space and time are fractured, and classical nudes and portrait busts that picture ideals of European beauty and power, thus representing a world where these ideals are valued. In the same vein, the images on Haida totem poles and Tlingit rattles are metaphors for a deeply integrated relationship between human and animal. An example of a visual model in contemporary art is Nene Humphrey's woven spheres discussed below, which are metaphorical depictions of patterns in our bodies and in our emotional and social lives.

Another place where art and science overlap is in the way many contemporary artists use formats from the sciences such as graphs, maps, diagrams, symbols, and other tropes. Using these formats is a popular creative strategy because it employs familiar images, styles, graphic devices, and codes of science to convey a storehouse of meaning. An example of this is *A01* from Hyungkoo Lee's *Animatus* series in which natural history–style illustrations of the bones of cartoon characters such as Bugs Bunny (see Figure 3.1) transpose a fictional character into the realm of real animals. Here we see how picturing a fictional character using a trope of biology and natural history raises questions about how current popular culture makes fictional animals as real as those that exist in nature. To be sure, Hyungkoo Lee is on to something; cartoon critters are far more familiar to us than animals in the wild.

TEACHING ART, KEEPING SCIENCE IN MIND

In teaching art, we must remember that making art can have its scientific aspects: its rational thinking, its precision, and its desire for a clear vision. We also must acknowledge the contributions of science that have influenced and inspired art over the years. Science brought to Europe a disposition toward skepticism, reason, and clarity of thought, and the practice of questioning, thinking critically, and testing (Ben-Ari, 2005; Derry, 1999; Newton, 2012). It also brought with it the valuing of sensory experience, of knowing ourselves and the world through

Figure 3.1. Hyungkoo Lee, *A01*, 2005.

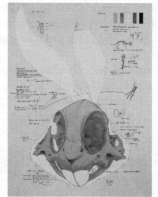

Pencil, ink, marker and acrylic on
paper, 109 x 79cm. © Copyright
Hyungkoo Lee. Image courtesy of
Gallery Skape.

sensation, thinking about what we sense, and putting our thoughts into action. Science generated the optimistic and creative notion that humans can understand their environment and themselves better, and they can take educated, thoughtful, creative action to improve their lives. Above all, science promoted the notion that humans could trust themselves to understand the world (Aicken, 1991; Newton, 2012). From the time of the Scientific Revolution and the Enlightenment, the arts have benefited from this mindset.

When we integrate art and science, we need to emphasize these key points: Art and science are both responses to ourselves, our experiences, and environment; they grew up together over the centuries as two divergent but complementary ways of thinking and doing; they both emerge out of curiosity and a sense of wonder; they are both experimental, improvisational, and open-ended; they share many conceptual strategies and methods; and they are the life's work of passionate, dedicated people. Lastly, science and art are both far from static; they are always in a state of disequilibrium and on the edge of the unknown. This is what generates change and keeps them alive and dynamic. As two sides of a coin, art and science complement and inspire each other. They are works in progress that do not compete with each other; rather they complete each other.

When you think about integrating science and art, consider the following points of integration:

1. Experiencing curiosity and wonder about the world and our place in it
2. Asking or raising questions; challenging foregone conclusions and habits of mind
3. Building upon past structures and knowledge to go into the unknown

4. Engaging in creative thinking, strategies, and process in both investigation and interpretation
5. Mixing logic and linear thinking with nonrational, nonlinear thinking
6. Applying ideas, structures, and methods of one area to another: metaphor and modeling
7. Making use of intuition, chance, mistakes, and the "prepared mind"
8. Engaging in improvisation and being flexible
9. Acting with perseverance and commitment
10. Experiencing the joy and pleasure in learning and discovery

ART THAT CONNECTS TO SCIENCE

Biology and Ecology: Creating Empathy and Concern

Understanding how living things connect and coexist is a primary theme of Amy Youngs's artwork. Out of this understanding, she believes will come empathy for other creatures and a concern for the environment. Youngs's work playfully explores this theme. For example, in Figure 3.2, *Holodeck for House Crickets* (2005), Youngs creates a safe and happy environment for insects bred for laboratories that cannot return to their native habitat. Her *Holodeck for House Crickets* is a hand-blown glass globe carpeted with leaves and grass with a moving image projected on the glass walls of trees blowing in the wind. As the house crickets enjoy themselves in their new home, Youngs amplifies and broadcasts their joyful chirping.

Youngs has also constructed many environments for living creatures that bring them and their role in our environment to our attention. For example, in *Intraterrestrial Soundings* (2004), she picks up and augments the noises worms

Figure 3.2. Amy Youngs, *Holodeck for House Crickets*, 2005.

Image courtesy of the artist.

make and provides bench-like worm-shaped amplifiers on which a "viewer" can recline while listening to the worms (see Figure 3.3). Similarly, in *Building a Rainbow* (2011), she exhibits a habitat for a rabbit that illuminates how rabbits participate in the nitrogen cycle; the rabbit eats, defecates, and fertilizes the plants that become his food (see Figure 3.4).

Figure 3.3. Amy Youngs, *Intraterrestrial Soundings*, 2004.

Image courtesy of the artist.

Figure 3.4. Amy Youngs, *Building a Rainbow*, 2011.

Image courtesy of the artist.

Integration (Purpose, Knowledge, Methods, and Forms). In the realm of *knowledge,* Youngs's work demonstrates how an artist takes a significant topic in science and relocates it in art. Youngs also makes the idea of interrelationships within nature and relationships of humans to animals come alive by engaging an audience with living organisms. Here she extends the *purpose* of science (to understand natural phenomena) to grasping phenomena in a visceral and experiential way (the purpose of art). In the realm of *methods,* Youngs researches her subject as a scientist would, and her artworks continue her inquiry as experiments into audience interactions with the organisms in the artwork. In all of her art, Youngs indirectly addresses the perspectives and methods of the biological and environmental sciences. In some pieces, she critiques science as cold and inhumane in its exploitation of animals (*Holodeck for House Crickets,* 2005) while in others she celebrates the curiosity and ingenuity that underlie scientific knowledge and investigation *(Building a Rainbow,* 2011).

Creative Strategies. In *Holodeck for House Crickets,* Youngs uses *projection;* she speculates what it must be like to be a house cricket. In *Intraterrestrial Soundings,* Youngs employs *amplification;* the artwork intensifies the sounds of worms to make the listener aware of these creatures. In *Building a Rainbow,* her creative strategy is *formatting;* Youngs arranges her work in the form of a student science project. In this way, she references science learning in schools.

Physics: Visualizing the Forces of Nature

Nathalie Miebach makes large multicolored, three-dimensional structures and environments that represent forces and patterns in weather. For example, *Changing Waters,* 2011 (Figure 3.5), is a large-scale installation that illustrates meteorological and oceanic interactions in the Gulf of Maine based on data from research buoys and weather stations. *Musical Score for Hurricane Noel,* 2010 and *Hurricane Noel,* 2010 (see Figures 3.6 and 3.7) depict weather data from the powerful hurricane that devastated parts of New England in 2007 (Miebach, 2012). While data may be the foundation of these works, Miebach transforms facts and figures into intertwining, whimsical lines and forms that blend basketry with weather maps. To underscore the patterns in natural forces, she also makes music using these data (see Figure 3.6).

Miebach's dynamic colorful installations make invisible forces visible and tactile, enabling the viewer to grasp and appreciate natural forces as interlocking, rhythmic patterns that weave, branch, expand, contract, and flow in space and time. Although her subjects may have dire consequences for humanity (as in *Hurricane Noel*), Miebach's works are beautiful and playful. And they communicate a deep awareness and appreciation of the complex, dynamic, often capricious forces that impact our lives and over which we have no control. What's more, Miebach gives us a fresh perspective on weather maps; our conventional symbols

Figure 3.5. Nathalie Miebach, *Changing Waters,* **2011.**

Image courtesy of the artist.

Figure 3.6. Nathalie Miebach, *Musical Score for Hurricane Noel,* **2010.**

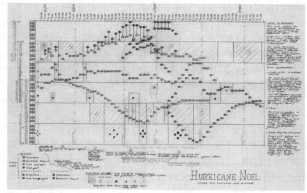

Image courtesy of the artist.

Figure 3.7. Nathalie Miebach, *Hurricane Noel,* **2010.**

Image courtesy of the artist.

for weather phenomena jump off the page or the TV screen into three-dimensional space, inviting the viewer to wander into a playground of whimsical structures in which every line, every dot, and every arrow has symbolic meaning.

Integration (Purpose, Knowledge, Methods, and Forms). Regarding *knowledge*, Nathalie Miebach demonstrates how artists depict and transform content from science. In making information and relationships among bits of information visible, tactile, tangible, and aesthetic, she draws her audience in and opens them up to thinking about critical issues. For example, in *Changing Waters* (see Figure 3.5), she focuses on the effects of global warming on weather patterns. On the level of *methods*, Miebach reveals how artists use structures from nature to organize their artwork. She also shows how mapping—a method and a *form* taken from the sciences and social sciences—can be used as a device for making meaning in art. In her mapping, Miebach references symbolism and *forms* in scientific illustration (weather maps). Each element of the sculptures and musical notations stands for some element in the weather. She also incorporates standard symbols from weather maps, connecting her work closely to scientific imagery. The beauty of Miebach's work reminds us of how visually engaging many scientific formats, such as maps, charts, and graphs, can be. Certainly, Miebach taps into the aesthetics of science, particularly the conjunction of aesthetic beauty with clarity and conciseness in transmitting meaning. In this way, she indirectly addresses the *purposes* of scientific formats: to record, to inform, and to propel further understanding.

Creative Strategies. Miebach uses the creative strategy of *reformatting*; she takes the format of weather maps in two directions; she maps weather information in the form of musical notations, thus transforming it into music, and she also makes information three-dimensional, shaping it into installations composed of woven basket–like forms.

Biology and History: Interconnections

What happens to us physically and mentally when we experience a great personal loss? What mechanisms do we use to help us cope? These are questions Nene Humphrey raises in her works *Circling the Center* (2012) and *Community Braiding* (2010), Figures 3.8 and 3.9. Humphrey is a multimedia artist with an abiding interest in the physiology of the brain. As a resident artist at Joseph LeDoux's neuroscience laboratory at New York University, she explores, alongside a team of neuroscientists, the amygdala, the seat of emotions in the brain. Here she peers through a high-powered microscope to draw very detailed renderings of the millions of intertwining neurons that make up this part of the body.

While she uses the tools and methods of neuroscientists, Humphrey approaches her research as an artist; she explores human experience, in particular how bodily structures respond to and affect human feelings and behavior. The

Figure 3.8. Nene Humphrey, *Circling the Center*, 2012.

Image courtesy of the artist and Lesley Heller Workspace, New York City.

Figure 3.9. Nene Humphrey, *Community Braiding*, 2010.

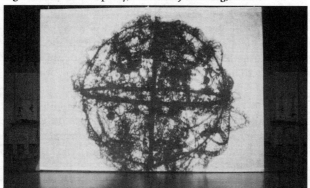

Image courtesy of the artist and Lesley Heller Workspace, New York City.

connections she draws in *Circling the Center* are between the neurological webs in the part of the brain that deals with sorrow and the intricate webbed braids mourners plaited in Victorian England to help them cope with their grief. The physical resemblance between the two webs immediately ties them together. Humphrey's work, however, makes deeper, metaphorical connections between the electrical impulses that ignite the neurons in the amygdala and the spirit that ignites a sense of community among braiding mourners. To convey this connection, performers make braids while animated images of magnetic resonance imaging (MRI) images, electronic circuitry, and Victorian mourning braids play on a screen, and tapes of serenading lab rats, ticking metronomes, and chanted braiding instructions permeate the air. With this weaving of sound, movement, and imagery, the work becomes a meditation on patterns—patterns in our bodies and patterns in our emotional and social lives.

This work is also a meditation on survival. Because the amygdala processes emotions such as grief and fear, it enables us to survive. The same is true of the personal and cultural rituals we perform around loss and grief. By integrating the physiological with the cultural, Humphrey makes these poetic connections, which are the hallmark of art (Sleigh, 2013).

Integration (Purpose, Knowledge, Methods, and Forms). Because she is so intimately involved with scientific research and knowledge, Humphrey's work alludes to the *purpose* of science: to find and explain physical phenomena. More importantly, her work exemplifies the core purpose of art: to find meaning in the knowledge we gather from science. Regarding *knowledge*, Humphrey plays with the knowledge of neuroscience and cultural history and, in so doing, generates knowledge about how humans function physically, emotionally, and socially. Regarding *methods*, in the first stages of her work, Humphrey mimics the methods of neuroscience and history, using tools from both (microscopes and primary historical sources) and doing copious research in both realms. In the greater part of her process, however, Humphrey's methods are purely those of art: weaving, braiding, performance, video, and sound. In regard to *forms*, Humphrey combines the imagery of neuroscience (MRIs) and the sounds of the lab with historical forms such as mourning braids.

Creative Strategies. Humphrey *mimics* researchers in neuroscience and history, using their methods and tools. She also *juxtaposes* scientific imagery with art imagery to connect scientific concepts with cultural concepts. Furthermore, she makes an *analogy* by comparing the electrical currents in the brain to the interpersonal currents that animate a social group.

REFERENCES

Aicken, F. (1991). *The nature of science.* Portsmouth, NH: Heinemann.
Baggott, J. (2012). *Higgs: The invention and discovery of the God particle.* Oxford, England: Oxford University Press.
Ben-Ari, M. (2005). *Just a theory: Exploring the nature of science.* Amherst, NY: Prometheus Books.
Beveridge, W. (1950/2004). *The art of scientific investigation.* New York, NY: Norton.
Bohm, D. (1998). *On creativity.* New York, NY: Routledge.
Cropley, A. (1992). *More ways than one: Fostering creativity in the classroom.* Norwood, NJ: Ablex.
Derry, G. (1999). *What science is and how it works.* Princeton, NJ: Princeton University Press.

Dyson, F. (2006). *Scientist as rebel.* New York, NY: New York Review Books.

Ede, S. (2005). *Art and science.* London, England: Tauris.

Fleener, M. J. (2005). Chaos, complexity, curriculum and culture: Setting up the conversation. In W. Doll, M. J. Fleener, D. Trueit, & J. Julien (Eds.), *Chaos, complexity, curriculum and culture* (pp. 1–17). New York, NY: Lang.

Gauch, H. (2012). *Scientific method in brief.* Cambridge, England: Cambridge University Press.

Gimbel, S. (Ed.). (2011). *Exploring the scientific method: A new approach to teaching and learning philosophy of science.* Chicago, IL: University of Chicago.

Gould, S. J. (1989). *Wonderful life: The Burgess Shale and the nature of history.* New York, NY: Norton.

Greene, B. (2003). *The elegant universe: Superstrings, hidden dimensions and the quest for the ultimate theory.* New York, NY: Norton.

Hazen, R., & Trefil, J. (2009). *Science matters: Achieving scientific literacy.* New York, NY: Random House.

Ingram, D., & Sykes, M. (2005). *An introduction to scientifically based research.* Washington, DC: National Assembly of State Arts Agencies.

Kirst, W., & Dickmeyer, U. (1973). *Kreativitatstraining.* Reinbek bei Hamburg, Germany: Rowohlt.

Lightman, A. (2006). *A sense of the mysterious: Science and the human spirit.* New York, NY: Random House.

Necka, E. (1986). On the nature of creative talent. In A. J. Cropley, K. K. Urban, H. Wagner, & W. H. Wieczerkowski (Eds.), *Giftedness: A continuing worldwide challenge* (pp. 131–140). New York, NY: Trillium.

Newton, R. (2012). *Why science? To know, to understand and to rely on results.* Singapore: World Scientific.

Next generation science standards. (2013). Retrieved from www.nextgenscience.org/next-generation-science-standards

Paul, R., & Elder, L. (2008). *The thinker's guide for students and faculty to scientific thinking.* Dillon Beach, CA: The Foundation for Critical Thinking.

Perkins, D. (1998). What is understanding? In M. S. Wiske (Ed.), *Teaching for understanding: Linking research to practice* (pp. 39–57). San Francisco, CA: Jossey-Bass.

Ricoeur, P. (1991). The function of fiction in shaping reality. In M. Valdes (Ed.), *A Ricoeur reader: Reflection and imagination* (pp. 117–136). Toronto, Ontario, Canada: University of Toronto Press.

Sleigh, T. (2013). Interview with Nene Humphrey. Retrieved from www.lesleyheller.com

Sullivan, G. (2010). *Art practice as research: Inquiry in the visual arts.* Los Angeles, CA: Sage.

Youngs, A. (2004). *Interterrestrial Soundings.* Retrieved from art.osu.edu/gallery-images

Youngs, A. (2005). *Holodeck for House Crickets.* Retrieved from hypernatural.com

4

The Social Sciences
Knowing Ourselves and Others

Julia Marshall

Social scientists are interested in people. Their concerns connect directly to the lives of students, and they probe the conundrums that befuddle them. What is unique about me? How do my culture, family, and peers influence my identity? How am I different from and/or similar to other people? Where do I fit in? Young people also wonder about the social world. How does society work? Who's got the power and why? What are the rules? Why are there rules? Do they ever change? How do I change them?

Social scientists believe that for us to answer these questions we must understand the mechanisms of the social world and also link the personal to the social. Sociologist C. Wright Mills (1959) coined the term "sociological imagination" to describe that ability to see how individual experience is shaped by social context. The social sciences foster this imagination; they not only develop the knowledge but also provide the structures and methods for coming to understand ourselves and others.

Contemporary art mines the same territory; it too probes and illuminates the social experience. Art also has a close but prickly relationship with the social sciences. While it benefits from its wisdom and has been known to pilfer its practices, art also critiques and parodies its mindsets and methods. Indeed, a crop of new forms of public, socially engaged art has emerged in the past 40 years that does these things. These new art forms marry the imagination of the artist with the sociological imagination, providing models of teaching and learning about the social world and social issues, and for performing social activism. As worthwhile as these art forms are, their practice is much richer with a foundation, an understanding, of the sciences that explain and conceptualize the areas these genres of art address. In this chapter, we provide the building blocks of that foundation, an account of what the social sciences contribute to our understanding of ourselves and how that understanding is applied in the world of contemporary art.

WHAT ARE SOCIOLOGY AND ANTHROPOLOGY?

The social sciences encompass an array of disciplines that study social life and the various ways humans interact and organize themselves. Among others, these disciplines include economics, archeology, material culture studies, visual culture studies, women's studies, media studies, ecology, psychology, political science, and cultural geography. These disciplines come under two overarching social science disciplines: sociology and social/cultural anthropology.

Sociology and cultural anthropology are fraternal twins; they are closely related but far from identical. While they share the same concerns, sociology studies social phenomena in large industrial societies while anthropology traditionally examines social life in small societies and focuses on multiple varieties of culture. For Westerners, sociology has historically been the science of "us," an examination of European/American society. Anthropology, on the other hand, was the study of the "other," or cultures outside the European/American realm. Today, however, as anthropology probes more and more into cultural pockets in large industrial societies, the two disciplines find themselves exploring similar territory (Monaghan & Just, 2000; Murphy, 1989). The two disciplines, however, differ in flavor. Sociology, although it boasts a current movement toward humanism, tends to be more scientific or positivist. Anthropology, for its part, acknowledges subjectivity in interpretation and borders on the humanities (Murphy, 1989).

As siblings, the two disciplines grew up at the same time; they first emerged in the early to mid-19th century with the drive to make social inquiry more structured, systematized, and scientific. Before this time, amateur enthusiasts explored social phenomena in their own rather unscientific ways. This is particularly true in anthropology where explorers, adventurers, and colonial bureaucrats kept accounts of their encounters in far-off places. With the establishment of sociology and anthropology as *sciences*, professionals replaced amateur enthusiasts, inquiry became more standardized, and theories were developed to explain evidence (Kendall, 2012; Monaghan & Just, 2000).

As *sciences*, sociology and anthropology struggle with the assumptions and expectations the term *science* implies. They require internally consistent theories based on evidence, inductive reasoning, and logic, as well as constant scrutiny of assumptions, methods, and conclusions. As sciences of human behavior, however, they must contend with a highly complex and variable subject that is less easily explained than phenomena in nature. That is to say, while all knowledge in the natural sciences is contingent and open to change, the knowledge of the social sciences is even more so. This means that generalizations in the social sciences are possible, but they are never ironclad, complete, or comprehensive (Bruce, 1999).

The two disciplines also grapple with checkered pasts. Sociology, with its initial stress on structure and stability, has been criticized for its support of the status quo and for Social Darwinism, which rationalized inequity and discrimination, while anthropology was early on associated with colonization and the subjugation of indigenous peoples by Western powers. As they evolved, however, the two disciplines have critiqued and repudiated erroneous theories of the past and moved on (Kendall, 2012; Kottack, 2011; Monaghan & Just, 2000).

Purpose of the Social Sciences

The purpose of the social sciences is to study human societies and social interactions to develop theories of how group life shapes human behavior and,
in turn, how individuals affect social life. Their goal is to uncover the hidden
social causes and structures behind collective life and social behavior and to
understand how individuals internalize cultural and social norms (Bruce, 1999).
Furthermore, today's social scientists see society and cultures as systems that
underlie all aspects of human life from individual consciousness and identity
to economics and commerce. Their purpose, therefore, is to understand those
systems (Murphy, 1989).

     For its part, sociology strives to shed light on particular social phenomena,
small slivers of behavior, in a large society (Murphy, 1989). In taking a microscope to social behavior or thinking that is familiar, "normal," or unconscious
and in digging deeply into the motivations and influences behind it, sociologists
enable us to see social phenomena more clearly and to understand it more thoroughly (Bruce, 1999). Anthropology also looks at social behavior and the factors
that cause it yet takes a different tack. It seeks to understand the totality of life
in a small society or group. The goal behind anthropology's holistic focus on
small societies is to reveal how cultural systems work, to discover the internal
logic of a culture (Monaghan & Just, 2000). Anthropology also investigates a
wide variety of societies and cultures. In doing so, it seeks to expose the common threads that connect us all to foster understanding of ourselves through the
in-depth, holistic understanding of others (Murphy, 1989). Consequently, both
social sciences share the overarching purpose of understanding ourselves—
sociology through making the familiar "strange," and anthropology by making
the "strange" familiar.

Methods of the Social Sciences

     Sociology. Sociologists employ four primary methods in conducting their
research. The first and most common method is the survey. Surveys entail interviews and questionnaires, often standardized to generate uniform and repli-
cable findings. Surveys are particularly useful in describing the characteristics of
large populations. Sociology's second method is analysis of existing data. Social
researchers often examine and analyze data from public records, official reports,
and raw information assembled by other researchers. A third method is experimentation, designed situations in which a researcher studies the impact of certain
variables on subjects' attitudes and behaviors. Experiments in sociology are used
to demonstrate cause-and-effect relationships. They are, however, rare and often
impractical due to logistics and ethical concerns (Bruce, 1999). All three research
methods are used in *quantitative* research, which produces statistical data through
analysis of numbers.

Sociologists also practice *qualitative* research, which explicates findings through narratives rather than representing it in numbers (Kendall, 2012). For qualitative research, sociologists employ the three methods described above and a fourth method, field research, which entails studying social life in its natural setting. This more informal research method can involve *participant observation*, in which a researcher engages in the activity under investigation, and *ethnography*, in which a researcher produces written descriptions of social situations, behavior, and thinking. Whether quantitative or qualitative, sociologists aim to perform research that is as objective, systematic, valid, and reliable as possible (Kendall, 2012). Although this fundamental orientation remains generally unchallenged and sociology stays more closely tied than anthropology to the natural science model, contemporary sociologists such as Peter Berger (1963) promote a more humanistic approach in sociology. This has resulted in an increase in qualitative social research with an anthropological and activist bent and the introduction of alternative experimental strategies including art-based research in education and psychology (Cahnmann-Taylor, 2008).

Anthropology. While anthropological research is predominantly qualitative, it also employs some quantitative methods, such as surveys. Although anthropology uses surveys and archival research like sociology, it differs from sociology in its concentration on fieldwork and ethnography (Monaghan & Just, 2000). Ethnographies in anthropology are personal accounts that often emerge from a sustained and intimate relationship between the ethnographer and those he or she is studying. These accounts are characterized by more active or engaged participant observation than we find in sociology with interviews that resemble free-form conversations more than formal, structured sociological interviews. Sustained and informal encounters have two benefits. First, they allow revealing moments to surface serendipitously. In anthropology, insights often come out of chance occurrences; therefore, an anthropologist's presence over time and his or her consistent attentiveness, flexibility, and ability to improvise are critical (Monaghan & Just, 2000). Second, sustained encounters also enable anthropologists to be fully immersed in a culture, to go deeply into cultural practices, and to be holistic and systemic in their thinking (Murphy, 1989).

As a core practice in anthropology, engaged ethnography, particularly the art of vivid portrayals and personal journaling, drives the discipline closer to literature. Certainly, many anthropologists since the time of Malinowski (1910s to 1930s) and Meade (1920s to 1940s) have embellished their ethnographies with colorful details and accounts of their personal experiences and responses to what they observed. Here ethnography borders on autobiography. Geertz calls this literary method "thick description" (Geertz, 1973). Since Geertz and his like (Clifford and Marcus), anthropology has taken an "interpretive turn," moving away from a scientific emphasis toward a more humanistic, literary approach (Monaghan & Just, 2000).

Cultural anthropology also remains a science, be it a "soft" science. As such, it constructs theories based on evidence. Its primary method of theory construction is *cross-cultural comparison*. Through comparing cultures, anthropologists find common patterns and identify differences in how these patterns play out in cultural practices (Monaghan & Just, 2000).

While mainstream anthropology relies on writing as a primary method in ethnography, anthropologists also engage in visual methods. Documentary film, video, and still photographs are popular means for capturing the details of life and discerning patterns in social behavior.

Forms of the Social Sciences

Forms in a discipline have two overlapping functions: They are the ways knowledge is represented, and they are tools for conceptualization and understanding. The forms in the social sciences generally correspond to their methods, and they reflect the respective viewpoints and goals of each branch. For example, sociology, which aims for a general take on a particular social phenomenon and often uses statistics, favors verbal analysis and theoretical writing along with graphs and charts that make statistics and ideas visible and comprehensible.

In contrast, anthropologists represent knowledge through comprehensive ethnographies and collections of imagery and objects. Both enable the ethnographer to go deeply into a culture and make cross-cultural comparisons among cultures. Collections, in particular, allow anthropologists to investigate visual symbol systems to unearth the meanings behind artifacts and also to construct a fuller picture of how these symbolic artifacts fit together in a cultural system.

A primary form or tool for research and development of ethnographies is the field study book. These books are a combination of notebook, sketchbook, and diary that mix visual data (photographs and sketches) with verbal descriptions, analysis, and personal reflections. Documentary films, video, and still photographs are also important forms of representation in anthropology. Not only are these forms important to mainstream anthropology with its verbal explanations but they also stand alone in a subset of the domain: *visual anthropology* (Schneider & Wright, 2010).

Knowledge of the Social Sciences

Knowledge in a discipline includes topics or information and the concepts that connect or explain them. The knowledge of the social sciences encompasses the entire human world and all of social experience. It is far too vast to cover here. We will, however, attempt to describe some of the more significant topics and concepts the two branches cover and point out information and ideas that are specific to each discipline.

Today, both anthropology and sociology focus on life in our modern global-ized world. In contrast to history, the study of the past, the social sciences focus primarily on the present (except for historical research in anthropology and ar-cheology). The subjects sociology addresses fall under the following themes: (1) culture, socialization, social structure, and social interaction; (2) social groups and formal organizations, deviance, and social control; (3) social inequality through social stratification, social class, race and ethnicity, gender, and age; (4) social in-stitutions that govern politics, the economy, marriage and family, education, and religion; and (5) social change in population and urbanization, technology, social movements, the environment, and human sexuality (Henslin, 2007). For its part, anthropology focuses on relationship structures such as kinship, lineage and clan, class, community, and nation-state, and it examines how concepts of ethnicity, race, social class, and nationalism build intragroup solidarity and create inter-group conflict (Monaghan & Just, 2000).

Together, the social sciences study humankind with the understanding that human beings are complex beings whose behavior and lives are governed by multiple personal, environmental, cultural, and social factors. Their knowledge, therefore, is primarily contingent, context-based, and always in flux. This is not to imply that the social sciences do not attempt to distill complex information down to general theories or comparisons. They do develop and have fundamental enduring concepts that support their evolving theories. The following is a short list of those key concepts.

Culture. One of anthropology's greatest contributions to our understanding of ourselves and others is its expansive definition of culture. Culture is all things human. It is the accumulation of all knowledge, beliefs, language, values, laws, cus-toms, art forms, material objects, and any other capabilities and habits acquired by humans over time as members of a society (Kendall, 2012; Monaghan & Just, 2000; Murphy, 1989). Moreover, culture is an integrated system; it is a web of meanings, values, and standards of conduct in which all strands or elements affect each other (Murphy, 1989).

Culture is not innate; it must be learned. Humans are socialized into a culture (or *enculturated*), and culture is passed from one generation to another or be-tween one person and another (Kendall, 2012). Culture also distinguishes humans from animals. Incapable of culture, animals are driven by instinct and governed by nature. Humans, on the other hand, have devised culture to provide the order required to constrain and direct behavior. This enables humans to rise above bi-ology (Bruce, 1999).

Social/Cultural Construction of Reality. Social scientists believe that culture goes far deeper than morals and models of behavior; it shapes the way we think and conceptualize the world and provides the symbols to communicate those conceptions. They also understand culture to be a human construct, an invention that, although it may have some relationship to outside reality, essentially exists in the human mind. Indeed, social scientists see society itself as a product of our collective mind (Cooley, 1902). Berger's theory of the *social construction of reality* takes this notion a step further, explaining reality as *intersubjective*. This means that something is deemed real or true when a majority of people agrees that it is (Berger & Luckmann, 1966). This collective agreement about reality is imbedded and manifested in culture. Consequently, culture determines reality, and it is the lens through which a society or social group, and the individual who lives within it, sees the world. We internalize culture, the lens, so thoroughly that it shapes our perceptions and personalities—our psychology (Bruce, 1999).

To share and build our collective reality, we need to communicate, and culture provides the means for doing this. These means of communication are symbolic. They include customary images such as religious or political symbols, and they include cultural practices such as rites and rituals; etiquette and customs; language; and cultural expressions like art, drama, and music (Geertz, 1973).

Cultural Relativism. If culture is a human construct based solely on a socially agreed upon concept of reality, it follows that no culture is closer to reality or truth than another. This is the central tenet of *cultural relativism*, a critical concept that gained acceptance in anthropology through the work of Franz Boas (1922, 1928). Cultural relativism suggests that cultures should not be judged in relationship to one another and that a behavior or belief must be understood within its own cultural context. This means that the values and beliefs of one culture, particularly that of the researcher, cannot be the basis of judgments about behavior in another culture, the one he or she studies. It also implies that there is no hierarchy of cultures; one culture is not the yardstick for other cultures or higher on a cultural scale (Monaghan & Just, 2000; Murphy, 1989).

Identity. The nature of individual identity is also a core theme in the social sciences because identity is understood to be socially constructed. The *sociopsychological* theory suggests that each individual's mind is the product of social interaction and relationships. One's identity, which is closely linked to mind, is also developed in this way. This means that our sense of who we are comes out of how others see us. Cooley (1902) called this phenomenon the "Looking Glass Self." It follows that, since each person has various relationships and interactions with multiple people, his or her identity is composed of a set of social identities, each developed in reaction to how others see him or her in social situations or relationships (Monaghan & Just, 2000). *Symbolic interactionist theory* (Goffman, 1959) builds on this concept, explaining identity and social systems in terms of drama. According to Goffman's theory, societies are collections of interconnected roles guided by stage directions in which each member plays a part and acts according to a script. The metaphor of drama or playacting implies that society establishes conventional roles and specifies how people behave as they enact them. There is little freedom to improvise. It also suggests that each individual's identity is developed as he or she acts out a role.

Change. Change is another motif in current social sciences; everything social scientists study changes over time. Therefore, they keep an eye out for new social and cultural developments and new twists on established ideas, and they study the nature of change itself. The social sciences have also been subject to change. Early on, many social scientists embraced Durkheim's notion that societies are self-perpetuating and static, and, for that reason, resistant to change. If change occurred, it was slow, and its evolution was always toward more complexity, with social roles becoming more diversified and based on work and class rather than on kinship and clan (Murphy, 1989). Social upheaval, rapid urbanization, industrialization, and advancement of technology, however, proved that societies, although resistant to change, could change relatively quickly. As life began to change fast, social theorists became interested in change itself. For example, theorists such as Mills, Weber, and Marx studied social evolution and saw it as the result of conflict over resources and power, and groups like social classes as the instigators of conflict and change (Kendall, 2012).

Today, sociologists and anthropologists not only understand the role of the group in upsetting the social applecart, they also acknowledge the influence of the individual. While they recognize the entrenched economic and social structures that inhibit extensive social transformation, they emphasize the malleability and dynamism of societies and the capacity of individuals to instigate change (Monaghan & Just, 2000). They believe that while a society's capacity to evolve and the ability of the individual to contribute to it vary from one system to another, every society transforms over time and each individual can contribute in a limited way to that evolution (Bruce, 1999).

Cultures also transform over time, and this process is incremental. That is because cultural change takes place within cultural constraints and parameters (Monaghan & Just, 2000). Indeed, culture, like society, is coercive; it sets the rules, terms, and limits of thought and behavior. There is a loophole, however. Although we are born into a culture and are limited by its forms and systems, each generation alters and shapes the culture it inherited, and individuals often provide the inspiration and leadership in this effort.

Anthropologists stress the living nature of culture, not only in the modern industrial world but also in indigenous societies. Highlighting the living nature of culture, many anthropologists have come to see it in terms of what Lévi-Strauss calls *bricolage*, as an organic entity that is perpetually revised through discarding and reinstating elements in ever-changing combinations (Monaghan & Just, 2000).

Cultural change, while it may come about through pressures and innovations by individuals or groups within the culture, most often is a result of *cultural diffusion* and *acculturation*, which are caused by outside influences. Murphy (1989) defines diffusion as the spread of cultural practices, beliefs, and expressions from one society to another. Diffusion occurs through contact between cultures. Acculturation is the learning of new ideas and practices and the psychological and cultural change that come with diffusion.

   Globalization. Cultural diffusion and acculturation are the primary processes behind globalization. While they have propelled social cultural change since human groups first encountered each other thousands of years ago, these processes are highly accelerated today (Pieterse, 2004). Globalization describes the dynamics of an emerging worldwide culture that is primarily North American in origin, flavor, and content (Berger & Huntington, 2003). As today's greatest expression of change, and the social phenomenon that is revolutionizing social, cultural, and economic life around the world, globalization is a primary preoccupation of the social sciences.

   Anthropologists have identified the primary mechanism behind globalization: *complex connectivity*, the situation brought about by a multiplicity of networks that enables massive flows of information and cultural exchange, and transformation (Tomlinson, 1999). They have also recognized different effects of globalization such as *glocalization* (local adaptations of global cultural forms) (Berger & Huntington, 2003) and *hybridity* (new mixed cultural forms) (Pieterse, 2004). Indeed, anthropologists understand all cultures to be hybrids (Murphy, 1989).

   Globalization highlights and amplifies the integrated nature of social life and culture, bringing us back to a central premise of the social sciences: Societies and cultures are *integrated systems* (Murphy, 1989). Globalization has produced an integrated transnational cultural, social, and economic system with smaller systems such as nation-states, local communities, families, and affinity groups nested within it. This has resulted in a new field of study in the social sciences, one that examines the dynamics of those systems in relationship to each other and their environments: *social ecology* (Murphy, 1989).

FUNDAMENTALS OF THE SOCIAL SCIENCES
AND INTEGRATION WITH ART

As you think about substantive multidimensional art-centered integrated learning and social studies, consider these fundamental ideas about the disciplines discussed in this chapter:

   1. Studying social structures and systems
   2. Seeking underlying behavioral patterns
   3. Generalizing from the specific
   4. Examining specific social phenomena across a large population

5. Exploring how social life shapes an individual and how individuals shape social situations
6. Seeking motives and reasons behind phenomena and behavior
7. Examining social constructs such as race, ethnicity, class, and community
8. Exploring how cultures and societies change
9. Studying culture and the ways it shapes our lives
10. Examining and contrasting culture in all its variety
11. Finding commonality among cultural practices
12. Engaging in holistic thinking about cultures and societies
13. Examining objects as evidence of social and cultural values and practices
14. Recounting experiences and impressions
15. Thinking empathetically

ART AND THE SOCIOLOGICAL IMAGINATION

Art intersects with the social sciences in many critical ways, and for this reason, we dedicate a long section to this topic. The most obvious connection between art and the social sciences is that art is a subject of the social sciences, particularly anthropology (Schneider & Wright, 2006). Social scientists recognize artworks as artifacts or evidence of cultural life, values, and worldviews. Art is also a material embodiment of symbols and systems of meaning. In other words, art not only represents cultural perspectives and concerns but it also embodies how a cultural group constructs meaning and communicates it symbolically (Geertz, 1973). Art, therefore, provides two kinds of information about a culture: "the what" or "content" of a culture and "the how" of a culture, the ways that content is presented. Art is, therefore, a particularly rich component of material culture (Prown, 2001), one of many kinds of visual expression investigated in *visual culture studies.*

While the social sciences help us to understand the social/cultural systems that shape art, they also influence art. Artists often look to social theorists for lenses on social phenomena they observe. Indeed, the art of an age is often an expression of the social theories in vogue at the time. We see this in the way many contemporary artists claim the influence of phenomenology and postmodernist theory, placing emphasis on experience and consciousness of that experience (phenomenology) and on varieties of experience (postmodernism).

The intersection of art and the social sciences also occurs in art's critique of the social sciences. Art criticizes sociology and anthropology to help us understand their downsides and what they reveal about Western culture. Its targets include sociology's scientific orientation, which, in seeking broad-based norms, can boil artistic taste and other social phenomena down to the most banal level (see Komar and Melamid below), and anthropology's tendency to "exoticize," aestheticize, pigeonhole, and frame non-European/American cultures in Western terms (see Michael Arcega below).

Although it can be critical of them, art shares purposes with the social sciences. For instance, artists often try to build understanding of human social life. To do this, they, like sociologists, defamiliarize the everyday, provoking reflection on social attitudes, practices, and relationships that are hidden or unconscious. Socially engaged artists also investigate social problems and what causes them and make social or political commentary, exposing social inequities and biases. Here building understanding coincides with "troubling" or troublemaking.

Art also works to make meaning of social phenomena. To make meaning is to draw connections, to put something in context, and to establish its relevance and significance. Art does this when it places things that seem abstract or disconnected from human experience into human terms. Like social scientists, artists locate these abstractions in their sociocultural context and point out their impact on individuals, societies, and cultures. The work of Chris Jordan, who makes abstract and unimaginable statistics about consumption and waste visible and, therefore, meaningful, is one example (see Chapter 8, "Mathematics").

Art often has purposes beyond those of the social sciences. While the social sciences aim to empower individuals and societies to understand themselves (sociology) and build empathy toward others (anthropology), art can transform understanding and empathy into action. Indeed, since the 1960s, many contemporary artists have seen art as a form of social action. This activism takes many forms that range from provocative events, to quiet personal and small-group performances, to urban renewal projects and street art, to disruptive interventions in civic and corporate environments. Even teaching art has been reframed as a form of social art action.

Variously called participatory, interactive, collaborative, relational, or socially cooperative art, the social activist genre of public art represents a "social turn" in the arts that is deeply influenced by the civil rights and feminist movements of the 1960s and 1970s and the liberatory pedagogy of Paulo Freire (Finkelpearl, 2013). It is art guided by artists in which audiences actively participate and, through participation, learn about ideas and issues of social consequence. This variety of art is particularly relevant to K–12 education because it seamlessly blends art and learning/teaching by taking methods and forms from education. An example of this genre is Futurefarmers' *Shoemaker's Dialogues* (2011) discussed below.

Socially engaged artists also derive inspiration and use methods from researchers in the social sciences. Often entering communities from the outside, they use the skills of anthropologists: listening, watching, and interacting. Like anthropologists, they encounter a community as outsiders and as participant observers. Furthermore, when they work on their own turf, they don the lens of the sociologist/anthropologist, stepping back to put their observations into a broader social framework.

Some artists have overtly taken on the role of ethnographer (Schneider & Wright, 2006, 2010). While this indicates a relatively new preoccupation in art and a new set of art skills, artists have a historical affinity with anthropology with its interest in the exotic, its openness to serendipity and improvisation, and its focus on visual culture and aesthetic forms. This new genre of artist–ethnographer does fieldwork in ways similar to those of an anthropologist, and this fieldwork is often in isolated places with various ethnic groups. An example of this is the work of Cuban American artist José Bedia, which is based on his experiences with Cuban Santeria and also references the Plains Indians, who were the subject of his extensive "field studies" (Schneider & Wright, 2006).

Another intersection between art and anthropology is their mutual use of *appropriation*. Appropriation is taking forms from another culture for one's own purposes (Schneider, 2006). Although appropriation can be seen as problematic, Schneider argues that appropriation is acceptable, even laudable, because it is a creative method for coming to understand a culture. In anthropology, appropriation entails documentation or reenactment of cultural forms; in the arts, it means reinterpreting those forms in one's artwork. A practice in art since the Impressionists first borrowed compositional formats from Japanese prints and Picasso copied African art, appropriation is also a time-honored learning strategy in art education.

Lastly, art and anthropology cross paths in their use of a common tool. Called a field study book in anthropology (and in the natural sciences), in art, this tool is variously identified as a sketchbook or research workbook. We commonly think of these books as places artists draft, render, and doodle, but often in contemporary art, they are much more than that. They are repositories of research—experiments, information, ideas, personal reflections, and insights—and they not only prepare the way for art projects, they also connect them. Schneider and Wright (2006) make the correlation between the research books artists use and the field study books of anthropologists and claim that they are anthropology's most valuable gift to the arts.

ART THAT CONNECTS TO THE SOCIAL SCIENCES

Critiquing Sociology and Popular Taste

Komar and Melamid's artworks often address history, politics, and ideology through a playfully ironic lens. In *People's Choice Project* (1993–), the team turned its iconoclastic eye on taste in art and did a sociological examination of the likes and dislikes of various cultures. Beginning with their original poll of 1,001 randomly chosen adults in the United States, the team conducted equally comprehensive scientific polls in Asia, Africa, and Europe. Before the project was completed, they had surveyed representative opinions of more than 2 billion people. With each poll, the artists analyzed the data about likes and dislikes in color, shape, imagery, scale, style, and composition and translated the data into two contrasting paintings for each country polled—one representing the most wanted and the other representing the least wanted art (Wypijewski, 1997; see Figures 4.1 and 4.2).

Figure 4.1. Vitaly Komar and Alexander Melamid, *America's Most Unwanted*, 1994.

Tempera and oil on canvas, 5 1/2 x 8 1/2 inches. Image courtesy Ronald Feldman Fine Arts, New York / www.feldmangallery.com

Figure 4.2. Vitaly Komar and Alexander Melamid, *America's Most Wanted*, 1994.

Oil and acrylic on canvas, dishwasher size. Photo by D. James Dee, Image courtesy Ronald Feldman Fine Arts, New York / www. feldmangallery.com

Integration (Purpose, Knowledge, Methods, and Forms). Komar and Melamid integrate art and social studies on a *knowledge* level by examining a social phenomenon: aesthetic tastes. They also critique the premise that social science can actually determine or measure anything as complex as social tastes or norms. Their generic paintings from all the cultures they studied suggest that any numerical analysis, no matter how statistically significant the numbers, will generate banal and meaningless insignificant generalizations. They also show that the questions asked by sociologists determine the findings. Here they challenge the *purposes* and the *methods* of sociology. As for integration on the level of *methods*, Komar and Melamid utilize techniques of sociologists such as polling, data collection, and statistical analysis as art-making strategies; they show how artists can play with the methods of a field to expose and critique it. They also use the *forms* of sociology: questionnaires and spreadsheets.

Creative Strategies. Komar and Melamid use the creative strategies of *mimicry* and *enactment*; they take on the persona of social scientists, and they use the methods of the social scientist: polling questionnaires, random sampling, and statistical analysis. The team also *formats*; they diagram the paintings that derive from the data they collected.

A Satirical Look at History and Cultural Lenses

As a keen social observer with a wry sense of humor, Michael Arcega explores cultural collisions, often alluding to ways Western culture has dominated non-Western cultures through creeping globalization—starting with conquest and colonization, continuing with representation of colonized societies through anthropology and museum collections, and culminating in contemporary tourist culture. To cast a critical eye on these subjects, Arcega's work relies on thorough historical research, precise craftsmanship, and iconoclastic humor. Indeed, Arcega is a sharp cultural critic with the sensibilities of a model maker and the mind of a comedian. This rich combination makes for seriously funny and beautiful works such as *El Conquistadork* (2011), a miniature exact replica of a 16th-century galleon constructed out of wood and sheathed in file folders (see Figure 4.3). Arcega launched his replica off the coast of Northern California to commemorate Spanish trade routes that linked North America, Mexico, and his native Philippines. The file folders not only kept the boat afloat but also have a conceptual function: to symbolize the business interests behind colonization (Arcega, 2006).

To call attention to the social construction of normality and the way Western culture has historically determined what is normal and what is not, Arcega resurrected a fictional ethnography by anthropologist Horace Miner titled *Body Ritual Among the Nacirema* (American spelled backwards; Miner, 1956) and made a series of artworks that bounced off Miner's original idea. Miner's casting of 1950s White American society as an esoteric tribe with mysterious and crazy beliefs and

Figure 4.3. Michael Arcega, *El Conquistadork*, 2011.

Image courtesy of the artist.

Figure 4.4. Michael Arcega, *Baby (Medium for Intercultural Navigation)*, 2011–2012.

Image courtesy of the artist.

Figure 4.5. Michael Arcega, *Dance Clubs*, 2008.

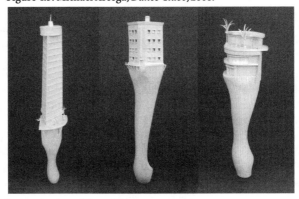

Image courtesy of the artist.

rituals satirized the way Western anthropologists tend to see the cultures they study as exotic and strange while missing the fact that Western practices and beliefs, when seen through the lens of outsiders, are equally as odd.

For his elaboration on Miner's article, Arcega explored current Nacirema culture. For this, he constructed another boat, *Baby* (2011–2012), a hybrid of a Native American kayak and a South Seas islands outrigger (see Figure 4.4). Arcega took *Baby* on a journey along the major waterways that cross the native habitat of the Nacirema, the trail of Lewis and Clark. On his journey, Arcega collected souvenir artifacts (ritual objects and symbolic representations of significant Nacirema sites). In an anthropology museum–style display of Nacirema culture titled *Baby and the Nacirema*, *Baby* and related souvenirs were exhibited alongside a series of artist-invented artifacts and a mobile of piñatas that symbolized cultural icons of the Nacirema. The piñatas included a giant, double-scoop ice-cream cone, the Statue of Liberty, and the Liberty Bell (Luggage Store, 2012).

To address globalization, Arcega updates or "globalizes" tribal artifacts from the South Seas islands. In a series of works for the de Young Museum in San Francisco titled *Homing Pidgin* (2008), Arcega responded to the museum's collection of Oceanic artifacts with works that include a giant hand-carved wooden spork (a utensil often found at McDonald's) and, as seen in Figure 4.5, a series of contemporary dance and spirit clubs, *Dance Clubs* (2008). Essentially wooden table legs with miniature architectural models of dance clubs (places for dance, mating rituals, and celebration) with flashing disco lights and dance music emanating from them, these are ritual objects for a contemporary global youth culture (Arcega, 2008).

Integration (Purpose, Knowledge, Methods, and Forms). It appears that Arcega's *purpose* is to shed light on the long history of Western cultural and economic colonization and on the collision and evolution of cultures that go along with globalization and conquest. The specific *knowledge* he addresses springs from his research into colonial history, anthropology, and the cultural artifacts of the Americas and the Philippines. As for *methods*, Arcega does historical research. As he states, "History tends to keep repeating, so I tend to mine history for content and try to apply it to current events" (Arcega, 2006). For *forms*, he creates modified versions of historical artifacts, architecture, vessels, and tools. In *Baby and the Nacirema*, the form he uses is that of the natural history display.

Creative Strategies. Arcega uses multiple creative strategies to convey his ideas. In *El Conquistadork*, he relies on the association between file folders and business to convey his message about commerce. This is an example of the *metaphor of materials*. In *Baby*, he *synthesizes* a kayak with an outrigger to make a *hybrid* that acts as a *metaphor* for intercultural communication (a way of navigating between cultures). In *Baby and the Nacirema*, he *mimics* the methods of anthropologists. In *Dance Clubs*, Arcega *juxtaposes* contemporary forms with traditional ritual forms.

Globalization: Culture Clash

Cultures once thought to be outside the long reach of globalization and, there-fore, untouched by its influence are no longer so. Globalization has seeped into the far corners of the Earth, bringing with it global popular culture and altering traditional ways of life. This is a theme of Ang Tsherin Sherpa's intricate, sump-tuous paintings. Sherpa was born in Nepal and trained as a traditional painter of Buddhist thangkas. Today, while he remains a thangka painter, he also uses his artistic training and knowledge of Buddhism to focus on contemporary life and culture. In this way, he shows in Figures 4.6 and 4.7 the discrepancy between the spiritual life that, as a young Buddhist, he attempts to sustain and the everyday life he lives as a citizen of the United States and the world (Picard, 2011).

Figures 4.6. Ang Tsherin Sherpa, *Untitled*, 2010.

Image courtesy of the artist and Rossi and Rossi.

Figure 4.7. Ang Tsherin Sherpa, *Derivative*, 2010.

Image courtesy of the artist and Rossi and Rossi.

Integration (Purpose, Knowledge, Methods, and Forms). The connection between Sherpa's work and the social sciences lies in the way he so clearly expresses a social/cultural phenomenon. Although his iconography is specifically Nepalese and Buddhist, his subject is pretty much universal; the clash he addresses is one many natives of traditional cultures face. Regarding *purpose,* Sherpa attests that his intention is to explore contemporary concerns and situations. The *knowledge* he draws on is his understanding of Buddhist spirituality and how the Buddhist belief system is embodied in its iconography. He couples this with his knowledge of contemporary global popular culture and its symbols. His *method* is to mix and match these images. The original images and the hybrid imagery he creates from them are the *forms* that convey his message.

Creative Strategies. Sherpa's creative strategies are *juxtaposition* and *layering*; he places the icons of one world in or next to the imagery of another and he superimposes them. The result is the viewer gets a little shock; these juxtapositions and layerings are surprising, ironic, and often quite funny. In reflection, they make a lot of sense; cultural life in our global world is full of ironic juxtapositions. In using this iconography, Sherpa takes full advantage of their inherent meaning; he constructs *analogies.* He also reveals hidden relationships. This is particularly true in *Derivative* (2009; Figure 4.7) where he superimposes a graph from a stock exchange upon the silhouette of the Buddha. The allusion to meditation and brain waves is hard to miss.

Socially Cooperative Art and Social Change

Rick Lowe is a "social practice" or a "socially cooperative" artist—an artist who understands his artwork as creative engagement with and intervention in the "real world." As discussed above, socially engaged art can mean many things. In Lowe's case, socially engaged art means an artist-initiated, "socially cooperative" urban redevelopment project that revitalized a neighborhood.

A resident of Houston, Lowe wanted to do something to enhance the lives of African Americans in his city. He discovered a block and a half of shotgun houses that were scheduled for demolition and then bought and refurbished them with the help of hundreds of volunteers from the surrounding community. Today, the original 22 houses have expanded to 40, and these buildings house artists' exhibition and residency spaces, office spaces, and low-income residential and commercial spaces (Thompson, 2012). In restoring the architecture and history of the community, and providing a site for art-centered dialogues and investigations into social issues, the project has brought the neighborhood back to life and become a national model for socially engaged art (see Figure 4.8).

What makes projects such as this art? This question has beleaguered and delighted social practice public artists for the past 30 years. While they have struggled for recognition in the art world, social practice artists have also happily taken art out of the art world and challenged every tenet of conventional art. Their works are often staged in public spaces far from museums and galleries, and these works seldom entail conventional art techniques and materials or produce tangible objects or images beyond simple documentation. To the artists and their public, however, this is art. The art lies in a work's ideas, the social dialogue and dynamics it promotes, and the performance of the "piece." It also resides in the learning and in the new perspectives and understandings that the work generates. In the case of *Project Row Houses*, however, some tangible aesthetic products, such as architecture and parks, exist. Also, *Project Row Houses* is connected to cultural symbols and art. Lowe was inspired by Houston artist John Biggers, whose iconic painting *Shotgun, Third Ward #1* (1966) portrays these small, narrow buildings as a symbol of African American life and heritage (see Figure 4.9). The real and functional shotgun houses of *Project Row Houses* are a living monument to African American resiliency and pride and a testament to Biggers's belief that art can have a positive impact on the world.

Integration (Purpose, Knowledge, Methods, and Forms). In addressing social issues head-on, intervening in social life, and engaging actively with communities, social practice art, such as *Project Row Houses*, seamlessly integrates with social studies in all four dimensions: purpose, knowledge, methods, and forms. In regard to *purpose*, Lowe shares with cultural historians and anthropologists the goal of deep understanding of a community and its social/cultural life. However, Lowe's ultimate purpose, toward which he applies this understanding, is to make positive social change through revitalizing and celebrating African American history and culture. The *knowledge* embedded in Lowe's work is historical (African American history) and cultural (the meaning of shotgun houses and the tangible effect refurbishment, community engagement, and the arts can have on a community). The *methods* Lowe used in developing the project are those of a city planner, architect, community organizer, historian, fundraiser, and visionary. Like many socially engaged artists, Lowe also acted as an ethnographer, a participant–observer, who studied his community while facilitating its transformation. In many ways, this was participatory research, inquiry instigated by community needs, conceived through community dialogue, and carried out by community members that results in communal self-awareness and action (Hacker, 2013). As for *forms*, while houses and parks constitute the visible form of the work, the most salient forms of *Project Row Houses* are invisible: the ongoing organization, the education programs, and opportunities provided to artists and the surrounding community.

Creative Strategies. Envisioning a revitalized neighborhood required *projection*: taking what exists, understanding its meaning and potential, and imaging what it could be. Making this vision a reality required all the creative skills and strategies required for complex problem solving.

Figure 4.8. Rick Lowe, *Project Row Houses*, 1993–present.

Photo by Eric Hester. Image courtesy of Project Row Houses.

Figure 4.9. John Biggers, *Shotgun, Third Ward #1*, 1966.

Image courtesy the John Biggers Estate.

Art as Pedagogy

Amy Franceschini is an artist/designer who, in 1995, founded Futurefarmers, a group of artists, designers, researchers, farmers, scientists, engineers, and illustrators who share a common interest in creating artwork that challenges current social, political, and economic systems (Futurefarmers, 2013). For this, the collective constructs works that are particularly interdisciplinary and integrative. In regard to interdisciplinarity, Futurefarmer works combine genres associated with the arts, such as performance and highly designed objects and installations, with related nonart activities, such as gardening and cooking. They also push the conventional boundaries of interdisciplinarity by inviting public dialogue and engagement through publications, dialogue on the Internet, lectures, forums, workshops, and events. In regard to integration, what makes Futurefarmers so integrative is the seamless way the collective pools their knowledge, skills, and resources with the expertise of outside practitioners to explore and play with critical issues that transcend disciplinary boundaries.

Shoemaker's Dialogues (2011) is one example of many Futurefarmer projects that hit all the bases. Taking place in the rotunda of the Guggenheim Museum in New York City, *Shoemaker's Dialogues* (as seen in Figure 4.10) brought Futurefarmers' down-to-earth, eclectic, and activist approach and aesthetic into a high art context. The center of the piece was a highly designed contemporary interpretation of Simon the ancient Greek shoemaker's workshop. Simon's atelier was allegedly the site of many of Socrates's dialogues; it was the place where the public could engage the philosopher and social provocateur to learn about the pressing issues of the day though questioning and dialogue. Following in the footsteps of Socrates, Futurefarmers transformed this spot in the museum into a public forum or classroom. Here they hosted dialogues and workshops with a labor historian, a geographer, and an anthropologist who discussed historical and social concepts related to shoes, feet, and labor. The collective also commissioned writers to create a series of "sermons" on various related topics.

Along with these didactic activities, the group also staged an event in which 22 people wearing shoes with printing blocks on their soles paraded and printed texts on long carpets of paper. Each component of this performance carried meaning. For instance, the printing ink was concocted from soot found in various places in New York City. Gathering that soot required historical research and fieldtrips to sites particularly affected by air pollution. *The Pedestrian Press*, as these printing shoes were called, made several forays into New York City, bringing the experience and the message of the work outside of the museum (Futurefarmers, 2013).

Integration (Purpose, Knowledge, Methods, and Forms). In engaging the *knowledge*, *methods*, and *forms* usually associated with geography, history, philosophy, anthropology, and other fields as foundations for their art, Futurefarmer projects exemplify the ultimate in integration. Furthermore, in blurring the lines between pedagogy and art, they provide us with models for art-centered integrative thinking and learning in the classroom. In particular, they integrate pedagogy into their projects; their works are essentially learning experiences around a critical issue in which teaching strategies, such as Socratic dialogues, lectures, and workshops, are conducted in the context of art. That is to say, these projects use the *methods* and *forms* of education, while they enhance them with the aesthetic and imaginative strategies of art. They also share the *purposes* of education: to inform and raise consciousness of critical issues, and to get people thinking, questioning, and communicating.

Creative Strategies. In *Shoemaker's Dialogues,* Futurefarmers employs many creative strategies, the most prominent being *mimicry* and *enactment* (they become

Figures 4.10, 4.11, 4.12. Amy Franceschini and Futurefarmers,
Shoemaker's Dialogues, 2011.

Images courtesy of the artists.

teachers and use pedogogical strategies; they also mimic the methods of anthropologists) and *layering* (they draw parallels between ancient and contemporary situations, methods, and ideas).

REFERENCES

Berger, P. (1963). *Invitation to sociology: A humanistic perspective.* New York, NY: Random House.

Berger, P., & Huntington, S. (2003). *Many globalizations: Cultural diversity in a contemporary world.* Oxford, England: Oxford University Press.

Berger, P., & Luckmann, T. (1966). *The social construction of reality: A treatise in the sociology of knowledge.* New York, NY: Random House.

Boas, F. (1922). *The mind of primitive man.* New York, NY: MacMillan.

Boas, F. (1928). *The anthropology of modern life.* New York, NY: Norton.

Bruce, S. (1999). *Sociology: A very short introduction.* Oxford, England: Oxford University Press.

Cahnmann-Taylor, M. (2008). Arts-based research: Histories and new directions. In M. Cahnmann-Taylor & R. Siegesmund (Eds.), *Arts-based research in education* (pp. 3–15). New York, NY: Routledge.

Cooley, C. H. (1902). *Human nature and the social order.* New York, NY: Scribner.

Finkelpearl, T. (2013). The art of social cooperation: An American framework. In T. Finkelpearl (Ed.), *What we made: Conversations on art and social cooperation,* (pp. 1-50). Durham, NC: Duke University Press.

Futurefarmers. (2013). *Shoemaker's Dialogues.* (2011). Retrieved from www.futurefarmers.com/#projects/shoemaker

Geertz, C. (1973). *The interpretation of cultures.* New York, NY: Basic Books.

Goffman, E. (1959). *The presentation of self in everyday life:* New York, NY: Anchor.

Hacker, K. (2013). *Community-based participatory research.* Los Angeles, CA: Sage.

Henslin, J. (2007). *Essentials of sociology: A down-to-earth approach.* Boston, MA: Allyn & Bacon.

Kendall, D. (2012). *Sociology in our times: The essentials.* Belmont, CA: Wadsworth.

Kottack, P. (2011). *Cultural anthropology: Appreciating human diversity* (14th ed.). New York, NY: McGraw-Hill.

Luggage Store. (2012). *Baby and the Nacirema.* Retrieved from www.luggagestoregallery.org/2012/09/baby-and-the-nacirema-by-michael-arcega/

Mills, C. W. (1959). *The sociological imagination.* Oxford, England: Oxford University Press.

Miner, H. (1956). Body rituals of the Nacirema. *American Anthropologist, New Series, 58,* 503–507.

Monaghan, J., & Just, P. (2000). *Social and cultural anthropology: A very short introduction.* Oxford, England: Oxford University Press.

Murphy, R. F. (1989). *Cultural and social anthropology: An overture.* Englewood Cliffs, NJ: Prentice Hall.

Picard, C. (2011). *Interview with Ang Tsherin Sherpa.* Retrieved from blog.art21. org//2011/01/12/active-blur-an-interview-with-tsherin-sherpa/4

Pieterse, J. N. (2004). *Globalization and culture: Global mélange.* Lanham, MD: Rowman & Littlefield.

Prown, J. (2001). *Art as evidence: Writings on art and material culture* (pp. 69–95). New Haven, CT: Yale University Press.

Schneider, A. (2006). Appropriations. In A. Schneider & C. Wright (Eds.), *Contemporary art and anthropology* (pp. 29–51). Oxford, England: Berg.

Schneider, A., & Wright, C. (2006). The challenge of practice. In A. Schneider & C. Wright (Eds.), *Contemporary art and anthropology* (pp. 1–27). Oxford, England: Berg.

Schneider, A., & Wright, C. (Eds.). (2010). *Between art and anthropology: Contemporary ethnographic practice.* Oxford, England: Berg.

Thompson, N. (2012). Rick Lowe: Project Row Houses. In N. Thompson (Ed.), *Living as form: Socially engaged art from 1991–2011* (pp. 256–257). Cambridge, MA: MIT Press.

Tomlinson, J. (1999). *Globalization and culture.* Chicago, IL: University of Chicago.

5

History
Making Meaning of the Past

David M. Donahue and Steven D. Drouin

Consider the following to assess the popularity of history. More than 2.5 million people a year visit the Alamo (The Alamo, 2012). Over 4.4 million visited the Vietnam Veterans' Memorial in Washington, DC, in 2009 (National Parks Traveler, 2010). *Titanic* was the first movie to break the billion-dollar mark in worldwide revenues (BBC News, 1998). Tom Brokaw's popular history book *The Greatest Generation* (1998) was a bestseller (Maryles, 2002). Seventy percent of the researchers at Britain's Public Records Office are engaged in genealogical research of their families (Fernández-Armesto, 2002). Viewers are fanatically loyal to *Mad Men* in part because of the show's obsessive attention to period detail from the 1960s.

These figures in the millions and billions point to our interest in the past, something that is not necessarily the same as history, particularly history as an academic discipline. Today, in common parlance, history is a word used to describe the discipline and the thing studied by that discipline, but originally, history was used only to describe the inquiry and the product of that inquiry. We might speak of the history of the United States or some other nation as something that exists apart from a particular historian's investigation or writings, but such use of the word "history" is relatively recent. We might also think of presidents and prime ministers as "making" history, but centuries ago, only historians "made" history, a field of study dedicated to searching for knowledge and truth, akin to what we today associate with science. History has two meanings. As the noted historian Bernard Bailyn stated, one meaning is "simply *what happened*" while another is "*knowledge of what happened*" (Bailyn, 1994, p. 7). It is this second sense of the word that defines history as a discipline and serves as the focus of this chapter.

WHAT IS HISTORY?

In the rest of this chapter, we focus on history as an academic discipline rather than the general past. We focus on the purpose, knowledge, forms, and methods of history as a discipline. We also explore what it means to understand the past and how integration with contemporary visual art can connect to such understanding.

Purpose of History

Referring not just to the school subject but also to the whole concept, Henry Ford once called history "bunk." In a nation of people like Ford who are consumed with the present and focused on the future, many would no doubt wonder about history's purpose. The historian Peter Stearns (2008) succinctly captures the value of studying the past: History helps us understand people and societies, how change happens, and how our world came to be.

Because we cannot learn everything about people and societies from controlled experiments (e.g., think of the ethics of an experiment on human coping in wartime), we use the past as a "laboratory" for understanding things about the human condition that could never be learned otherwise. As a laboratory, the past serves as evidence for understanding how humans behave in societies and why we lead our lives the way we do. Because the past is connected to the present, we study the past to better understand current concerns and one of the constants of our life—change. Our gaze into the past to understand the present might take any number of directions. For example, those seeking to understand the current state of schooling in the United States might study the development of the public school system's curriculum and its connection to the economy; or perhaps immigration, urbanization, and assimilationist education policies; or even schools as workplaces in connection with ideas about gender. These examples illustrate how history can reflect varied perspectives and questions, each leading to different tensions and epistemological struggles. All these examples would illustrate that ours is not the only era of remarkable change.

A comprehensive overview of the discipline's history is beyond the scope of this chapter; other books delve into the topic in detail (e.g., Burrow, 2008; Wells, 2008). A look at several historians from different eras illustrates how the purpose of history is always subject to questioning and evolution, as are the knowledge and methods of the discipline.

From ancient times through the middle of the 20th century, history generally focused on the political, diplomatic, and military matters of peoples and nations. Such histories contributed to the development of people's identities and often provide examples for moral reflection (Stearns, 2008). Writing in the 5th century B.C., Herodotus chronicled the wars between the Persians and Greeks while Thucydides covered the Peloponnesian War between Athens and Sparta. Both men are considered "fathers" of history, each representing a different approach to understanding history. Herodotus's purpose was to record stories, even those of uncertain veracity. He wrote, "I must tell what is said, but I am not at all bound to believe it" (1987, p. 521). Herodotus cared about factual truth; however, he also cared about how people remembered the past, or what is sometimes called "memory," which is seen as a less factually accurate account of the past compared to history. By contrast, Thucydides's purpose was to record what actually happened in his history. He included multiple and conflicting perspectives to present what he considered a true account of complex phenomena, keeping his own opinions at bay. He was interested in chronology and causation, and he focused on human choices and actions rather than those of the gods to explain what happened on Earth.

Jumping all the way from ancient Greece to 19th-century Berlin, we see the "professionalization" of history and the beginning of an academic discipline led by Leopold von Ranke. Over his long life, spanning most of the century, he wrote enough to fill 60 volumes with his collected works. Like his predecessors, Ranke focused on political and military history, but he is remembered more for his contributions to how history is conducted than for what he wrote. He became what some would call the "father" of "scientific" history, showing how the past really was the goal of academic historians. In his first book, he wrote the maxim for which he is best remembered: "To history has been assigned the office of judging the past, of instructing the present for the benefit of future ages. To such high offices this work does not aspire: It wants only to show what actually happened" (Ranke, 1824/1909, page n.a.).

Starting in the 1960s, history shifted focus from its attention to politics, wars, and diplomacy to social and economic aspects of the past. Many historians working in this era paid attention to class conflict and drew on social science theories like Marxism to explain the past. They believed their explanations of politics, society, and the economy of the past could inform present-day decisions about policy and legislation. Also at this time, technology gave historians new ability to analyze large data sets, and with it the hope of being able to use quantitative paradigms to develop even more convincing arguments about the causes of historical change.

E. H. Carr, a British historian focused on the Soviet Union, is best remembered for an influential piece of historiography, *What Is History?*, published in 1961. In it, he contradicted Ranke, who believed historians should be impartial analysts of facts from archives and secondary sources. Carr's statement, "Study the historian before you study the facts" (1961/1987, p. 23), acknowledged that historians are humans with biases and agendas and that their choice of facts from the past and, therefore, their interpretations reflect those biases and agendas. He believed historians should check those biases but did not pretend they could abandon them as they sought answers to enduring questions with which societies struggle in the present and may struggle in the future.

Contemporary historians have less faith in being able to explain causality, and instead their purpose is to make meaning of the past. Most recently, historians have sought to understand the role of culture and gender in society. Cannadine (2002) describes the attention to gender as "the recovery of the lives and experiences of one half of the world's population, based on the recognition that gender was not merely a useful, but arguably an essential category of historical analysis and comprehension" (p. x). Contemporary historians focus on people, particularly "the humble, ordinary people, history's obscure, the losers and bystanders in the process of historical change" (Cannadine, 2002, p. 8). Rather than seeing their work as having implications for current policy, current historians instead hope to instill appreciation for the diversity of humanity, thus fostering greater tolerance for different cultures and beliefs.

While the purpose of history—along with ideas about its knowledge and methods—has evolved over the centuries, new purposes have not necessarily replaced old ones. While history of gender and sexuality are more popular today, historians have not abandoned political history, for example. The history of history can be compared to *pentimento*, where old work is visible under newer layers of paint. The discipline today includes historians working on older and newer areas of interest and on works that combine both.

Historical Knowledge

The scope of historical knowledge can seem boundless. One of the most common complaints of K–12 teachers is "covering" it all—too much content and too little time. At the college level, the array of courses is like a banquet with more offerings than can ever be consumed. The history department at the University of California, Berkeley, for example, lists 816 undergraduate courses! (University of California, Berkeley, 2012). These include courses on nations (from Brazil to Yugoslavia), specific times and places (Berkeley in the 1960s, the ancient Mediterranean), people (African Americans, Latin American women), ideas and institutions (from apartheid to Zionism), and phenomena (sexuality, hunger, medicine, and emotions). Indeed, is there anything without a history?

History as a discipline draws on wide-ranging knowledge from discrete facts to overarching theory. Addressing all this knowledge in one chapter is impossible, and instead we focus on several broad areas of knowledge that are also relevant to teaching K–12 students about history. These broad areas can provide entry points for substantive multidimensional art-centered integrated learning because they also speak to tensions and questions considered by artists as much as by historians.

Facts and Stories. If people have a complaint about learning history in elementary or secondary school, it often sounds something like this: "I hated learning all those names and dates. History was just a bunch of facts." Indeed, those names and dates from history textbooks probably were just facts, not historical facts. A fact is something that happened in the past, but it becomes a historical fact when a historian uses it as part of an argument. History textbooks are often devoid of arguments, so the information they present can be called facts, but not necessarily historical facts.

The notion of historical facts is complicated even more, however, by questions of "truth." Fernández-Armesto (2002) cautions that the only facts about the past "that we do know objectively, and with certainty, are facts only about the sources"

(p. 155). In other words, we can know what a diary, tax register, ship's log, or presidential address says, but not the reality beyond those artifacts, because everything else is reconstructed by historians in the present. Consider Laurel Thatcher Ulrich's *A Midwife's Tale* (1990), which reconstructs the life of Martha Ballard, who lived in a Maine village in the late 1700s and early 1800s. In this case, the only "fact" is her diary, little more than a record of the services she provided. However, historians do not limit themselves to facts. They create lively narratives of the past. In the case of Ballard, Ulrich engaged in what historian John Lewis Gaddis (2008) calls a "thought experiment" in the present or "an exercise in historical paleontology" (p. 41) to give greater meaning and context to the diary from the past. Ulrich placed the facts from the diary in the context of all else that was known about the times to paint a full picture of Ballard's world and worldview.

History is a story or a narrative created from facts, and that narrative requires invention and imagination. People do not live in stories. Creating those stories is the work of historians drawing on the raw material of the past. Whereas stories connote fiction for many people, the stories about the past that historians write are arguments based on evidence. Historians are not novelists, though like all good writers, historians do have a voice, perspective, or personal point of view, which comes out in their work. Contemporary historians do not ascribe to the ideals of "scientific" or positivist study of the past, but they have not given up on the idea of striving for truth. As Megill (2007) writes, history is not only narrative but truthful, "which does not mean 'true' in any absolute sense, but does mean 'justified,' by a mode of justification appropriate to history. The alternative to the view that history is truthful narrative is one form or another of history-as-propaganda" (p. 11) or history to prove a point, usually about the present or future. To avoid propaganda while still claiming a voice, historians reflect on their biases and preconceptions and articulate the assumptions and purpose behind their work.

"Pastness" and Presentism. Historian Bernard Bailyn (1994) writes that "the past is not only distant but different, and it takes a great effort of imagination and substantial knowledge to get back into such remote experiences" (p. 53). Perhaps the effort required to inhabit the past accounts for the difficulty of avoiding what historians call *presentism*, or the tendency to use ideas from the present to interpret the past. Using ideas from the present, whether they are about human rights or hygiene, can distort our understanding of the past. At its worst, presentism can be used to interpret the past as a way to justify our own beliefs about the present or explain why the present was inevitable.

Perhaps our desire to learn from history accounts for presentism. We seek antecedents to our present and hope to find people before us who faced the same decisions so we can learn from their experience. Historian Gordon Wood (2008) offers caution about learning from the past: "I don't believe that history teaches a lot of little lessons to guide us in the present and future" (p. 6). He goes on to offer how we might benefit, however:

Knowledge of the past can have a profound effect on our consciousness, on our sense of ourselves. History is a supremely humanistic discipline: it may not teach us particular lessons, but it does tell us how we might live in the world. (p. 6)

If historical understanding is not learning a series of lessons but instead developing historical consciousness, then we must understand the past on its own terms, put information about the past into the context of the past, and appreciate that the past is like traveling to another country with different customs, beliefs, perspectives, even different sounds and smells. Understanding the past on its own terms poses what Bailyn (1994) describes as "a moral problem, because to explain—in depth and with sympathy—is, implicitly at least, to excuse" (p. 58). He offers the example of Thomas Jefferson and his attitudes toward slavery as an example of this moral conundrum.

In a similar vein, Bailyn (1994) recommends that to understand the past on its own terms, we should appreciate our ignorance of the future. No one, past or present, knows what will happen in the future. When students of history possess such dispositions and understanding, then they have moved beyond presentism to an appreciation of the pastness of the past, or an understanding of the past on its own terms. Such knowledge is not esoteric or without utility. Looking at the past as a different world and understanding it on its own terms can help us understand certain truths about the past, present, and future. For example, even if identities and knowledge are culturally constructed, the process is extraordinarily complex and not easily changed or manipulated. Change happens, but not according to desires or plans.

Chronology, Causation, and Meaning. Social scientists look for root causes of social phenomena. In the language of social science, these roots are *independent variables,* and the other aspects of phenomena that change as a result of them are *dependent variables.* Social scientists "control" variables to isolate causes that might be statistically significant. By contrast, to historians, all variables are dependent. John Gaddis (2008) calls this an ecological view of reality where variables cannot be controlled. This view has important implications for how historians think about causation.

Although historians use chronology to create narratives of the past, the first event in a chronological narrative is not necessarily the cause, in any linear fashion, of the next event, particularly when historians are looking at large-scale change such as in national history. Links that might be clear when we seek to explain the relationship between touching keys on a pad and seeing words show up on a screen are much harder to define when the outcome we seek to explain is the rise of Nazism or the end of the Cold War and everything is somehow related to everything else.

Although causation is murky, historians do make important distinctions. They think about major and minor causes as well as immediate, intermediate, and distant causes. For example, most immediately, Prohibition ended because of the 21st amendment to the U.S. Constitution. Less immediately, the inability to enforce the 18th amendment, which created Prohibition, led to its demise. Even more distant, some might argue, humans' unending thirst for alcohol led to its failure. Historians also consider the difference between general and exceptional causes, the former setting "necessary" conditions for change and the latter being the "sufficient" condition for change. They also consider counterfactuals. Could things have been otherwise? In answering this question, historians think about a variety of possible explanations to help establish causation (Gaddis, 2008).

Generalization and Specificity. One of the greatest challenges historians face is the tension between generalization and specificity. Since the past entails every thought and action of every being in a particular moment, re-creating in textual form even a small window of time proves virtually impossible. Inevitably, some aspects of reality are left out. Therefore, all history is an abstract reconstruction of the past. Historians embrace this limitation.

Just as the portrait painter Luc Tymans does not necessarily attempt to achieve photographic realism (see Figure 5.1), but a unique understanding of a subject, historians seek to portray the past in a way that best exemplifies what they have learned (Furay & Salevouris, 2000). The challenge then is to find the balance between generalizations and specificity.

Figure 5.1. Luc Tuymans, *Portrait*, 2000.

Image courtesy of David Zwirner, private
collection, New York.

Part of the beauty of history is that good history is rooted in the particularities of a situation. Thus, while no steadfast laws of history exist, Gardiner reminds us that what does "exist are historians writing upon different levels and at different distance, historians writing with different aims and different interests, historians writing in different contexts and from different points of view" (Gardiner, 1963, p. 109). The result of the interplay between these layers of histories is a generalized knowledge that approaches truth.

Historical Forms

Historians generally work with words. Their work can take the form of a monograph examining a specific historical event or a biography of a historical personage— for example, Robert Caro's multiple volumes about Lyndon Baines Johnson. Just as often, these works focus on less-well-known persons whose stories serve as cases of larger historical phenomena. For example, Isabel Wilkerson's *The Warmth of Other Suns* (2010) tells the in-depth stories of three African Americans to illustrate on a personal level the Great Migration, the movement of millions of African Americans from the South to cities in the North, Midwest, and West.

Historians also work to synthesize the work of many other historians. They do so to provide overarching narratives, to help make sense of large periods of time or nation-states. Doing so is not easy or without obstacles. Making broader generalizations into a single narrative typically proves difficult. Such broad generalizations can be found in the framework of Arnold Toynbee's 12-volume work *A Study of History* (1934–1961), which spans 20 human "civilizations" and 6,000 years. Aware of the limitations in such a vast undertaking, renowned historians Will and Ariel Durant, who themselves wrote their own multiple volume *The Story of Civilization*, wrote, "History smiles at all attempts to force its flow into theoretical patterns or logical grooves; it plays havoc with our generalizations, breaks all our rules; history is baroque" (Durant & Durant, 1961, p. 267).

Beyond books, the work of historians can also make its way into the form of museum exhibits, film documentaries, and architectural preservation. Stearns (2008) makes the point that all these forms of history have an aesthetic as well as an educational function, for stories told well can be beautiful. He notes that "history as art and entertainment serves a real purpose" (p. 3) because it can prompt readers to immerse themselves in the distant pasts and imagine worlds different from our own.

Historical Methods

The methods of history as a discipline are about more than remembering. Historians might remember many people and events from the past, but the methods of the discipline rely on thinking, not memory, specifically the ability to think skeptically, argumentatively, synthetically, and empathetically.

Thinking Skeptically. Historians are skeptical. For that reason, they do not take historical artifacts at face value. Instead, they are always evaluating sources and the information they contain. First, historians evaluate a source in light of whether it is relevant in helping to answer a question that they are investigating. They select some sources based on their relevance and ignore others.

Once they have evaluated the relevance of sources, they have only just begun thinking skeptically. As Evans (1999) writes, "The language of historical documents is never transparent, and historians have always been aware that they cannot simply gaze through it to the historical reality behind" (p. 90). No source has a "true" meaning. Instead the historian has to interrogate the writer, the writer's context, and the intended reader to make meaning of a source document.

Historians use a wide variety of questions to evaluate sources and explain how the answers to these questions are key to interpretation (Howell & Prevenier, 2001). Historians consider the reliability of the source. Questions that might help them evaluate reliability include the following: Was the source created intentionally or not? What was the psychological state of the author? To what extent might the author's reporting have been selective? What prejudices might an author have? Who else might have influenced an author? Was the author witnessing something firsthand? Contemporary historians, unlike their 19th-century counterparts, would not necessarily consider firsthand accounts to be more reliable.

Historians consider the times and society in which the author wrote. Was the author able to report freely? On what terms would the author understand what was going on? Was the author qualified to make sense of something? How did the author's culture, politics, or personality shape the source?

Finally, historians consider the source in light of other sources. What other facts are known? What do other sources say? Does a large number of sources agreeing on something make those sources more reliable? Historians' skepticism would lead them to question the majority as much as the minority.

Thinking Argumentatively. Historian Allan Megill (2007) writes, "Historians cannot simply *assert* that such and such claims are true about the past. Rather, they must put forward arguments and evidence that justify our agreeing that the claims in question are true" (p. xii). In this sense, historians' argumentation is not about engaging in constant disputes with other historians but rather about how they convince others—historians, students of history, even the general public—about their interpretations. Historians make claims about the past. They offer evidence to support those claims and provide warrants connecting that evidence to the claims.

Historians argue for why some events in the past are more significant than others. They make arguments for why an event was a watershed—or not; why a chunk of the past can be labeled as a specific period in history with a start and end date; why some themes rather than others reverberate through an era and help us understand it; why they see a pattern in the past where others might see only chaos; and why they believe something was a cause of something else.

Thinking Synthetically. Historians are rarely interested in facts for their own sake. Instead they are interested in what Ranke called the "interconnectedness" of facts (Evans, 1999). This interconnectedness is what makes facts significant and meaningful. While historians can relate information about a document, understanding its connectedness to the larger context almost always requires synthesis using invention and imagination. Because of this need to imagine and invent, no history is entirely factual. Put another way, Davidson and Lytle (1986) write, "History is not something that is simply brought out of the archives, dusted off, and displayed as 'the way things really were.' It is a painstaking construction, held together only with the help of assumptions, hypotheses, and inferences" (p. vii). Facts are not history. Instead they are the raw material from which a story is told.

Thinking Empathetically with Historical Perspective. Because historians want to understand the past without judging it by contemporary standards, they think empathetically. They take a generous perspective that seeks to understand people in the past in the context of the past. Wood (2008) beautifully describes the nature of what it means to think empathetically, writing,

> To be able to see the participants of the past . . . in the context of their own time, to describe their blindness and folly with sympathy, to recognize the extent to which they were caught up in changing circumstances of which they had little control, and to realize the degree to which they created results they never intended. (p. 11)

In a similar vein, Bailyn (1994) describes empathetic thinking as not assigning heroism or villainy to people in the past, remaining sympathetic to the accounts of those on the losing side of past struggles, and appreciating the role of contingencies and accidents in shaping history, rather than ascribing sole responsibility to the choices of those living in the past.

UNDERSTANDING HISTORY

Most K–12 students learn history from textbooks that "typically focus tightly on facts, events, and people, and not the kinds of questions, decisions, and heuristics historians employ in their day-to-day practice," like thinking skeptically, argumentatively, synthetically, and empathetically (Paxton, 1999, p. 317). Not surprisingly, such texts impoverish students' understanding of historical complexity and nuance and mislead them about what it means to understand history. Learning from such books, students may see history as a series of disconnected facts and fragmented knowledge or believe that *the* objective historical truth exists and can be known. Whereas textbooks simplify the past into one grand narrative, historians go out of their way to complicate their understanding of the past by raising questions, developing alternative interpretations, framing context in multiple ways, and understanding the past on its own terms (Lienhardt & Young, 1996).

TEACHING HISTORY

The teaching of history in K–12 schools has been based on a set of principles that do not always match the purpose, knowledge, forms, and methods of the discipline described so far. Perhaps the oldest reason for teaching history has been to help students memorize content knowledge and develop discipline-based skills. Memorizing knowledge at the fact level has been emphasized by those who want to create "cultural literacy" and cohesion among people sharing a common history (Hirsch, Kett, & Trefil, 2002). Advocates of discipline-based skills instruction favor educating students as historians who "do not cover information, but rather uncover it" (Gibb et al., 2002, p. 177) and who learn the methods and habits of mind of the profession.

A second purpose for teaching history has been to develop critical thinking skills in students. Critical thinking has been embedded in history classes to decrease teaching "inert" or decontextualized knowledge (Wright, 2002) and increase students' ability to make connections among facts, broader themes, and their own lives. Others have emphasized critical thinking as part of a "less is more" approach by "shifting from an emphasis on teaching data to teaching thinking" (Gibb et al., 2002, p. 177).

A final purpose for teaching history in schools has been to foster democratic citizenship. The notion of learning history to promote civic education is longstanding. Two schools of thought exist on the use of history for civic education: traditionalists and progressives (Parker, 1996).

Traditionalist history educators have emphasized a more passive civic participation, with education focusing on developing an understanding and appreciation for democratic government and individual rights. This emphasis can be exemplified by local statutes such as the 1994 Lake County, Florida, School Board policy regarding the teaching of history:

> This instruction shall also include and instill in our students an appreciation of our American heritage and culture such as: our republican form of government, capitalism, a free enterprise system, patriotism, strong family values, freedom of religion and other basic values that are superior to other foreign or historic cultures. (Glazer, 1997, p. 1)

In contrast, the progressive wing of history for democratic education advocates fostering a more active form of citizenship and learning. While knowledge of history and current government is essential, inspiring "public agency—people's capacities to act with effect and with public spirit" is equally if not more essential (Boyte, 1994, p. 417). Such citizenship does not end with merely voting for representatives but entails living a life of participation, or as Dewey called it, creative democracy (1939/1976), where students carve out a space of action between themselves and government (Parker, 1996). As such, progressive historical education takes on a social justice character, seeking to empower both teachers and students as agents of change (Ayers, Kumashiro, Meiners, Quinn, & Stovall, 2010).

FUNDAMENTALS OF HISTORY AND POINTS OF INTEGRATION WITH ART

As you think about art-centered integrated learning and history, consider these fundamental ideas about the discipline discussed in this chapter:

1. Understanding change
2. Telling stories
3. Exploring memory
4. Seeking truth
5. Distinguishing between pastness and presentism
6. Appreciating chronology, causation, and meaning
7. Generalizing from the specific
8. Thinking skeptically
9. Thinking argumentatively
10. Thinking synthetically
11. Thinking empathetically

Each idea represents a "big" idea—a purpose, focus, or method—in history as well as a possible point of integration between history and contemporary visual art. As you explore these points of integration, consider where the ideas overlap between history and visual art and where they diverge, where historians and artists share ways of thinking or explore similar ideas, or where they are in tension. For example, like a historian, Do Ho Suh explores the terrain of specificity and generalization or abstraction. His work, shown in Figure 5.2, *Who Am We?* (1997), conveys a composite or general picture of his generation drawn from thousands of yearbooks to describe the history of the Korean people, a process and product not unlike that of a historian sifting through numerous documents.

As an artist who works with glass, Josiah McElheny, also addresses history. In *Modernity circa 1952, Mirrored and Reflected Infinitely* (2004), he grapples with historical memory and how the past reverberates into the present. For this, he re-creates primary sources: old-fashioned glass containers. To convey his take on history, the artist places these flasks and bottles in a case, much like those in history museums, where the transparency of glass, the reflective quality of mirrors, and the infinite ricochet of reflected imagery and light allude to the prism of memory and history. Both artists, in different ways, suggest the wide array of possibilities for integrating contemporary art with history.

Figure 5.2. Do Ho Suh, *Who Am We?*, 1997.

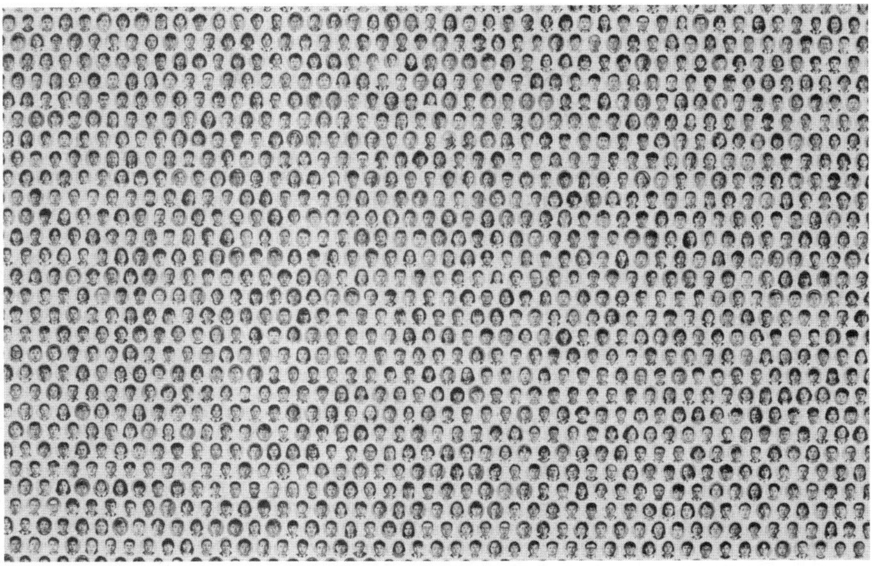

Wallpaper, dimension variable. Image courtesy of the artist and Lehmann Maupin Gallery, New York and Hong Kong. © Do Ho Suh.

ART THAT CONNECTS
TO HISTORY

History Is Alive

In her collection of photographs, *Using History*, Greta Pratt confronts American history as it "lives" today. Each photograph shows how modern-day Americans remember, memorialize, reinterpret, refantasize, and relive great historical events and idolize larger-than-life figures of American history. Many of these works are ironic, even funny; many are disturbing; some are touching. At their best, they are all three. Take, for example, a picture of a Lincoln impersonator stepping into an RV that is painted log cabin–style, or the portrait of two young children dolled up as parade floats: the girl as a cowgirl, the boy as totem pole (see Figures 5.3 and 5.4).

While these two pictures may raise a smile or make us uneasy, Pratt also presents us with the truly surreal. Consider the TV newsman reporting on a battle reenactment as if it were a real live war (see Figure 5.5).

Figures 5.3 and 5.4. Greta Pratt, *Using History*, 2005.

Images courtesy of the artist.

Figure 5.5. Greta Pratt, *Using History*, 2005.

Image courtesy of the artist.

What do these photographs tell us about current American popular culture and its romance with the past? For one, they imply that a lot of us love history—a mythological sort of history—the kind that has a fixed stock of iconic events and characters, which we can cozy up to, fantasize about, play with, and use for our own purposes. This is history seen through the misty, myopic eyes of a love-struck public trying to connect to its past. For another, they suggest that, in this passion for our past, Americans make a spectacle of it. We make pilgrimages to historic sites, play at reenactments, concoct historical theme parks, and resurrect "history villages." With this treatment, history becomes a boisterous stage show with all its rough patches and unpleasantness left out of the script.

In documenting this spectacle, Pratt shows us how American history is warped and woven into popular culture and how it is jerry-rigged to serve to further political agendas, make us feel good about our past, sell merchandise, build patriotism, and/or help us construct our personal and collective identity.

Integration (Purpose, Knowledge, Methods, and Forms). In regard to *purpose*, Pratt is clear about why she made these photographs. She asserts that she wanted to capture the ways Americans memorialize the past in order to understand how she and we remember history. Pratt's goal was also to penetrate the surface and unearth what this commemoration means about us. "My intention with these images is to address how the culture and morality of today are reflected in what we commemorate about the past" (Pratt, 2005, page n.a.). Pratt also shows *how* we venerate those chosen subjects. Her photographs, therefore, are a cultural study of both what we love and how we show that love. Her social commentary is particularly incisive and sharp in her depiction of the "how."

Pratt's *methods* and *forms* are those of a photojournalist. Photojournalism requires research and being on the spot to capture events as they unfold. It also calls for attention to detail with an eye on the full picture. Pratt began her research for *Using History* and related projects by visiting sites commonly studied in elementary schools: Plymouth Rock, Jamestown, Gettysburg, Mount Vernon, and other "holy" sites of American history. At those places, she employed the keen eyes and ears of an anthropologist.

Creative Strategies. Pratt's journalistic, anthropological eye is tempered by the eccentricity of her perspective and the subtle humor, irony, and empathy she conveys in her photographs. The primary creative strategies in her work are *juxtaposition* and *layering*: odd and ironic pairings and overlays of historic and contemporary icons. The twist here is that Pratt does not create her photographs by using these strategies as much as by noticing and capturing them with her camera when they occur.

Evoking History

Ann Hamilton creates grand multimedia installations that engage the senses and mind on multiple levels. Using cloth and other materials, spoken and written texts, animals and actors, her installations immerse viewers in aesthetic experiences that make historical and literary ideas come alive (Smith, 2012). Hamilton's background is in textiles and that heritage permeates every aspect of her work, from the physical and tactile qualities of her materials to her interweaving of repetitive movements and patterns. Hamilton's disposition to weave is also true of the conceptual aspects of her projects, particularly the metaphorical connections she makes between materials and ideas. Over her long career, Hamilton has also been an "integrator"; she has explored the realities behind historical texts, the wisdom of poets and philosophers, and the concepts and tropes of science. Here we will focus on two of her explorations of history and how it echoes in the present.

In *indigo blue,* Hamilton tackles neglected history. This installation (see Figure 5.6) was originally created for the 1991 Spoleto Festival in Charleston, South Carolina, and was restored and installed in 2007 in the San Francisco Museum of Art (Hamilton, 2011). The original installation was composed of two parts: a massive mountain of 18,000 folded blue work shirts and pants on a raised platform and an ongoing performance by an actor sitting at a table erasing texts from history books. The site was a dark, dingy, empty factory dating from the 1800s when the textile industry drove the economy of South Carolina. In researching Charleston and thinking about the history that the city prefers to present to tourists, Hamilton decided to cast a light on the less celebrated history of Charleston: the lives of those who labored long hours in Charleston's factories. The work shirts and pants, and the labor it took to fold and stack them, serve as metaphors for the original laborers and their work. The vastness of the pile of work clothes also alludes to the oppression of the working class during the industrial age. Indeed, this huge heap looks like a mass grave. Also, the connection to historical forgetfulness is made clear by the erasing of history texts by an actor sitting adjacent to the pile.

Fast forward to the winter of 2012–2013 and Hamilton's multisensory installation, *the event of a thread,* in the Park Avenue Armory in New York City. When a viewer entered the armory hall, he or she was immediately drawn in by the sights

Figure 5.6. Ann Hamilton, *indigo blue,* 1991/2007.

Commissioned for "Places with a Past: New Site-Specific Art at Charleston's Spoleto Festival." Mary Jane Jacob, curator, Charleston, South Carolina, May 24–August 24, 1991. Materials: blue work clothing, steel and wood base, wood table, chair, light bulb, books (military regulation manuals, blue bindings), saliva, pink pearl erasers, erasures, net sack, soybeans. Collection of San Francisco Museum of Modern Art. © Ann Hamilton. Image courtesy of Ann Hamilton Studio.

and the sounds. Placed by the entrance was a table with actors reading texts from Aristotle to pigeons nesting in wooden cages. Floating across the midsection of a cavernous hall was a white silk curtain that rose, fell, and billowed as visitors floated through the air on swings. Because the swings controlled the movements of the curtain, the give and take of the ropes physically connected visitors to the curtain and to each other. This sense of interconnectedness was heightened by the sound of actors' voices reading Aristotle's texts emanating from speakers placed around the room and mingling with viewers' conversations and laughter. In this playful yet meditative spectacle, the cavernous hall became a park, a place for visitors to interact and share a rare aesthetic experience. The link to history emerged in this communion. The vast space was once the drill hall of a 19th-century armory and was used for practicing military marches and maneuvers. It was the place where soldiers came together to build brotherhood by performing military rituals. The artist's goal in *the event of a thread* was to weave a similar thread of fellowship among those who inhabited the hall in the artwork (Hamilton, 2013), this time around the rituals of a work of art and the fun of playground (see Figure 5.7).

Integration (Purpose, Knowledge, Methods, and Forms). Hamilton taps into the primary *purpose* of history: to remind us in the present of the events, people, and ideas that preceded us, thus connecting the past to the present. While historical *knowledge* is the foundation and springboard of her work, Hamilton does not dwell on it. Her work is not didactic but experiential; her history lessons come alive through poetic, aesthetic, embodied experiences. In regard to *methods*, Hamilton, like historians, researches primary sources. She also interprets her findings, as a historian would do; she synthesizes "historical facts." As an artist, she

Figure 5.7. Ann Hamilton, *the event of a thread,* **2012.**

Park Avenue Armory, New York City. Photo by Thibault Jeanson,
unless otherwise noted. Commissioned by Park Avenue Armory.
Image courtesy of Ann Hamilton Studio.

is free to illuminate these facts in fanciful ways. Regarding *forms,* Hamilton often uses historical or philosophical texts, whether she is erasing them or reading them aloud.

Creative Strategies. Although she uses multiple creative strategies, *metaphor* is Hamilton's primary method for creating meaning. Often her metaphors lie in the materials or objects she uses (blue work shirts in *indigo blue* or swings and ropes in *the event of a thread*) and movement (erasing in *indigo blue* and swings flying in *the event of a thread*). She also *juxtaposes* objects, materials, people, and animals with movement, sounds, and smells. All of these ingredients serve to *embody* and *amplify* ideas and feelings.

Media and Historical Understanding

Wang Du takes his images of current events and historical figures right off the front pages. In *Défilé (Parade)* (2000), he transforms photographs of protesters, policemen, soldiers, and military hardware from protests in China into large-scale three-dimensional sculptures (see Figure 5.8). These sculptures are not realistic in any conventional sense, but hyperrealistic; the one-point perspective of photography is exaggerated to heighten the drama of a photograph and draw attention to how media images inflate and distort our impressions of political and historical phenomena (Absolutearts, 2005).

Wang Du also addresses the way media hypes political and historical figures through relentless replication of their images. In *Absolute Image* (2011), the portrait of Osama bin Laden is repeated over and over in a circle and strewn with photocopies of articles about bin Laden. What's more, Wang Du alludes to how the media (and history) can whitewash or recast historical figures. bin Laden is portrayed in the style of a classical Greek bust (see Figure 5.9). This gives him a certain caché, a gloss of heroism. Furthermore, the busts of bin Laden are snow white—scrubbed clean and polished. With this work, Wang Du raises this question: Could bin Laden, with his notoriety cleansed and recast, eventually become a historical figure worthy of commemoration?

Integration (Purpose, Knowledge, Methods, and Forms). Regarding *knowledge,* Wang Du depicts events, movements, and people of social and historical significance that make up the knowledge of history. He also addresses how we understand these figures and events through the hyperbolic lenses of the all-pervasive media. In doing so, he questions the *purpose* of media and the history they generate. Is the purpose to inform public opinion or to shape it? In regard to *methods,* the artist acts as a social researcher and critic; he researches, collects evidence, discerns patterns, and reveals and critiques those patterns. Although his target is the media, he is a media person in his own right; he, too, creates exaggerated images. Indeed, he "re-mediates" mediated imagery, further distorting it and taking

Figure 5.8. Wang Du, *Défilé,* **2000.**

Mixed media, variable dimensions. Image courtesy Galerie Laurent Godin, Paris.

Figure 5.9. Wang Du, *Absolute Image,* **2011.**

Thirty plaster sculptures, gouache, variable dimensions. Image courtesy Galerie Laurent Godin, Paris.

it out of context to make his point. That is to say, he uses the *forms* found in the media. Furthermore, in *Absolute Image,* he makes use of an iconic form from art history, the classical bust.

Creative Strategies. Wang Du *reformats* media imagery into large-scale sculpture. He *juxtaposes* printed media with the images that come from it.

Layering Past onto the Present

Walking often is a contemplative experience that affords us time to follow our thoughts as we follow a trail. When walkers are free to meander, they often wander through their minds as much as they stroll through space. Walking is, indeed, a twofold experience that takes us both into the mind and through physical places (O'Rourke, 2013). Janet Cardiff and Robert Bures Miller draw on these ideas when they send their audiences on walks. Their walks are not meanders, but directed, narrated journeys back in time that take us into our collective mind, in particular our memories and our fantasies about the past. These walks occur in historical sites. For example, in *Jena Walk (Memory Field)* (2006), the artists led visitors on an audio journey over a battlefield in Germany where the Prussian army and Napoleon fought 200 years ago. For this walk, visitors wore headphones to listen to re-created sound effects of 19th-century battle scenes. As they strolled, time slipped from one century to another and walkers became aware that they were traversing the landscape as others had done for centuries, thus achieving a heightened sense of being in the present.

Cardiff and Miller also design video tours that incorporate music, sound effects, and actors playing out vignettes. One such tour, illustrated in Figure 5.10, was the *Alter Bahnhof Video Walk* (2012), a tour of a railroad station created for dOCUMENTA 13 in Kassel, Germany. As visitors walked through the station, they watched on iPods a video that had been filmed in the exact same places they visited along their way. When they followed the moving images on the iPods and tried to sync them with what they were seeing in their environment, a peculiar confusion of reality occurred, and past and present came together. This sense of overlapping past and present was heightened and given poignancy when the tour came to a memorial to Jews who were sent off to concentration camps from this station during World War II. It was from this point that the walkers entered into the dark history that lingers over this building (Cardiff & Miller, 2013).

Figure 5.10. Janet Cardiff and Robert Bures Miller, *Alter Bahnhof Video Walk,* **2012.**

Still frame from representational video of the walk. Image courtesy of the artists.

Integration (Purpose, Knowledge, Methods, and Forms). Cardiff and Miller's stated *purpose* is to give their audiences the dual experience of being in a liminal space where the present collides with the past, and a heightened sense of being alive here and now is realized. The *knowledge* the artists address is of European history—its significant places and events. They also draw on an understanding of how we experience time, place, and memory—concepts associated with the humanities and psychology. The *methods* they use include researching history, much as historians do, and writing scripts, setting up vignettes, and audio- and video-taping. Their *forms* are guided tours.

Creative Strategies. In Cardiff and Miller's walks, video images and sounds are *juxtaposed* with physical experience in a real place. The artists *amplify* experience through these juxtapositions. They also use narratives to elicit fantasies and memories and to bring their audience along.

REFERENCES

Absolutearts.com. (2005). Recent work by Wang Du (2005-11-19 until 2006-03-05). Retrieved from www.absolutearts.com/artsnews/2005/11/21/33480.html

The Alamo. (2012). *The Alamo visitors.* Retrieved from www.thealamo.org/visitors/over view.php

Ayers, W., Kumashiro, K., Meiners, E., Quinn, T., & Stovall, D. (2010). *Teaching toward democracy: Educators as agents of change.* Boulder, CO: Paradigm.

Bailyn, B. (1994). *On the teaching and writing of history.* Hanover, NH: University Press of New England.

BBC News. (1998). *Titanic sinks competitors without a trace.* Retrieved from news.bbc.co.uk/2/hi/59913.stm

Boyte, H. (1994). Review of *Civitas: A framework for civic education. Teachers College Record, 95,* 414–418.

Brokaw, T. (1998). *The greatest generation.* New York, NY: Random House.

Burrow, J. (2008). *A history of histories: Epics, chronicles, romances, and inquiries from Herodotus and Thucydides to the twentieth century.* New York, NY: Knopf.

Cannadine, D. (2002). Preface. In D. Cannadine (Ed.), *What is history now?* (pp. vii–xiv). New York, NY: Palgrave Macmillan.

Cardiff, J., & Miller, G. B. (2013). *The Alter Bahnhof Walk* (2012) *& The Jena Walk (Memory Field)* (2006). Retrieved from www.cardiffmiller.com/artworks/walks/#

Carr, E. H. (1987). *What is history?* (2nd ed.). London, UK: Penguin Books. (Original work published in 1961)

Davidson, J. W., & Lytle, M. H. (1986). *After the fact: The art of historical detection.* New York, NY: Knopf.

Dewey, J. (1939/1976). Creative democracy: The task before us. In J. Boydston (Ed.), *John Dewey: The later works, 1925–1953* (Vol. 14, pp. 224–230). Carbondale: Southern Illinois University Press.

Durant, W., & Durant, A. (1961). *The story of civilization* (Vol. 7): *The Age of Reason begins*. New York, NY: Simon & Schuster.

Evans, R. J. (1999). *In defense of history*. New York, NY: Norton.

Fernández-Armesto, F. (2002). Epilogue: What is history now? In D. Cannadine (Ed.), *What is history now?* (pp. 148–161). New York, NY: Palgrave Macmillan.

Furay, C., & Salevouris, M. J. (2000). *The methods and skills of history: A practical guide* (2nd ed.). New York, NY: Harlan Davidson.

Gaddis, J. L. (2008). *The landscape of history: How historians map the past*. New York, NY: Oxford University Press.

Gardiner, P. (1963). *The nature of historical explanation*. London, England: Oxford University Press.

Gibb, D., Adam, R., Delaye, D., Goodhew, T., Matsen, L., Ramsey, T., & Rona, L. (2002). Teaching thinking. *The History Teacher, 35,* 175–200.

Glazer, N. (1997). *We are all multiculturalists now*. Cambridge, MA: Harvard University Press.

Hamilton, A. (2011). Interview with Ann Hamilton on creating *Indigo Blue*. Retrieved from www.marthagarzon.com/contemporary art/2011/01

Herodotus. (1987). *The histories*. (D. Grene, Trans.). Chicago, IL: University of Chicago Press.

Hirsch, E. D., Kett, J. F., & Trefil, J. (2002). *The new dictionary of cultural literacy: What every American needs to know*. Boston, MA: Houghton Mifflin.

Howell, M. C., & Prevenier, W. (2001). *From reliable sources: An introduction to historical methods*. Ithaca, NY: Cornell University Press.

Lienhardt, G., & Young, K. M. (1996). Two texts, three readers: Distance and expertise in reading history. *Cognition and Instruction, 14* (4), 441–486.

Maryles, D. (2002, March 18). Few surprises in the winners' circle. *Publishers Weekly,* 249 (11). Retrieved from www.publishersweekly.com/pw/print/20020318/36667-few-sur prises-in-the-winners-circle.html

Megill, A. (2007). *Historical knowledge, historical error: A contemporary guide to practice*. Chicago, IL: University of Chicago Press.

National Parks Traveler. (2010). *By the numbers: Vietnam Veterans Memorial*. Retrieved from www.nationalparkstraveler.com/2010/05/numbers-vietnam-veterans-memorial5901

O'Rourke, K. (2013). *Walking as mapping: Artists as cartographers*. Cambridge, MA: MIT Press.

Parker, W. C. (1996). "Advanced" ideas about democracy: Toward a pluralist conception of citizen education. *Teachers College Record, 98,* 104–125.

Paxton, R. J. (1999). A deafening silence: History textbooks and the students who read them. *Review of Educational Research, 69,* 315–339.

Pratt, G. (2005). *Using history*. Gottingen, Germany: Steidl.

Ranke, L. (1909). *The history of the Latin and Teutonic peoples from 1494 to 1514*. London, England: G. Bell & Sons. (Original work published in 1824)

Smith, R. (2012, December 7). The audience as art movement: Ann Hamilton at the Park Avenue Armory. *The New York Times*. Retrieved from www.nytimes .com/2012/12/07/arts/design/ann-hamilton-at-the-park-avenue-armory .html?pagewanted=all&_r=0

Stearns, P. N. (2008). Why study history? *American Historical Association*, 1–7. Retrieved from www.historians.org/pubs/Free/WhyStudyHistory.htm

Toynbee, A. (1934–1961). *A study of history* (Vols. 1–12). New York, NY: Oxford University Press.

Ulrich, L. T. (1990). *A midwife's tale: The life of Martha Ballard, based on her diary, 1785–1812.* New York, NY: Knopf.

University of California, Berkeley. (2012). *Undergraduate courses.* Retrieved from history.berkeley.edu/undergraduate/courses?field_term_tid=All&field_courseyears_tid=All&field_couretypes_tid=All

Wells, C. (2008). *A brief history of history: Great historians and their epic quest to explain the past.* Guilford, CT: Lyons Press.

Wilkerson, I. (2010). *The warmth of other suns: The epic story of America's great migration.* New York, NY: Vintage Books.

Wood, G. (2008). *The purpose of the past: Reflections on the uses of history.* New York, NY: Penguin Books.

Wright, I. (2002). Challenging students with the tools of critical thinking. *The Social Studies, 93,* 257–261.

6

Geography

Making Meaning of Location and Place

Julia Marshall

Where is Zambia? How far is it from the Sierra Mountains to the Pacific coast? How big is Argentina? These are questions geography answers—questions of absolute location, relative location, and scale, questions we expect geography to grapple with. Geographers, however, tackle other questions, ones that are more complex, social in nature, and close to students' direct experience. What makes a place a home? How does living in a suburb differ from living in a city? How do location, climate, and human intervention affect a landscape? Yes, geography is a social and a natural science as well. It is the science of human experience and action related to landscapes and places (Holt-Jensen, 2009).

Geography explores the relationship between the Earth and its peoples through the study of *space*, *place*, and *environment*. It is the consummate science of synthesis because it connects the natural and social sciences so seamlessly in its examination of humans and their environment, and in the mix of methods and thinking it uses to carry out that study (Holt-Jensen, 2006). Geography is also distinctive because it is a transdisciplinary field, one that bridges and meshes disciplines, incorporates integrated thinking and research, and also has a distinct lens on the world (Klein, 2000), a lens that looks at phenomena—both physical and human—in terms of location, place, human–environment interaction, movement, and region. Geography, therefore, is important to any discussion of integrated learning because of its inherently integrated, transdisciplinary nature. Geography intersects with art in a variety of significant ways. Contemporary artists explore many of the concepts of geography, and they make great use of geography's premier form: the map.

Geography is also of critical importance to young people living in a highly integrated world. As citizens of the global community, they need to know about the factors that shape their world, such as who the powers in the world are and where they are, the size of the Pacific Gyre and how it came about, where their clothes and mobile devices come from and who makes them, and how and why what happens in China, India, or Iran affects their environment and way of life.

WHAT ARE PHYSICAL AND HUMAN GEOGRAPHY?

There are two branches of geography: physical and human geography. While physical geography focuses on the natural environment (how the climate, vegetation and life, soil, water, and landforms are produced and interact), human geography considers the human environment (cultural, social, and political factors related to location, space, place, and environment; Holt-Jensen, 2009). Each of the two branches of geography can be divided into subdisciplines. For example, two of the subdisciplines of physical geography are biogeography and climatology. For its part, human geography has subdisciplines such as economic geography and political geography.

Physical and human geography have had a long and bumpy life together beginning with the ancient Greeks, who mapped and wrote topographical descriptions of the known world, and continuing in the Middle Ages, when pilgrims needed maps to get them to their destinations. At these times, the human and physical pieces of geography were integrated. This was not true, however, by the time of the Renaissance, when geography became critical to global exploration. It was then that the difference between a social science and a natural science became clearer. From then on, it was evident that the two versions of science called for different methodologies and that the knowledge they constructed was dissimilar—the natural science producing verifiable "hard" facts or certainty about the natural world, and the social sciences constructing knowledge about its complex human subjects that is "probabilistic" and conditional. This tension, however, has not caused a full divorce in geography; it just split the field into two branches, linked together by their mutual geographical vision of space, location, and place and their integrated vision of the interaction between humanity and nature.

Today, that integrated vision is more important than ever as physical and human geographers turn their attention to the big issues and problems that face our planet: pressures on global resources, population growth and change; globalization in economics, technology, and culture; global politics and power relationships; and poverty, hunger, and climate change, to name a few. The "cultural trend" in geography since the 1980s, which turned human geography's focus toward society, ethnicity, gender, nationality, and politics, has today been joined by a rising concern with the global natural environment, especially climate. Geographers, both human geographers and physical geographers, are there to lend their distinctive methods, forms, and knowledge to the effort of understanding and solving these complex and daunting problems. In fact, geography has a new subdiscipline, ecogeography, a holistic approach specifically focused on these concerns (Holt-Jensen, 2006).

Purpose of Geography

Geography in general is a very practical science. From its inception, it has supplied the tools and knowledge for real-world activities such as commerce, economics, exploration, travel, science, war, and politics—any endeavor that requires knowing where things are, how big they are, how far they are apart, what zone or region they reside in, or how to get there from here. Geography, however, goes deeper than mapping out locations, states, regions, or landforms. It also makes in-depth studies of human life and natural phenomena and how they play out in locations. Geography, therefore, is about understanding deeply the phenomena it locates— how these phenomena are related, spatially and conceptually, and how they interact and influence each other.

Knowledge of Geography

The knowledge of a discipline incorporates both facts or information and the concepts that connect or explain them. In all disciplines, concepts provide the frame or lens through which topics are viewed. This is, of course, true of geography.

The facts or information of physical geography include what geographers call "abiotic" and "biotic" factors. Abiotic factors are such things as geological formations, soil, climate features, and ocean currents. "Biotic" factors are living organisms such as vegetation, animals, and humans as biological creatures. The information of human geography is that of the social sciences seen through a geographical lens. This means that geography looks at human phenomena in terms of physical, psychological, social, and political location (Holt-Jensen, 2006).

While geographers examine disparate questions, themes, and topics, the core of their work concerns how geographic concepts inform or help to explain different processes that shape the everyday world (Knox & Martson, 2012). Some of these key concepts are *place*, *space*, and *scale*. Other critical concepts are *location*, *region*, *movement*, and *human–environment interaction*. These concepts help to structure geographic analyses.

At its most basic level, *location* refers to where something lies according to specific geographic coordinates on the Earth's surface. In other words, location is where something is and can be pinpointed precisely. *Space* has to do with relative location. The study of space explores relationships between places and patterns of activity arising from the use people make of physical settings where they live and work (Holt-Jensen, 2006). Space, therefore, integrates relative location, human activity, and movement between locations. It is a concept that refers to the three-dimensional context, or container, in which life takes place (Gregory, 2009).

Scale is the concept of relative size. The idea of scale may refer to a point on a map relative to its actual size on the Earth's surface. It can also refer to the size of an issue, question, or spatial unit being analyzed. The concept of scale also comes into play when geographers study how a certain phenomenon can take place at different magnitudes. For example, geographers use the notion of scale to understand how a social movement or a phenomenon related to climate or ecosystems can occur in a tiny region and also around the world (Montello, 2001).

Two other concepts in human geography are particularly critical and timely: *movement* and *human–environment interaction*: movement because it describes the passage of human populations and the practices and processes that animate, shape, and inform everyday life, and human–environment interaction because it describes our collective impact on nature and its effect on us. The geography of globalization is particularly concerned with these two concepts.

Of all the concepts geographers employ to analyze and frame their inquiries, the concepts of *region* and *place* are the most complex and integrative. And of these two concepts, place is the most poetic and humanistic; it refers to the meaning a site has for those who encounter or live in it. A "sense of place" emerges when a meaning is attached to a location (Gatrell & Elliott, 2009). Because meaning is about human understanding, place is a complex and integrative concept. It considers people, culture, history, sensory experience, imagination, symbolism and myth, and the physical properties of a location. As a concept that takes all of this into account and taps into human experience, imagination, and aesthetics, place is a much-visited theme in literature, architecture, design, and art (Holt-Jensen, 2009).

The concept of *region* also exemplifies the science of geography at its most integrated because it shows how geographers dig deeply into one area to construct a complex, holistic understanding of it. A region is a specific area or zone on the Earth's surface. It can be a small area or a large area within a state or a grouping of states (Knox & Martson, 2012). What makes a zone a region is its specific and distinctive characteristics. Regional geography, a specific kind of geography, presents a total integrated picture of a region and what makes it distinctive (Holt-Jensen, 2009). In this way, geography mimics anthropology, which studies specific cultures in the same holistic way.

Forms of Geography

The map is the geographer's most useful resource and form of expression (see Figures 6.1 and 6.2). The map is also a particularly useful tool; not only can it represent locations and relationships in space but geographers use maps to show how ideas and phenomena are related and how phenomena change over time. We may think geographers use and produce maps exclusively, but they also work with tables, diagrams, and written accounts, including ethnographies and regional analyses (Holt-Jensen, 2009).

Methods of Geography

Physical geographers do field studies in which they apply methods, such as photo documentation, soil description and sampling, stream gauging, channel surveying, field mapping, water quality sampling, vegetation characterization, and spatial sampling. They also do statistical analysis of their findings, and map the

Figure 6.1. Wm. Darton and W. R. Gardner, *New and Improved View of the Comparative Heights of Principal Mountains and Lengths of Principal Rivers in the World,* 1823.

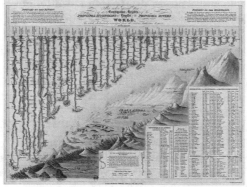

This image was provided to Wikimedia Commons by Geographicus Rare Antique Maps, a specialist dealer in rare maps and other cartography of the 15th, 16th, 17th, 18th and 19th centuries, as part of a cooperation project.

Figure 6.2. A. J. Bormeester, *Nova Totius Terrarum Orbis Tabula,* 1684.

This image was provided to Wikimedia Commons by Geographicus Rare Antique Maps, a specialist dealer in rare maps and other cartography of the 15th, 16th, 17th, 18th and 19th centuries, as part of a cooperation project.

phenomena they study using conventional cartographic methods and modern technology, such as GPS (Global Positioning System), new climate and weather field instruments, and remote sensing devices.

For their part, human geographers use a wide range of methods in carrying out their research and analysis in the field, and these are much the same as those used in the social sciences. They include survey research. Survey questions are most frequently answered in quantifiable or numeric ways, and they are designed to collect a large amount of information over a short period of time. Because survey methods are most often quantifiable, the methods and tools that human geographers use to analyze survey data are designed to look at numeric patterns conveyed in statistics. Quantitative survey methods also may be of use for conducting comparisons.

Human geographers do qualitative research as well. Qualitative methods in human geography include interviewing individuals and focus groups and use of ethnographic methods. These methods for data collection are designed to obtain more nuanced information. In their use of these methods, both quantitative and qualitative, geographers resemble sociologists.

Human geographers also resemble anthropologists in doing ethnographic research into cultures and cultural phenomena. For this, they use interviews, surveys, and participant observations to gain in-depth knowledge of the communities they research. Ethnographers also write detailed fieldnotes that emerge from their observations and experiences in the field. The resulting data are then used as a basis for analysis and description.

Human geographers, like their colleagues in physical geography, map out their findings to see how information fits together and to convey that information graphically. Indeed, mapping locations, relationships, and processes in nature and in human life creates and conveys the "geographical lens."

Aesthetics of Geography

Maps are geography's primary aesthetic expression. Who doesn't love to look at maps? How intriguing it is to see how the countries of Africa, Asia, or South America fit together, or where Magellan reached the Pacific Ocean. What fun it is to locate oneself on a map, dream of where you might go, and plot out a path to get there. Maps spur the imagination; they may be abstract representations, just colors, shapes, and lines that have little to do with reality on the ground, but they inspire exploration and adventure, real or imagined. Maps, therefore, engender pleasure and interest. Also, they are often beautiful with their lines, forms, and colors, and other visual qualities that map lovers and artists alike savor. Beyond their beauty, maps are representations of information, whether of facts, relationships, movement, or concepts. Maps carry meaning through numbers and geometry and through cartographic symbols and conventions that are decodable. At their best, maps possess the clarity and conceptual "fit" that characterize aesthetic experience in the sciences, mathematics, and art. Indeed, as visual imagery and symbols that integrate math and science with visual pleasure and impact, and conceptual fit and clarity, maps are truly *the integrated aesthetic form.*

What about the other things geographers do? Aesthetics is also about making meaning on a deep level, and geographers do that in their in-depth analysis of interrelated causes behind natural and social phenomena and in their explorations of meaning behind a place. Geographers also think deeply about how our minds work when they connect and contrast the basic ways we perceive a site. Their work highlights the contrast between the abstract and distilled nature of a map of a place and the onsite reality of that place, which we can only grasp through the embodied experience of being there. Here geographers cross over into the realm of the arts and aesthetics as they delve into the nature of symbolic representation versus real lived, sensory experience.

FUNDAMENTALS OF GEOGRAPHY AND INTEGRATION WITH ART

As you think about art-centered integrated learning and geography, consider these fundamental ideas about geography discussed in this chapter:

1. Seeking underlying patterns in nature and human life
2. Exploring the world as a system composed of a natural system and a social/cultural and political system
3. Inquiring into how a natural environment affects human life
4. Examining how human needs and actions impact the natural environment
5. Studying change in cultures and societies and the landscapes they inhabit
6. Exploring movement between and among places and spaces
7. Thinking spatially; seeing spatial relationships
8. Examining how symbols, numbers, and other conventions represent ideas and information
9. Investigating how direct experience of something is different from "reading" an abstract graphic representation of it

CONTEMPORARY ART AND GEOGRAPHY

When we think of the integration of art and geography, the mind naturally turns to maps. Perhaps this is because maps are often visually stunning. Indeed, cartographers have throughout history applied artistic skills and techniques to boost a map's effect (Harmon, 2009). As images that have conceptual utility and visual impact, maps have spawned a generation of map-based, map-inspired contemporary art. Harmon maintains that since the 1960s, more and more artists have been making maps and using maps in their artwork. She identifies the following reasons for this: First, artists have found cartography to be a rich vein of concepts and imagery to mine; second, they have found that cartographic rules afford them a set of assumptions to utilize and disrupt; and, lastly, maps are an adaptable visual and conceptual form that welcomes appropriation.

Maps also act as metaphors for activities such as seeking location, experiencing displacement, ordering chaos, exploring scale relationships, and charting new landscapes. Maps can also frame statements about politics, territoriality, and other notions of power and projection. For example, Joyce Kozloff uses maps to illustrate what people know, alluding to knowledge as the foundation of human imagination and culture and of political and economic power. In her *Knowledge Series* (1999), Kozloff renders historical maps on globes to illustrate what people knew about world geography at different times and in different places throughout history. In picturing this knowledge, she taps into how knowledge limits, expands, and shapes worldviews (see Figures 6.3 and 6.4).

Furthermore, many artists use maps to convey their political and social messages. Today, especially, artists use maps to respond to social, cultural, and economic globalization to help themselves understand cultural change. While maps signify and organize meaning, artists also use maps not for what they signify but for how their systems and forms can be adapted to an artist's purposes (Harmon, 2009).

When considering art and geography, landscape is another art form that comes to mind. From Paul Cézanne's many renditions of Mt. Ste. Victoire, to Frederic Church's monumental landscape paintings of the South American wilderness, to Andrew Wyeth's dry, earth-hued depictions of weatherworn fields in

Figure 6.3. Joyce Kozloff, *Knowledge #74: 1561,* 1999.

Watercolor, plaster and rope on cardboard, with porcelain base, 9 7/8 inches diameter. Image courtesy of the artist and DC Moore Gallery, New York.

Figure 6.4. Joyce Kozloff, *Knowledge #76: 1602,* 1999.

Watercolor and acrylic, plaster and rope on cardboard, with porcelain base, 9 11/16 inches diameter. Image courtesy of the artist and DC Moore Gallery, New York.

Maine and Pennsylvania, to Grant Wood's cartoon-like pictures of the soft rolling hills of Iowa, landscape has been about the power of place. This includes urban landscapes as well, such as Edward Hopper's haunting depictions of interior and exterior scenes in New York.

Although landscape is still a viable form, artists have pioneered other ways to explore urban landscapes—looking to re-present places, as opposed to representing them. For example, the "Situationists," a group of artist–geographers in the 1950s and 1960s, walked and explored Europe's fabled cities to experience the urban environment. The Situationists placed a great emphasis on firsthand, sensory, and conscious experience of a place. They also examined the way the mind forms its understanding of a location through moving through it. This they called *psychogeography*. To practice psychogeography, the Situationists perfected the art of "drifting," meandering in an improvisational way, finding the unexpected by going to unforeseen places without a plan and learning along the way. The map of their journeys emerged in the act of drifting as the Situationists traced the route of their travels (O'Rourke, 2013). These wanderings as learning experiences tap into geography's concern with movement through space to places and are reminiscent of the art research journey process described in Chapter 2.

The Situationists' early expeditions inspired a slew of map-based, performance-based contemporary art forms that explore location, movement, and place, including art that uses GPS and other new mapping or locative technologies (O'Rourke, 2013).

ART THAT CONNECTS TO GEOGRAPHY

Technology, Location, and Place

With a background in videogames and design software, Aram Bartholl is a tech artist who does not create art for computer screens but instead makes art about the social/cultural impacts of digital technology. One of Bartholl's concerns is the way virtual space has expanded to create an immaterial world as experientially real as any physical place in the "real world." In his *Map* project illustrated in Figure 6.5, he takes this concept to the streets, showing how virtual space overlaps and shapes our perceptions and experiences of "real" places. With a simple witty gesture, he makes that superimposition palpable; he installs a 20-ft-tall (approximately 6.1-m-tall) Google map pin in the exact spot Google cites as the center of a city. These pins are placed in diverse cities such as Taipei, Taiwan; Berlin, Germany; and Szczecin, Poland. On encountering one of these familiar icons, one can't help but recognize the conflation of place and map, and the invisible net of virtual systems becomes apparent . . . and quite funny.

Figures 6.5. Aram Bartholl, *Map*, 2006–2010.

Photo by Aram Bartholl. Image courtesy of DAM Gallery.

Bartholl is also concerned with the way digital technology is evolving, fearing eventual loss of our autonomy and privacy, as flash-drives and exterior hard-drives are replaced by corporate-controlled storage banks called "clouds." In *Dead Drops*, he stages a counter offensive by cementing USB flash-drives into walls to create a network of communication hubs far from the clouds, the Internet, and the purview of "Big Brother" technology (see Figure 6.6). In the beginning, each of these flash-drives was empty except for instructions on how to use it and participate in the piece. As time goes by, people plug their computers into these devices to download and share information, writings, and images—in short, to communicate. While an act of defiance or intervention, *Dead Drops* also embodies Bartholl's primary theme; it represents another collision of the virtual world with the material world in the way it generates a network of communication based on actual sites in a city. Houses become data storage spaces, and the physical network that is a city becomes a virtual one as well (Glover, 2011).

Integration (Purpose, Knowledge, Methods, and Forms). Bartholl's stated *purpose* is to alert us to social realities. The *knowledge* he taps into is of technology, the way technologies affect us, and how communication networks work. Bartholl is also a keen observer of community and social life, and his knowledge about contemporary life is anthropological in flavor. While he focuses on digital phenomena, his *methods* are not computer based, but the techniques of a participant–observer in the mode of anthropology. Bartholl is essentially a social practice public artist who studies contemporary culture and social life and either informs his public or collaborates with them. In his attention to geographical/virtual space, Bartholl thinks like a geographer, exploring social phenomena in terms of place and geographical location. As for *forms,* the physical or visual forms Bartholl works with are city sites and buildings, computer devices, digital icons, and maps. His invisible forms are community and virtual networks.

Figure 6.6. Aram Bartholl, *Dead Drops*, 2010.

Photo by Aram Bartholl. Image courtesy of DAM Gallery.

Creative Strategies. In both *Map* and *Dead Drops*, Bartholl's primary strategy is *juxtaposition*: placing an image or device in surroundings where both the inserted object and its new environment are understood in relationship to each other. This *recontextualization* points out the many layers of reality we live in today.

Playing with Place, Space, and Borders

Maps are useful tools that can convey an abundance of information. Often that information is based on reality; maps visualize real territories. However, maps can also depict imaginary territories. Lordy Rodriguez knows this well, and he uses the language of maps to mix reality with fantasy and to reconfigure the world. As a first-generation Filipino American, Rodriguez is keenly aware of boundaries and displacement, and this drives his interest in shifting places around, drawing new borders, and realigning regions. In his many fanciful, mixed-up maps of the United States, Rodriguez does just that. In *America (Key Map of States and Their Capitols)* (2006), for instance, he places Texas on the East Coast and Pennsylvania on the West Coast, and everything else wherever he likes (see Figure 6.7). Cultures and peoples, territories and places, become jumbled and relocated. Their new locations and borders seem to tell us that the America of today has a new map—a new set of alignments.

In *America (Key Map of States and Their Capitols)*, Rodriguez also includes five new states: Internet, Hollywood, Monopoly, Disney, and Territory. These new territories, of course, are not real geographic territories but mythical places or states of mind. This confusion of the geographical (physical) and the virtual (mental or imaginary) is amplified and made clearer in Rodriguez's map of the Internet, *Internet 2.0* (2007) (illustrated in Figure 6.8), in which a virtual territory is isolated and represented as a real, physical place.

Although Rodriguez's newly configured worlds spring out of his own capricious whims, *America (Key Map of States and Their Capitols)* and *Internet 2.0*

Figure 6.7. Lordy Rodriguez, *America (Key Map of States and Their Capitols)*, 2006.

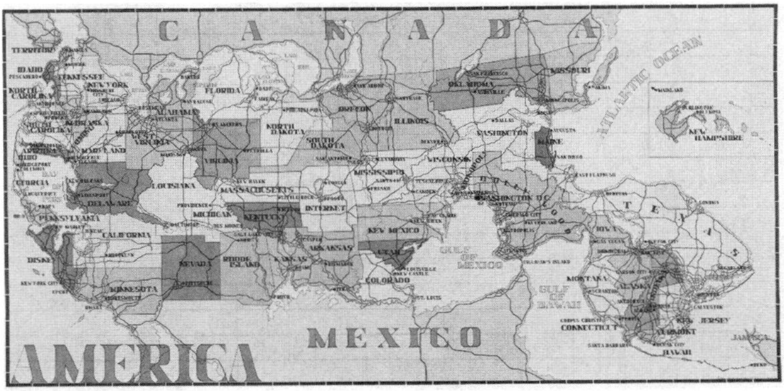

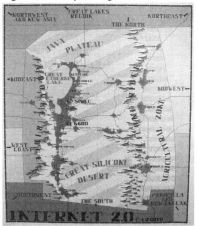

Image courtesy of the artist.

Figure 6.8. Lordy Rodriguez, *Internet 2.0*, 2007.

Image courtesy of the artist. Collection of the San
Jose Museum of Art, San Jose, California.

address some real phenomena and carry a dollop of social commentary. The five
additional states in *America (Key Map of States and Their Capitols)* mark particularly "American" states of mind, as real to many Americans as Minnesota or Maine.
Indeed, they represent American values and show how important those values are.
Why else would they merit their own regions? For its part, *Internet 2.0* represents
a more global reality and set of values; the World Wide Web is the real world now,
with all its interconnectivity and commercial reach. Both artworks, therefore,
make a social comment and are indicative of many of Rodriguez's maps that poke
fun at American society and the global culture that surrounds it.

While all his maps are visually tethered to real geography, in his latest works, Rodriguez drops the texts and symbols of cartography and fills his territories, still recognizable as real places, with colorful abstract patterns. An example of this is Figure 6.9, *United States Map II (Not States)* (2010). Here the United States becomes a crazy quilt of stripes, dots, curvy lines, and plaids—a metaphor for a diverse, multifaceted America. Rodriguez is playing here with form and concept, and that's a beautiful thing.

Integration (Purpose, Knowledge, Methods, and Forms). "Being from an immigrant family, finding my social place in the U.S. and how I represent that, has always been personally important to me" (Rodriguez, 2013). Understanding his location, and thus his identity, is an original *purpose* behind Rodriguez's work. Other purposes appear to motivate the work as well: the desire to represent the fluidity and arbitrariness of political and cultural boundaries and also to capture the flexible, idiosyncratic nature of the mind (Raud, 2004). To accomplish this, Rodriguez draws on his *knowledge* of American geography, politics, and culture, and his knowledge of cartographic iconography and conventions. As for *methods*, Rodriguez researches the physical and cultural territories he pictures by making extensive road trips. He also uses the mapping techniques of cartographers. Rodriguez's *forms*, of course, are maps and the texts, symbols, colors, lines, and shapes they employ to represent everything related to spaces and places.

Creative Strategies. Five creative strategies animate Rodriguez's paintings. *Reformatting* (using the format of the map from geography), *juxtaposition* (reshuffling sites and territories), and changing *scale* (making things relatively larger or smaller) are the most apparent strategies the artist uses. These strategies enable the artist to picture in visible, concrete ways the ineffable, invisible workings of

Figure 6.9. Lordy Rodriguez, *United States Map II (Not States)*, 2010.

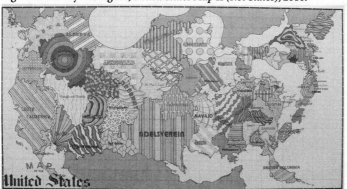

Image courtesy of the artist and Hosfelt Gallery.

politics, culture, and the imagination. Principally in his later more abstract work, Rodriguez *edits* (takes out the extraneous details) and *abstracts* (pares down "real" shapes to their essential forms). Here he takes full advantage of the map as a visually stunning aesthetic form.

REFERENCES

Gatrell, A., & Elliott, S. (2009). *Geographies of health: An introduction*. Malden, MA: Wiley-Blackwell.

Glover, I. (2011). Artist profile: Aram Bartholl. Retrieved from rhizome.org/editorial/2011/aug/24/artist-profile-aram-bartholl

Gregory, D. (2009). *The dictionary of human geography*. Malden, MA: Wiley-Blackwell.

Harmon, K. (2009). *The map as art: Contemporary artists explore cartography*. New York, NY: Princeton Architectural Press.

Holt-Jensen, A. (2009). *Geography: History and concepts*. London, England: Sage.

Klein, J. (2000). Voices of Royaumont. In M. Somerville & D. Rapport (Eds.), *Transdisciplinarity: Recreating integrated knowledge* (pp. 3–13). Oxford, England: EOLSS.

Knox, P., & Martson, S. A. (2012). *Human geography: Places and regions in global context*. New York, NY: Pearson.

Montello, D. (2001). Scale in geography. In N. J. Smelser & P. B. Baltes (Eds.), *International encyclopedia of the social and behavioral sciences* (pp. 13501–13504). Oxford, England: Pergamon Press.

O'Rourke, K. (2013). *Walking and mapping: Artists as cartographers*. Cambridge, MA: MIT Press.

Raud, C. (2004). Lordy Rodriquez. Retrieved from www.stretcher.org/features/lordy_rodriguez_new_states/

7

Creative Writing
The Long and Winding Road

Rick Ayers

Creative writing allows us to document our reality and dissect the stories and metaphors that frame our lives. By its nature, such writing helps us complicate our thinking about where and how we fit in, what we are, and where we are or might be heading. Creative writing can open that negotiation in a way that is inventive, restorative, perhaps even transformative. Daniel Alarcón (2010), speaking of creative writing, observes,

> If the American Dream is to have any relevance at this late date, it must be elastic, renewable. It must be . . . an intensely personal construct; a negotiation with reality, with tradition, with one's own past and family history and, in no small part, a wager on the future. (p. xv)

In the explorations below, I will raise some key observations and questions about the practice and discipline of creative writing—what authors do—and then follow with some considerations about creative writing in schools.

For many writers, the practice of creative writing becomes an orientation and a discipline that not only serves communication with others but also primarily and initially generates their own thinking and reflection process. Creative writing is never just technique or style; it is in the first place a way of being and thinking and then communicating through language about philosophical, political, social, and personal matters.

Perhaps more than any other discipline, however, the practice of creative writing has no road maps or algorithms. It is a matter of trial and error, of intuition and inspiration. For some writers, a regular discipline of hours at the desk is crucial; for others, ideas and formulations are best discovered in solitary or social pursuits away from the writing itself. Some emphasize the craft and hard work; others insist that it is a matter of letting the muse of inspiration come. However, for all, it is a winding and uncertain process, one that adheres to the style and temperament of each individual writer. It is a matter, as Miles Horton says, of making the road while walking it.

WHAT IS CREATIVE WRITING?

The raw material of creative writing is most obviously language. But language is itself always and necessarily plastic and malleable. Writing is contingent on many things including historical flow, economic condition, and the social and cultural context of the writer. Creative writers sometimes insist on mixing vernaculars precisely to decenter the dominant discourse—as Junot Díaz has done brilliantly in his Pulitzer Prize–winning *The Brief Wondrous Life of Oscar Wao* (2007). Here formal English shares the page, even the same sentence, with Spanish, Ebonics, science fiction and fantasy references, and Dominican slang.

Creative writers have license to adopt multiple voices and multiple dictions, they may make up words, and they may even cross over to nonword sounds and exclamations. But always it is language, it is the word—written, spoken, and shared—that is at the heart of creative writing.

Besides eliciting flights of imagination, creative writing allows the writer to understand and wield the power of story, the importance of connecting with others through compelling narratives that fulfill particular expectations of story. Unlike most expository writing, creative writing has an experiential side. Expression and dialogue are crucial to the process, for creative writing is never an act of solitude, of hidden texts, of retiring into oneself. It is always a performance that demands an audience and seeks to move others. Creative writing generally enlists a broad audience, not simply the judging eye of a single reader. The power of story stands as a bastion against our anxiety about the future and uncertainty about the rules of the game in the culture. For, in creative writing, we can try on our own rules, explore other possible futures.

Creative writing, beyond the stories it tells, allows us to experience and experiment with the plasticity of language, the way the sounds and patterns and juxtapositions of a composition may communicate meaning that is beyond the literal meaning of the words.

Creative writing is not simply a matter of doing whatever comes to mind. The written piece starts often in subjectivity, but it must make itself into an object, must find coherence and definition in a product that can be shared either orally or on paper. While there is no constraint on the judgment of the author, there must be constant engagement with others and an iterative process in construction of an effective written piece. In creative writing, the author constructs a feeling–thought, which is both sensuous and imaginative. The piece may seek to express ambiguity, but it is not sloppy or random. The meaning of the piece is not arbitrary. Moreover, only the audience makes meaning from the creative piece, so the author must interact with the audience to qualify, or perhaps even to learn, what the piece means.

Purpose of Creative Writing

The practice and the teaching of creative writing—how to define it and how to pursue it—is a contested field in every way. The Scottish romantic novels of Walter

Scott were embraced by slave owners in the 19th century as the model of chivalry; endless war epics have enchanted militarists. I argue here, however, that there is tremendous anti-authoritarian, democratic, and even healing potential in the practice of language arts.

The very act of "creative writing" is an extension of storytelling, songs, and language play that goes back to the beginning of human history. It only became "creative writing" when the technology of writing was invented. Yet the deployment of language for aesthetic purposes is central to all cultures. While early writing, such as Chinese court records, Cretan Linear B, and Mayan stelae, preserved official decrees and records, evidence of creative and secular vernacular utterances is present whenever ancient sites are preserved, such as the neighborhoods of Pompeii. While writing in Europe was the province of the religious orders through the Middle Ages, the invention of moveable type by Gutenberg led not only to translations of the Bible into local languages but to the proliferation of novels, poems, and gossipy broadsheets wherever presses made an appearance.

Sanity is generally thought to be a person's ability to tell an ongoing story about his or her life, to narrate that life as it is lived. The loss of that capacity is seen as insanity or dementia. Creative writing contributes to the construction of culture through the linking of these internal stories and narratives of individual lives to the shared stories and narratives of society. In addition, creative writing sets out to make the familiar strange, calling on people to think in new ways about their world and their endeavors.

Creative writing has also been proposed as an authentic form of research. Leavy (2013) proposes that deeper truths can more often be accessed through fiction than through traditional research. She draws on the work of Barone and Eisner (1997), who explore the notion of arts-based research and assert that such writing is characterized by the following:

1. The creation of virtual reality.
2. The presence of ambiguity.
3. The use of expressive language.
4. The use of vernacular language.
5. The promotion of empathy.
6. The personal signature of the researcher/writer.
7. The presence of aesthetic form. (p. 214)

Applying these elements, creative writers can lay claim to their own contribution to knowledge of the world as well as the generation of new theory to explain the world.

Creative writing activates the participation of all people to make their own contribution to culture. It is a practice in debate with the elite notion of high culture, arguing instead for a broad democratic engagement in public discourse (Finkelstein, 1984). In the modern era, the arguments for creative writing went hand in hand with the celebration of public art such as mural work of the Mexican

Revolution. Such an approach represented a criticism of the museum housing of art, where pieces would all be collected in one place to be passively admired.

Creative writing, by the very freedom it allows and even demands for the writer, is based on the premise that individual and community experiences are valid and worthy of exploration. It rests on assumptions about humanity—that the world is not made up of settled and autonomous facts but, rather, that new worlds are constantly in the making, that the emotional landscapes and analytical constructions of young people make a contribution. Aspiration, desire, moral re-flection, and ethical action existing in the human heart are thus encouraged and brought to light. As such, creative writing propels the humanity of writers and readers and contributes to a democratic impulse, the expression of truths from below.

Forms of Creative Writing

Creative writing embraces a wide range of forms and genres. The personal essay combines expository and creative writing. Generally, when we think of the creative work in writing, expository and advocacy writing are not considered. Some forms, however, such as the personal essay, combine expository and creative writing. Although writers constantly blur and cross over the lines between genres, typically the following forms are central to creative writing: memoir, personal essay, short story, novel, drama, and poetry. Each of these, we know, is divided into numerous subgenres.

The complicated process of anointing some works as worthy and classic and others as lesser contributions—the process of canonization—reflects the power relationships of those who define culture more than some intrinsic value of the work. Or, to put it another way, creative writing is often divided, in production as well as in consumption, between different classes and groups in society. Jacqueline Susann romantic novels are snapped up at the grocery store, African American novels of Iceberg Slim are popular in urban centers, the *Harry Potter* series sweeps through the youth population, and David Foster Wallace titles are popular among academic readers. Nevertheless, a constant cross-fertilization and conversation goes on between and among all of these domains.

While it is impossible to propose exhaustive treatment on each of the genres, a few salient descriptions and questions are in order.

Memoir. While the traditional autobiography is purported to simply tell one's own life, perhaps emphasizing lessons learned or accomplishments achieved, the modern memoir is regarded as more of a creative project. In it, the writer draws from his or her life but is granted license to re-create dialogue and to take imagina-tive asides, for the memoir is not simply a record; it is the rendering of a moment or series of moments, the development of a theme, and the proposal of a disposi-tion toward the world.

Personal Essay. Two other genres of composition that fit, at least partly, under the rubric of creative writing are personal response essay and journalistic writing. Early in secular composition, it was considered a radical departure to introduce the "I" pronoun (Montaigne, 1580/2012). First-person writing has since been incorporated into the "personal essay," which serves as a kind of bridge between creative and expository writing (Lopate, 1994). Such writing takes as its subject matter actual events, texts, or cultural productions; it is not simply a flight of fancy but deploys considerable elements of creativity and draws from personal experiences and point of view. With the rise of New Journalism in the 1960s—which itself was a reaction to the inauthentic voice of objectivity in establishment media—such writers as Joan Didion and Hunter S. Thompson exploded the impersonal voice in reporting and celebrated creativity and personal perspective.

Short Story. Generally creative writers pursue a theme through a series of short stories, whether it is social issues, linked characters, a place or time, or even philosophical pursuits. While short stories may seem simpler to construct than novels—there are fewer words to compose, for one thing—writers find the form to be deceptively complicated. The work of taking the reader into another world, another set of circumstances, values, and feelings, is much more difficult without the luxury of long exposition.

Novel. Extended stories go back to the earliest epics, from *Gilgamesh* to *The Iliad*. Probably the earliest written story that can be called a novel is the Japanese *The Tale of Genji* by Lady Murasaki Shikibu from the 11th century. While a number of tales of chivalry arose in Europe from the 15th century, many consider Miguel de Cervantes's *Don Quixote of La Mancha* the first European modern novel. Generally, a novel includes a central character, as well as others, whose personality is explored in depth, a sequence of events over time, and a story arc—from a problem statement to a resolution. Often novels contain digressions, psychological dimensions, parallel plots, stories within stories, and multiple points of view.

The subgenres and divisions within the novel are endless with some of the larger categories being the literary novel, mystery, science fiction, historical, and comic. Novels also follow national or regional trends and inclinations, such as the testimonial and magic realism novels of Latin America. Many argue that a powerful novel better captures the reality of a period than the writing of contemporary political analysts (Leavy, 2013). This can be seen, for example, in comparing the way Conrad captured the reality of imperialism in Africa in *Heart of Darkness* versus the kind of analysis advanced by his contemporary historians in 1900.

Drama. Dramatic production goes back to the earliest human cultures and is found in rituals and religious practices as well as in secular entertainments. From the Mahabharata in India, to the drama contests in Greece, to the griot performances in West Africa, communities found theatrical productions to be a site for gathering to laugh and cry, to consolidate their social identity, and to consider dilemmas. Creative playwriting (and screenplay writing) is as varied and complex as is our global society. For example, while a modernist playwright produces plays experimenting with thin and obscure plotting, such writers as August Wilson and David Simon have returned realism—a kind of gritty and textured realism—to the stage and screen.

Poetry. Poetry or verse began as public performance and is still considered a performative, as well as written, art. The border between songwriting and poetry writing is thin and often crossed. Poetry is a form of writing that is easy to recognize yet hard to define. Generally, a creative writing piece is a poem when the language is compact and layered with meaning. Poetry sometimes, but not always, uses verse (meter and rhyme). And for many, poetry is considered the most creative, the most aesthetically rich, form of creative writing.

The poet has to wield language, which is a tool for objectivity, for representation of facts. He or she must use this tool as an object, an end in itself, to express something that is more on the affective, sensual side of experience. When one analyzes a poem, seeking to draw out the plot or the "message," too often this means stripping it of the ineluctable power of the way the poem is made. If the message suffices to explain the poem, it would be easier to get rid of the poem and simply share the message. However, that would never be satisfactory. The poem does something more. In struggling to write a poem, we begin to appreciate the aesthetic that comes out of the language and yet is beyond the literal meaning of the words. Hence, the classic book on understanding poetry by John Ciardi (1975) is called *How Does a Poem Mean?* By switching out the expected question, What, Ciardi asks us to consider the effects of sound, subconscious resonance, and metaphor in making a poem work. Because the meaning of a poem is so deeply embedded in the culture that produced the writer's language, the translation of poetry is the most difficult, some would say hopeless, of tasks.

Methods of Creative Writing

One writer takes walks or otherwise distracts attention until inspiration comes; another insists that the key is to sit down in the morning and work, write, until 6,000 words are on the page. Some want the muse to land unexpectedly on their shoulders; others want to wrestle her down and demand ideas. How a person goes about the business of creative writing is as varied as the practitioners. Moreover, the question of writing as an individual pursuit or as a matter of social engagement is a result of the various inclinations of those who write. Some well-known elements in the methods of creative writing include the workshop, engagement with other literature, and publishing.

Workshop Process. Much has been written and debated about the question of whether creative writing can be taught as a discipline for professional writers.

Novelist John Barth (1985) responds with an emphatic affirmative. There are over 800 degree programs in creative writing in the United States. Many student and professional writers participate in writing workshops, either as support for their own craft or as a vocation to sustain themselves while helping others with their writing (Myers, 2006). Such writing handbooks as *Writing Down the Bones* (Goldberg, 1986), *Bird by Bird* (Lamott, 1994), and *So You Want to Write* (Piercy & Wood, 2005) are often the staples of writing workshops. While skeptics point out that very few participants in graduate writing workshop programs become professional writers, such a proposition is as ridiculous as suggesting that students should only study music if it leads to a professional career in the field.

Keys to creative writing workshops are the prompt and the group feedback. The prompt is whatever gets the writing going, whether it is another text or artifact, a question or a challenge, or simply an assignment. Many writers draft without self-editing, making a best effort at capturing the feeling and ideas they want to convey. Writing freely, sometimes even in a stream-of-consciousness way, releases authors from the self-doubt, hesitation, and artificiality that so often surrounds school writing.

Writers need feedback. Some feedback comes from friends, colleagues, and editors. However, many turn to the workshop as an effective strategy for creative writing feedback. Generally, the writer takes the "author's chair" and reads his or her piece, or part of the piece, out loud. Those who listen are taught how to give encouraging, content-rich, and deep feedback. In the workshop approach, both the author and the audience are exploring the elements of effective communication and powerful writing.

Sometimes the writing style, or tone, of participants in one workshop will start to converge in a common one. Workshop writing is sometimes criticized as producing too many eager authors who show off a kind of self-congratulatory cleverness of their prose or verse but have little to say. Thus a tension exists over what constitutes a legitimate contribution to the cultural discourse and what is simply styling.

While the workshop is writer centered, it is not writer led. The distinction points to the role of the workshop leader. Simply imagining that writers will find a way to produce great writing on their own is a romanticization of the process. The task of the workshop leader is to guide the discussion and even to teach students how to be an attentive audience that gives helpful feedback.

After critique, the authors go back to edit, redraft, and reframe their pieces. If they care to, some writers may start over. And, depending on how major the piece is in the writer's process, it could go through numerous drafts and numerous workshop presentations. This process is so common in creative writing that workshop has become a verb and an author can be said to have "workshopped" a piece.

Writing and Literature. Strong writing is closely connected to reading and a robust reading program of peer and published pieces. Thus the engagement with literature is crucial to the creative writing project. Texts can serve as models or can be places to generate ideas and challenges for the creative writer.

How this works can be seen in the ways that media literacy and video production classes work hand in hand. Students who are studying film and video are often required to make their own short videos. The tasks involved in video making—idea creation, storyboarding, casting, framing, shooting, editing, sound integration, and presentation—all have parallels in creative writing. Video makers become more adept at deconstructing and critiquing an electronic text when they have worked to produce their own videos. And so it is with writers.

Writers learn to pay attention to the process of creating a text—making it possible for them to read as writers (Prose, 2007). Writing is in many respects a matter of imitation, as phrases and tropes move from one text to another. It is also a project of engagement, response, and even critique of previous writers. Bloom (1973) asserts that all literary texts are a response to those that precede them. He calls this relationship the "anxiety of influence," the tension of reading, misreading, responding to, and reframing previous works. Further literary theory, from critical to postmodernist to post-structuralist, surrounds writers and creates the context for their new contributions. As such, the creative writer is engaged in a massive public discourse, a cultural discourse that engages millions of people around the world in reading, writing, critiquing, imagining, rethinking, and starting anew.

Publishing. The poet Rainer Maria Rilke (1993) declares a deeply personal goal for writing, one that is oblivious to audience: "Go into yourself. Search for the reason that bids you to write. Find out whether it is spreading out its roots in the deepest places of your heart" (p. 16). In creative writing, generally writers do not agree with this turn inward. In spite of the romantic appeal of Rilke's words, they mask the public purpose that is present even for him, the communicative purpose of creative writing. Writers may do a good deal of self-exploration, and some may prefer solitude and withdrawal during some phases of the writing process. But ultimately creative writing is to be shared.

Central to the creative writing approach is the issue of publishing—how will works be shared with the world? For many writers, the creative process goes on for years before they are ready to share publicly. For others, they believe they have something that will be welcomed and important in the literary world but they can't find an outlet, a publisher. With the old system of large publishing houses and their editors no longer controlling the bulk of publishing, writers often turn to self-publishing options or create their own small presses. Moreover, the world of response and criticism has changed greatly in the Internet world. Instead of a handful of cultural gatekeepers at the major newspapers and magazines, writers can get word out through social media and blogs. Indeed, many creative writers have their own blogs in which they discuss other works, political issues, and their own ongoing writing projects.

Tools of Creative Writing

The tools of creative writing can be refreshingly minimal. Writers can deeply engage in creative writing with simply some paper and a writing implement. Computers have made an appearance in the creative writing process and can certainly be useful, again for sharing texts and accessing other texts. Many writers find, however, that the physical booklet, the journal, is a more personal tool and should be at least part of the repertory of the writing life. Such journals often are like student chapbooks or taggers' graf books. Writers jot down bits of overheard dialogue, paste in artifacts from their lives, record ideas and questions, and elaborate on thoughts for future projects.

While creative writing is often accomplished with the writer's addressing a blank piece of paper, existing texts are critical tools for expanding imagination and inspiring interesting writing. Such texts might include other books, stories, and poetry; personal letters and family histories; photographs (from photograph books or from family); artworks (public art as well as pieces from books); films and video; and just about anything else that makes up the writer's world.

Another useful practice for a creative writer is to get away from the world altogether. Writers are often inspired to deeper writing if they take a walk to a coffee shop, ride the bus to another part of the city, sit outside in a park, or even go on a writers' retreat. All the sensory and community experiences on such a voyage provide another text for writers to respond to as well as stimuli to trigger memories or imaginative flights.

Knowledge of Creative Writing

When an author is writing, he or she must be focused not just on the craft—the form—of the writing but on an idea, a thing, a subject of some sort. Thus, authors have to know or be engaged in the world as well as in the aesthetic use of language and the craft of the profession. Writers, then, are embedded in the discourse of their times even as they work to surmount, extend, or add to this ongoing discourse. The discourse of a time and place, therefore, is an area of knowledge for creative writing. Another area is a writer's interior discourse—the writer's conversations with himself or herself.

HIP-HOP: YOUTH AS CREATIVE WRITERS

One of the salient literacy practices of current times impacting young writers today is hip-hop. According to Hoch (2007), hip-hop comes out of many traditions, African and Caribbean storytelling and art, multiracial and multiethnic communities, appropriation of European customs, a legacy of political and gang organizing, the rise of supply-side economics and the undermining of the urban infrastructure in the 1980s, and accelerated technology. He argues that some of the aesthetics of the hip-hop generation include the following:

1. Codification of language (spoken and written), dress, gestures, and images.
2. Call and response.
3. Sociopolitical context and legacy (post–civil rights/'70s nationalism/ Reaganomics).
4. Metaphor and simile.
5. Illusion (magic).
6. Polyculturalism (immigrant and migrant).
7. Battle, braggadocio (competition).
8. Lack of safety, barriers, and boundaries (stage).
9. African and Caribbean diaspora performing traditions.
10. Lack of resources and access.
11. Reappropriation of materials, technology, and preserved culture.
12. Urban blight.
13. Criminalization of poverty.
14. Criminalization of culture. (p. 354)

It is within these traditions and forces that hip-hop creative writers draw on current social knowledge and literacy practices, as well as their cultural and intellectual affordances. They draw on the knowledge of their times as part of their work and contribute to building knowledge with their work. And, indeed, all writers work in this cultural context.

Young people find endless opportunities to do creative writing outside of school. This is writing that is not prompted or demanded, that does not earn the author a grade or a paycheck. It is only written for the purpose of communicating with others. And in many cases, it is written against the best advice of composition teachers. Examples of this kind of out-of-school writing include slam poetry (Yedidia, 2006), hip-hop, notes and chapbooks (Finders, 1997), digital media and radio productions (Soep & Chávez, 2010), online blogging and hybrid literacies (Hull & Schultz, 2002), zines, and other types of "street scripts" (Mahiri, 2004).

Youth cultural productions, especially in creative writing, are always shaped by traditions and styles that come from outside of school. For example, in school slam poetry competitions in the late 1990s, teachers urged students to follow a modernist, nonrhyming approach to composition. But students were familiar with the rhyming couplets of hip-hop and stuck to that approach. Confronted with young people passionately engaged with deep creative writing, many English teachers found themselves declaring that they could not teach anything; the students were ahead of them in understanding this genre.

Moreover, the integration of hip-hop and other youth culture in creative writing class represents an example of young people's deploying culturally relevant pedagogy (Ladson-Billings, 1995) and cultural modeling (Lee, 2007) in their own meaning-making.

Creative writing also exists in a zone of tension with other disciplines because of the way culture has been framed. In current social discourse, personal freedom has come to mean self-dependence instead of connectedness and being together in community. As Maxine Greene (1988) argues, education talk is "intertwined with talk of economic competitiveness, technology, and power" (p. 1). And students are encouraged, instead of interpreting and imagining possible lives, to "attend to what is 'given' in the outside world . . . to accede to the given, to view what exists around us as an objective 'reality,' impervious to individual interpretation" (p. 7). In this context, the invitation to inhabit the perspective of others, to take flights of fantasy, to expand and explore in the arts, offers the possibility of new ways of seeing the world and new possibilities for changing it.

In the best of circumstances, arts organizations and schools break down or blur the borders between disciplines so that they can be in dialogue with each other. Instead of students' going from creative writing class to art class, in creatively organized schools, the writing and art teacher can work together, devising joint activities based on word and image. Even when such direct integration is not possible, students in visual arts class can always advance their literacy through writing in response to art, through the creation of artist statements, and through writing exercises as precursors and warm-ups for visual art tasks.

Students find that the habits of mind they develop in one area of the arts are easily transported to others. The questions of authenticity and personal vision, of audience and publishing, of critique and cultural discourse—all these and others are freely engaged in the literary and visual arts.

INTEGRATION OF VISUAL ART
AND CREATIVE WRITING

Creative writing—the telling of stories, the creation of narratives and verse—is fundamental to what it means to be human, and the existence of such practices goes back to the beginning of the species. Every human being exists within culture and also creates culture through engagement with a culture's ongoing discourse. The representations of this discourse—the stories, narratives, and verses—are all about people who participate by repeating the creations of others, as well as adding their own. A culture that engages its participants in creative writing is one that honors the capacity of people to participate vigorously and with confidence.

Of all the disciplines, creative writing lends itself most naturally to integration with visual arts. All of the elements discussed above, from self-exploration to responding to canonical texts, from student agency to effective teacher coaching, from personal expression to connecting with audience, apply equally to visual arts and creative writing. At their cores, creative writing and visual arts are disciplines of the imagination (Greene & Heath, 2012).

In some cases, the terms that are used to describe postmodern, hip-hop, and youth-centered writing production can apply across platforms to visual arts. For example, collage is the practice of taking bits of writing or rhythm from one site to another and remixing with other pieces; the concept of reappropriation has to do with taking another work and repurposing it for a new piece. Mixing, sampling, digitizing, all of these youth literacy practices also find a way into visual art. The work of Enrique Chagoya and Kerry James Marshall shows how closely such narrative strategies are reflected in visual art. In Chagoya's case, the artist depicts the ongoing story of U.S. cultural and economic imperialism by appropriating and collaging imagery from indigenous Mexican cultures, in particular Aztec codices, and U.S. popular culture. In his later work (*What Appropriation Has Given Me, from Beyond*), Chagoya focuses on more modern Mexican images and appropriates the style, imagery, and likenesses of Frida Kahlo and Diego Rivera, juxtaposing them with images of popular snack foods and Mickey Mouse's hand to make a satirical statement about the U.S. commercialization of Mexican culture (see Figure 7.1).

In a similar vein, Kerry James Marshall appropriates imagery to tell an African American story. In Figure 7.2, *Visible Means of Support, Monticello* (2009), Marshall borrows a trope from popular culture, the "connect-the-dots" genre of drawing, and uses it to reveal the hidden story of slavery behind cherished American historical sites such as Monticello (SFMoMA, 2009).

Figure 7.1. Enrique Chagoya, *What Appropriation Has Given Me, from Beyond*, 1992.

Image courtesy of the artist.

Figure 7.2. Kerry James Marshall, *Visible Means of Support, Monticello,* **2009.**

Acrylic on PVC, 48 x 59 inches (unframed). Inventory #KM09.018. © Kerry James Marshall. Image courtesy of the artist and Jack Shainman Gallery, New York.

ART THAT CONNECTS TO CREATIVE WRITING

Words, Objects, and Poetry

There is a deep connection between poetry and visual art. Is it that art can be lyrical and evocative like poetry? Is it that poetry can be mysterious, even puzzling like art? Both are true. But what lies beneath those connections? Perhaps it is how art and poetry both tap into what we know, what we have experienced, and what we dream about, and then they send us either to new worlds or back into ourselves.

It seems both poetry and art are springboards; they start with something we can grasp, say a word or an image, and propel us forward into the ineffable. In this way, they evoke the unsaid and the unseen through what is said or what is seen. The "said" and "seen" are, therefore, the catalysts of poetry and art. They are also the building blocks.

In poetry, the blocks are words. Words are how we anchor the ineffable, because words root us back into the "substance" of our experience. As poet Caroline Marshall (2013) writes, "In their music and many associations, words enable a return to the concrete substances of which experience is composed because they are the *names* we give those substances" (p. 1). Through words we revive experience—we hear the gurgle of laughter down a hall, feel the subtle give of a key on a keyboard, smell the aroma of coffee, see a jet drawing a line across the sky—we attach our wordless thoughts or experiences and restore to consciousness the sensory experiences that compose our memories.

In art, the building blocks (or anchors) are visual imagery and physical objects. For artist Doris Salcedo, physical objects have the power of poetic words. Just as words in poetry take us beyond words, her objects take us beyond objects. This is because Salcedo's objects are *found* objects. Found objects are closer to the words of poetry than objects created by an artist because, although they might do so, poets do not often *create* words to anchor or express thoughts and experiences, but *find* words to do so.

Salcedo's work is filled with lonely, enclosed, and closed found objects, and it speaks through these objects of her personal experiences and her sense of loss. As a native of Colombia, she has witnessed political terror and the disappearance of many people, including friends and family. Her *Atrabiliarios* (1992, 1997) is a collection of shoes once worn by women who disappeared in Colombia. Here each discarded shoe summons the presence of the woman who wore it (see Figure 7.3).

Salcedo does not merely collect shoes, just as a poet does not simply collect words. Poets and artists make something of and with their building blocks. In *Atrabiliarios*, Salcedo encases the shoes in niches along a wall, covering them with a thin, gold, translucent skin. Encased and obscured, the shoes become metaphors for the people who once filled them; they become ghosts in gauzy coffins.

While words and metaphors are at the core of poetry, the way words link together, how they sound, and how they flow bring resonance to a poem. Marshall (2013) writes,

> The music of language (consonance, alliteration, assonance, and onomatopoeia, the cadences and rhythms created by syllables) all work on the senses and quicken the impulse to remember, to recall images and other recollections of experience, and to explore the feelings and thoughts they conjure. (p. 1)

Figure 7.3. Doris Salcedo, *Atrabiliarios*, 1993.

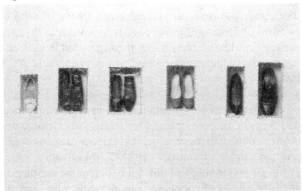

Wall installation with drywall, nine shoes, cow bladder and surgical
thread in 6 niches, 25 1/2 x 70 x 5 inches / 64.8 x 177.8 x 12.7 cm.
Image courtesy Alexander and Bonin, New York.

This is the power of form. Poetry is composed of words clustered into phrases, sentences, or stanzas—words given form by the poet. Form is also core to visual art, and in art, form is how objects and images are arranged. In Salcedo's *Atrabiliarios*, the simple way the niches of shoes are lined up on a wall is an example of form. Here, repetition of slightly varied objects suggests a lineup and anonymity and allows the viewer to inspect each niche as an object unto itself and as part of a whole. We see here how form in art embodies meaning.

Gabriel Orozco also plays with the idea of evocative, meaningful form. In his *Chicotes* (2010), illustrated in Figure 7.4, he arranges pieces of exploded tires in a spare, almost scientific, grid-like arrangement. What is Orozco up to here? Returning to the poetic principles of art—the power of objects and form—we gather that Orozoco is using these means to conjure experience, in this case an encounter with an urban street. In gathering the everyday detritus of the street and arranging it in a simple, direct—even clinical—fashion, Orozco is enabling us to really see it, to smell it, and to be seduced by its raw beauty. The textures, colors, and shapes of these ragged, rutted shards ground us in the street while the copiously arranged clusters and patterns they lie in allow these humble but beautiful objects to transcend their material being. Indeed, they become abstract and majestic. This is how art, like poetry, takes the mundane and pulls it into the ineffable.

Why do we call attention to poetry? What is the lesson we learn about art? Simply put, the lesson is about the essence of art. Art, like poetry, is about

Figure 7.4. Gabriel Orozco, *Chicotes* (detail), 2010.

Rubber tires. Dimensions variable. Image courtesy of
the artist and Kurimanzutto, Mexico.

transforming the material, the tangible, the "substance" of our lives into meaning. We look to poetry to understand art because poetry of all the writing forms reveals this most clearly and directly. That is to say, poetry gives us the words to anchor our experiences of art. And poetry can help us explain art to those we teach.

Graphic Fiction

Packard Jennings is a social critic and activist. Known for his "interventions"—performance artworks that take place in public places and draw attention to social issues—he is also a storyteller, and this is where his art overlaps with creative writing. In a series of six posters, *Postcards From Our Awesome Future*, Jennings collaborates with Steve Lambert to imagine and illustrate a future ideal San Francisco where transportation is a thrilling entertainment, animals replace humans, and abandoned recreational facilities accommodate a new, healthier lifestyle (see Figure 7.5).

Jennings also tells tales on his own. Inspired by illustration in advertising and comic strips, Jennings tells stories in a pop culture style. In *Becalmed*, his comic strip for *Creative Time Comics* (see Figure 7.6), Jennings imagines sailors on an 18th-century schooner discovering a treasure box at sea. This treasure is not the kind we would expect in the 1700s, but a gift from the 21st century: a pile of plastic litter. Using the storytelling conventions of the comic strip, Jennings conjures the past to make a point about the present.

Integration (Purpose, Knowledge, Methods, and Forms). At the dimension of *knowledge*, Jennings addresses social and environmental issues, common subjects of science and literary fiction. The artist reveals how stories engage audiences and, once they are engaged, challenge them to think about critical realities. This appears to be Jennings's *purpose*. Jennings also makes another connection to literary fiction; he uses the popular literary genre of sailing stories, stories of adventure in which sailors escaped civilization, to show that today this escape is no longer possible.

Regarding *methods*, Jennings mimics journalists in researching a subject before he tells a story. In the case of *Postcards From Our Awesome Future*, he and Lambert interviewed architects, city planners, and transportation engineers, who were asked about what they would do if there were no budget constraints or bureaucracy to obstruct them. In terms of *form*, Jennings employs the visual vocabulary and formats of graphic novels and comic books.

Creative Strategies. Jennings *projects* ideas into another time and then envisions their effect. This strategy of projection is at the heart of science fiction and historical fiction. Jennings also *formats*, using the pop culture format of the comic book to tell his story. In *Postcards From Our Awesome Future*, Jennings and Lambert *mimic* journalists in interviewing experts.

Figure 7.5. Packard Jennings and Steve Lambert, *Postcards From Our Awesome Future,* **2007.**

Funded by the San Francisco Arts Commission.

Figure 7.6. Packard Jennings, *Becalmed,* **2010.**

Commissioned by Creative Time.

Metaphor and Autobiography

Do Ho Suh is a global artist who leads a nomadic life. Born in Korea and now living in New York, Suh addresses big ideas through the lens of his personal experience. The meaning of home in a global mobile society is one of Suh's prevailing themes. In many of his works, his home, whether it is the traditional Korean house he grew up in or one of his many apartments in the United States, acts as a metaphor for his itinerant life and the sense of displacement he feels or the memories that make him who he is. To Suh, home is what you take with you and what makes you who you are. To convey this idea, Suh makes exact replicas of his past homes. Many of these structures are tents made of diaphanous, translucent silk, the materiality of which conveys the notion of memory and identity as both elusive and portable (see Figure 7.7).

Suh also constructs his homes in conventional building materials, and these homes are often landing on or crashing into other buildings. We can interpret these images in many ways. Is Suh's wedged Korean house, *Bridging Home* (2010), a metaphor for an unsettling arrival in a foreign land (see Figure 7.8)? Is his home that hangs awkwardly like an unwanted appendage in *Fallen Star* (2009) a metaphor for his sense of alienation (see Figure 7.9)? Look closely at the parachute in *Fallen Star*, and you will see that it is a deflated silk version of his native home.

Integration (Purpose, Knowledge, Methods, and Forms). Regarding *knowledge*, Suh's theme of home and its sister motif, identity, are common subjects in literature. Furthermore, Suh's work is autobiographical, and biography is a prominent literary *form*. In *Bridging Home* and *Fallen Star*, Suh also makes a literary reference to Dorothy's runaway house in *The Wizard of Oz*. Suh's work addresses

Figure 7.7. Do Ho Suh, *Seoul Home/L.A. Home/New York Home/Baltimore Home/London Home/Seattle Home/L.A. Home*, 1999.

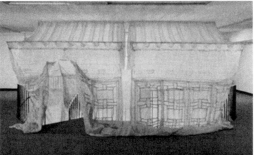

Silk with aluminum frame. 149 x 240 x 240 inches. Image courtesy of the artist and Lehmann Maupin Gallery, New York and Hong Kong. © Do Ho Suh.

Figure 7.8. Do Ho Suh, *Bridging Home,* **2010.**

Steel structural frame with sub timber frame, Filcor 45 FRA EPS,
bonded to 19mm marine plywood, painted finish. Dimensions:
House (1:1 scale) suspended between buildings that are 4.23
meters apart, lowest point 3.52 meters above ground and highest
point 10.326 meters above ground. Installation view at the
Liverpool Biennial 2010. Image courtesy of the artist and Lehmann
Maupin Gallery, New York and Hong Kong. © Do Ho Suh.

Figure 7.9. Do Ho Suh, *Fallen Star 1/5,* **2008–2009.**

ABS, basswood, beech, ceramic, enamel paint, glass,
honeycomb board, lacquer paint, latex paint, LED lights,
pinewood, plywood, resin, spruce, styrene, polycarbonate
sheets, and PVC sheets. 131 x 145 x 300 inches. Image
courtesy of the artist and Lehmann Maupin Gallery, New
York and Hong Kong. © Do Ho Suh.

the *purposes* of literature; it illustrates how both literature and art put a human face on social issues, trends, and forces through telling stories of individuals whose lives are affected by them. Suh also draws parallels with literature in his attention to detail. His works are exact replicas of real buildings, and this attention to detail relates to literature; details often make stories engaging, real, and meaningful. In fact, in art and literature, abstract ideas often dwell in the concrete. Where Suh's work intersects most prominently with language arts is in his use of metaphor. Metaphor is usually thought of as a literary device, a poetic way to describe something verbally. However, metaphor is also a powerful means for making meaning in visual art; it is both a *method* and a *form*. In integrating at the level of *methods*, Suh, like his counterparts in literature, does his homework; he researches every detail of his subject matter.

Creative Strategy. Do Ho Suh's work is *metaphorical;* he uses architecture and materials as metaphors to embody his concepts.

REFERENCES

Alarcón, D. (2010). Things get interesting. In Students of John O'Connell High School, *We the dreamers: Young authors explore the American Dream* (pp. viii–xvi). San Francisco, CA: 826 Valencia.

Barone, T., & Eisner, E. (1997). Arts-based educational research. In R. M. Jaeger (Ed.), *Complementary methods for research in education* (pp. 73–116). Washington, DC: American Educational Research Association.

Barth, J. (1985, June 16). Writing: Can it be taught? *The New York Times*. Retrieved from www.nytimes.com/books/98/06/21/specials/barth-writing.html

Bloom, H. (1973). *The anxiety of influence.* Oxford, England: Oxford University Press.

Ciardi, J. (1975). *How does a poem mean?* Boston, MA: Houghton.

Díaz, J. (2007). *The brief wondrous life of Oscar Wao.* New York: Riverhead Books.

Finders, M. (1997). *Hidden literacies and life in junior high.* New York, NY: Teachers College Press.

Finkelstein, B. (1984). Education and the retreat from democracy in the United States, 1979–198? *Teachers College Record, 86*(2), 275–282.

Goldberg, N. (1986). *Writing down the bones: Freeing the writer within.* New York, NY: Shambhala.

Greene, M. (1988). *The dialectic of freedom.* New York, NY: Teachers College Press.

Greene, M., & Heath, S. B. (2012). Rebellions, breakthroughs, and secret gardens: The arts and imagination. In H. Kohl & T. Oppenheim (Eds.), *The muses go to school: Inspiring stories about the importance of arts in education.* New York, NY: New Press.

Hoch, D. (2007). Toward a hip-hop aesthetic: A manifesto for the hip-hop arts movement. In J. Chang, *Total chaos: The art and aesthetics of hip-hop* (pp. 349–364). New York, NY: Basic Civitas Books.

Hull, G., & Schultz, K. (2002). *School's out: Bridging out-of-school literacies with classroom practice*. New York, NY: Teachers College Press.

Ladson-Billings, G. (1995). Toward a theory of culturally relevant pedagogy. *American Educational Research Journal, 32,* 465–491.

Lamott, A. (1994). *Bird by bird: Some instructions on writing and life.* New York, NY: Anchor.

Leavy, P. (2013). *Fiction as research practice.* Walnut Creek, CA: Left Coast Press.

Lee, C. D. (2007). *Culture, literacy, and learning: Taking bloom in the midst of the whirlwind.* New York, NY: Teachers College Press.

Lopate, P. (1994). *The art of the personal essay: An anthology from the classical era to the present.* New York, NY: Teachers and Writers Collaborative.

Mahiri, J. (2004). *What they don't learn in school.* New York, NY: Lang.

Marshall, C. (2013). *Writing to learn what you know.* Unpublished manuscript.

Montaigne, M. (2012). Of practice. In C. Klaus & N. Stuckey-French (Eds.), *Essayists on the essay* (pp. 1–7). Iowa City: University of Iowa Press. (Original work published 1580)

Myers, D. G. (2006). *The elephants teach: Creative writing since 1880.* Chicago, IL: University of Chicago Press.

Piercy, M., & Wood, I. (2005). *So you want to write: How to master the craft of writing fiction and memoir.* Fredonia, NY: Leapfrog Press.

Prose, F. (2007). *Reading like a writer: A guide for people who love books and for those who want to write them.* New York, NY: Harper.

Rilke, R .M. (1993). *Letters to a young poet.* (M. D. Herter Norton, Trans.). New York, NY: W. W. Norton.

Yedidia, D. (2006). *Hearts sized like cities: The Youth Speaks anthology.* San Francisco, CA: First Word Press.

8

Mathematics
Logic and Imagination

Ruth Cossey and David M. Donahue

Mathematics contributes to answering questions in almost every field of human endeavor. Anyone in doubt should consult the National Science Foundation's (2013) webpage on mathematics discoveries, which includes a story about how a University of Houston mathematician's model provides insight into better stents for heart patients. Other stories describe the connection between discoveries in math and searching for a cure for cancer, improving 3-D movies, and creating synthetic brains from carbon nanotubes. While these contributions are of little surprise to mathematicians, to those whose only exposure to the discipline was their elementary and high school education, such stories may indeed be revelations.

WHAT IS MATHEMATICS?

Mathematics in K–12 schools is often taught as if the discipline were nothing more than a series of disconnected facts to be memorized or discrete skills to be mastered. In fact, mathematics allows us to investigate the logical consequences of theories across the disciplines and apply the outcomes of such investigation imaginatively to applications ranging from filmmaking to surgery.

The rest of this chapter reintroduces mathematics to artists, art educators, and disciplinary outsiders. It explores what it means for learners to develop mathematical understanding, ways that understanding is fostered by new common core standards in mathematics, and how art-centered integrated learning enables learners to see mathematics in a fuller way—to recognize the logic, imagination, and aesthetic sensibility that underlie the discipline.

Purpose of Mathematics

Mathematics is a field of study that goes back to ancient times. Not surprisingly for a discipline so old, knowledge in the field is vast and its purposes varied. Most readers are familiar with the kinds of mathematics making up the school curriculum. These include the oldest types of mathematics such as arithmetic, algebra, geometry, trigonometry, and calculus for which many students understand a practical purpose. Some readers may be less familiar with newer areas of study within mathematics like topology and game theory, which also help solve practical problems. Not all mathematics, as we shall see, is predicated on solving practical problems, however. Mathematicians also engage in problems for the sheer beauty and challenge of math.

The earliest purpose of mathematics was to give numerical representation or value to quantities of things in the world—to quantify and to work flexibly with those quantities: to count, add, subtract, multiply, and divide quantities represented by numbers. Up to about 2,500 years ago, mathematicians, like those in Egypt, primarily studied numbers and arithmetic. Algebra, or the study of operations and relations, can be traced to contributions made by ancient Egyptian, Babylonian, Greek, Indian, Arab, and Muslim mathematicians and represented the next stage of development in mathematics (Devlin, 1994). Algebra enables us to access unknown quantities. An algebraic equation sets up a relationship between known quantities and an equivalent correlation with an unknown quantity. The equation, therefore, is like a puzzle in which one piece is missing; when we know the values of the other parts, we can figure out the value of the missing piece.

Geometry, or the study of shape, size, space, and the relative position of objects, extended the focus of mathematics, starting in the West around 500 B.C. The purpose of geometry is to map out space in numerical relationships and to enable the computation of relationships in space. For example, Pythagoras's theorem provides us with a formula for calculating the length of the sides of a right triangle. Another geometric formula using *pi* enables us to figure out the circumference of a circle if we know the diameter. Geometry, therefore, solves space-related puzzles; through its formulas, we can access unknown information.

The parallel growth of astronomy during this time created a number of geometric problems as astronomers followed the positions of stars and planets. The desire to map the locations of stars led to the development of trigonometry, or the study of triangles and the relationships among their sides and angles. Therefore, the purpose of trigonometry is to enable the calculation of unknown distances between entities that cannot be easily measured, such as the distance between planets.

By the mid-1600s, Newton and Leibniz created calculus to study motion and change. Calculus allows mathematicians to gain precise understandings of very small differences or the sum of infinite numbers. With calculus, mathematicians could now study everything from the motion of the planets to the flow of liquids and the expansion of gases. Thus far, mathematics was used to solve problems involving tangible variables and factors in the natural world of physics, chemistry, astronomy, geography, biology, and so on, or in the social world of commerce, public health, and politics. By the 18th century, mathematicians became interested in mathematics itself, or "pure mathematics," to study entirely abstract concepts. Why study pure mathematics? What is the purpose? Perhaps the purpose is to transcend practical application, to experience the pure pleasure of calculating, puzzle solving, and coming to understand how things fit together. This is where the aesthetics of math become most apparent. Such a focus stands in contrast to applied mathematics, or the mathematics used to solve problems in science, engineering, and business. Applied and pure mathematics rely on each other, however. Often, applied mathematics draws on insight from pure mathematics, and pure mathematics finds its inspiration in the real world.

In the last 100 years or so, mathematicians have explored the world of pure mathematics, but they also have developed multiple mathematical theories that have practical purposes—for example, game theory. Drawing on calculus and probability, game theory is an important field in applied mathematics that allows mathematicians to develop models of how rational—and not rational—persons interact with each other. These models can be applied literally to playing games such as chess or poker but also to more complicated "games" such as the diplomatic relationships among nations or buyers and sellers in the marketplace. Indeed, economists frequently use game theory as part of their work. Sometimes mathematics *is* art as in the case of work illustrated in Figure 8.1 (constructed through mathematical formulas) by Erik and Martin Demaine in computational origami, or the mathematical study of bending and folding.

As you think about the vastness of mathematical purposes, remember that mathematics is ultimately about solving problems (quantifying tangible and intangible things, finding numerical and spatial relationships, calculating unknown quantities)—whether they are applied or pure—across disciplines, whether in

Figure 8.1. Erik and Martin Demaine *[0162]*
***Green Balance,* 2011.**

Photo by Erik Demaine and Martin Demaine. Used
with permission of the artists.

sciences like astronomy or physics, social sciences like economics, or even the arts where mathematicians contributed to our understanding of perspective, composition, and aesthetic relationships in space. As mathematician and philosopher Alfred North Whitehead pointed out, it is through mathematics that "the stars are weighed and the billions of molecules in a drop of water are counted" (Whitehead, 1958, p. 1).

Knowledge of Mathematics

In the last 100 years or so, mathematical knowledge has exploded. Devlin (1994) calculates that at the beginning of the 20th century, all the world's math knowledge fit into 80 books, compared to the 100,000 volumes it would take to contain mathematical knowledge at the beginning of the 21st century. During that same time, the distinct areas of study in mathematics mushroomed from a dozen to around 70. Many of the recent areas of specialty in mathematics, like topology and game theory, are related to the earlier fields that make up the school curriculum. Emerging from geometry, topology is the study of continuously deforming objects and their properties. To understand a continuously deforming object, think of a circle that can be turned into a triangle by pulling on the circle to make corners and sides. Topologists study abstract shapes, including objects in four dimensions to, as one mathematician describes it, "deepen our understanding of everything we can imagine, with the idea that this is the starting point in becoming a more enlightened species" (Iga, n.d.).

Each area of mathematics from algebra and geometry to topology and game theory has its own key knowledge, ideas, and concepts. Math as a discipline, however, has a few overarching concepts, and these provide some of the most fruitful areas of knowledge for substantive multidimensional art-centered integrated learning. These key concepts include patterns, abstraction, and aesthetics.

Mathematics as the Study of Patterns. Devlin (1994, 2000) describes mathematics as the study of patterns, and he sets out the broad terrain of these patterns:

> numerical patterns, patterns of shape, patterns of motion, patterns of behavior, and so on. Those patterns can be real or imagined, visual or mental, static or dynamic, qualitative or quantitative, purely utilitarian or of little more than recreational interest. They can arise from the world around us, from the depths of space and time, or from the inner workings of the human mind. (Devlin, 1994, p. 3)

Clearly, patterns refer to more than visual patterns, and they do not need to be anchored to any single context (Thurston, 2011, p. xi). Devlin here uses the term as a mathematician would to imply order, structure, and logical relationships, all of which fit under the rubric of patterns. The wide-open scope of seeing and understanding patterns everywhere is why mathematics is a discipline applied to so many questions. Like reading and writing, mathematics is an important inter-disciplinary tool for understanding the world. Some readers may be surprised to think of mathematics as the study of patterns; they may be wondering, Isn't math about numbers? Even numbers, however, are about patterns. The number one can represent the pattern of "one-ness."

Studying patterns allows people to see the world differently. For example, observers of patterns can see fractals when they look at trees and Fibonacci numbers when they look at nautilus shells (see Figure 8.2). They can hear patterns in music that might not otherwise be heard if they had not thought about it mathematically.

Observing patterns can serve our ability to solve problems and to do so in multiple ways. For example, at the ballpark for the home team, you might see 100 sections of seating, each with 20 rows and 10 seats across. Or you might see 20 rings of 1,000 seats. Each of these patterns provides a way of being able to make a reasonable, pardon the pun, ballpark estimate of how many people the stadium holds when full. As a child, the noted mathematician Carl Friedrich Gauss used his ability to see patterns to impress his teachers with the feat of adding all the numbers from 1 to 100 in just a few seconds. He did so by creating a pattern of 50 pairs, grouping 1 with 100, 2 with 99, and so on for 50 pairs, each adding up to 101, yielding 5,050, or the result of 50×101 (Hersh & John-Steiner, 2011). The implication of defining mathematics as the study of wide-ranging patterns is that *how* a topic is studied is more important than *what* is being studied. This is, in effect, what makes a topic "mathematical" and will be described in the next section.

**Figure 8.2. Fibonacci Numbers
Superimposed on Shell.**

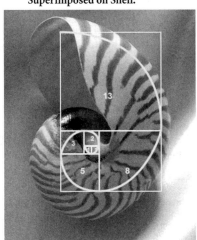

Mathematics and Abstraction. Studying patterns can mean making connections and solving problems in the real world. It can also mean extending these connections and solutions to the abstract because patterns exist everywhere and mathematicians are interested in developing general rules and principles from consideration of specific problems. As Whitehead (1958) points out, two plus two is four whether applied "to apples and to angels, to the ideas of the mind and to the bones of the body. The nature of things is perfectly indifferent" (p. 2). In other words, mathematicians consider the purely logical consequences of observing a pattern. Once someone understands that 2 + 2 = 4, that person understands that in every case of two things combined with two other things, the result will always be four things.

This abstract quality of mathematics is an important concept in the discipline. Typically, mathematicians engage in abstract thinking after observing a phenomenon and noticing a pattern:

> Then comes the abstraction of that pattern to a mathematical object or structure, say the concept of a natural number or of a triangle. As a result of studying that abstract concept, the various patterns observed might lead to the formulation of axioms. At that point, there is no longer any need to know about the phenomenon that led to these axioms in the first place. Once the axioms are available, everything can proceed on the basis of logical proofs, carried out in a purely abstract setting. (Devlin, 1994, p. 55)

This process allows mathematicians to understand properties and general ideas about phenomena apart from reference to particular instances, though mathematics can be applied to particular instances. Davis and Hersh (1998) describe two ways mathematicians make phenomena abstract. One is "idealization," or stripping away irrelevant details, and the second is "extraction," or focusing only on the essential features of a problem. Mathematicians can even make abstractions about patterns that happen in mathematics, thus adding a layer of abstraction upon abstraction. As we can see, mathematics is abstract in two ways: It abstracts from actual phenomena, and it deals with objects that are not necessarily concrete and tangible (Gowers, 2002).

Interestingly, the increased attention to abstraction in mathematics took place during the early 20th century, an era when artists such as Piet Mondrian "idealized" and "extracted" to produce abstract art, distilling the complex forms they observed down to austere lines, forms, colors, and compositions. Later, this trend toward abstraction evolved into the minimalism of artists such as Carl Andre, whose work consists of multiple simple geometric shapes in repeated patterns. These simultaneous developments in art and mathematics demanded "greater effort on the part of anyone who wants to understand the work" in either field (Devlin, 1994, p. 55). As with abstract art, putting in the effort to understand abstract concepts in mathematics leads not only to deeper understanding of the concepts but an affective or aesthetic appreciation of them, too.

Mathematics and Aesthetics. Mathematics, perhaps more than most disciplines, is often compared to art and music and described as having an aesthetic quality. Math is even called "beautiful" by its practitioners and theoreticians (Hersh & John-Steiner, 2011). Bertrand Russell (1919) wrote,

> Mathematics, rightly viewed, possesses not only truth, but supreme beauty—a beauty cold and austere, like that of sculpture, without appeal to any part of our weaker nature, without the gorgeous trappings of painting or music, yet sublimely pure, and capable of a stern perfection such as only the greatest art can show. (p. 60)

British mathematician G. H. Hardy (1940/1992) spoke in equally stirring terms about beauty and math:

> The mathematician's patterns, like the painter's or the poet's, must be beautiful, the ideas, like the colours of the world, must fit together in a harmonious way. Beauty is the first test; there is no permanent place in the world for ugly mathematics. (p. 85)

In contrast, Hersh and John-Steiner (2011) remind us not to overemphasize aesthetics or beauty in the discipline. After all, they write, "The truth is that a mathematician striving to solve a problem does not worry much about making it come out beautiful," noting that "anything that works is welcome" (p. 61). Other mathematicians may subsequently try to refine a proof or make it more beautiful, but there is no assurance that it will work. They cite the "quadratic formula" as a prime example of something mathematical that is basic to the discipline but decidedly "not beautiful!" (p. 61).

Although mathematical formulas may not always be beautiful, that does not mean they are not aesthetic. That is because aesthetics encompasses much more than beauty. As art education theorists Parsons and Blocker (1993) suggest, aesthetics also includes *pleasure*, *interest*, and *fit*. In the case of the quadratic equation, its aesthetic value lies not in its elegance or beauty but in how it fits the task—in the way it works.

How do the aesthetics of math correspond to art? Let's start with beauty. According to Gowers (2002), "Beauty in mathematics is not the same as beauty in music, but then neither is musical beauty the same as the beauty of a painting, or a poem, or a human face" (p. 51). Notions of beauty in mathematics and art are not the same thing either. Most mathematicians seek "beauty" in the sense that beauty is equated with truth. Mathematicians seek truth, not just truth beyond a reasonable doubt as in other disciplines, but truth that something can be proved beyond all doubt. This search for truth stands in high contrast to art, especially contemporary art. As art theorists Sian Ede (2005) and Graeme Sullivan (2010) maintain, current art does not concern itself with anything close to a provable "truth" or even a grand narrative or theory; its concern is with messing with "truths"—complicating them, making them complex. If beauty is truth (as in math), you won't find that kind of beauty in art.

Beauty in art is often a more complex thing. In the main, contemporary artists do not strive for classical "beauty"—beauty defined by classic notions of harmony, balance, proportion, and symmetry (valued in math)—as an end unto itself. Artists do, however, often use such beauty to draw a viewer in so they can hit them with a message, sometimes a very ugly one (see Chris Jordan below). Similarly, if beauty is clarity, as it is in math, you can find it in contemporary art, but probably not as much as you will find ambiguity.

The aesthetic factor you will find consistently in art and math is *fit*. Fitness, or the capacity of an artwork or a math formula or theorem to suit a purpose—and to suit it in the most economical of ways—is one place where the aesthetics of math and art intersect. Fit, therefore, is simplicity (a value in math). Both art and math attempt to convey complex ideas in the simplest of ways. We find this quality in many of the artworks presented in this book.

Another place of confluence between math and art is *interest*. Mathematicians and artists are passionately interested in the questions they pursue and in their practice. Moreover, they want to engender interest in their audience. Still another site is *pleasure*. Perhaps the greatest motive for doing math or making art is the pleasure of the process, the joy of discovery, the shaping of something (whether it is a formula or a sculpture) into something that *fits*. Pleasure also lies in the thrill of knowing there is always something more to learn. As Gowers (2002) writes, "Mathematical proofs can provide a similar pleasure (to art) with sudden revelations, unexpected yet natural ideas, and intriguing hints that there is more to be discovered" (p. 51).

Forms of Mathematics

In math, as in all disciplines, the forms are tools. Symbols play an important role in helping mathematicians express abstract ideas; they are the forms, or tools, or "language" of the discipline. Frequently, these symbols make mathematics seem mysterious and inscrutable to those just entering the discipline, "but that is not because [the symbols] are difficult in themselves. On the contrary, they have invariably been introduced to make things easy" (Whitehead, 1958, p. 40). The symbols represent simplifications or abstractions of complex ideas. Think for example of the complex idea represented by the symbol 0, standing for zero.

Symbols are used in equations or formulas. For example, consider the economy of meaning packed into an equation like $a = b$. While we might not know the exact value of a or b, we do know that they are equal to each other. Symbols allow us to describe and analyze general patterns; for example, the symbolic phrase $a + b = b + a$ describes the commutative law of addition or the general pattern that when two numbers are added together, the order of those numbers does not affect the result.

Symbols are part of another form used in mathematics—theorems. Theorems are mathematical statements that are proven using previously established mathematical knowledge, including other theorems. The way of establishing a mathematical theorem is through a proof. The proof is another form or tool in mathematicians' toolkit. Proofs are logical arguments establishing the truth of a theorem. Mathematical proofs are deductive, meaning that the conclusion is based on a series of assumptions or conditional statements. IF a = b and b = c, THEN a = c. As you can see, theorems combine symbolic thinking as well as natural language. The estimation of theorems can change over time. What was once considered a difficult and important theorem may become easy and unimportant in a later time. Theorems also have an aesthetic quality and may be described as elegant, for example.

While symbols are not math, any more than notes are music, skill at reading symbols in math is more crucial to understanding the discipline than being able to read music is crucial to making meaning from music. After all, listeners can make meaning after hearing the sounds without reading the notes. The same is not true of mathematics (Devlin, 1994).

Methods of Mathematics

Mathematical methods are more than operations like addition and multiplication, and each area of mathematics has its own way of operating. What unites all these methods, however, is the way mathematicians think, particularly how they use logic, imagination, or intuition and think flexibly.

Thinking Logically. Courant, Robbins, and Stewart (1996) call mathematics "an expression of the human mind [that] reflects the active will, the contemplative reason, and the desire for aesthetic perfection." (n.p.). They continue, "Its basic elements are logic and intuition, analysis and construction, generality, and individuality. Though different traditions may emphasize different aspects, it is only the interplay of these antithetic forces and the struggle for their synthesis that constitute the life, usefulness, and supreme value of mathematical science."

While intuition may lead mathematicians to consider initially a particular solution to a particular problem, ultimately the discipline requires rigorous adherence to logic. This is what allows mathematicians to observe patterns, develop models about the world based on those patterns, and claim their models are true. While practitioners of other disciplines can never say with certainty that something is true, mathematicians can do so because their clear and logical thinking lays out the conditions and assumptions under which something can be said to be true. For example, if a > 2, then it is always true that a + 1 > 2. As Gowers (2002) writes, mathematicians

> are rarely satisfied with the phrase "it seems that." Instead they demand a proof, that is an argument that puts a statement beyond all possible doubt. . . . The fact that disputes [about truth] can in principle be resolved does make mathematics unique. (pp. 36–40)

At the same time, most mathematicians today are not writing proofs. Rather, they are working to "solve problems to whatever degree of accuracy or certainty is required" (Devlin, 2011, p. 32). In fact, experimental mathematics, the kind that uses computers to look for patterns to support mathematical assertions, is often trial-and-error searching. With this use of experimentation and observation, mathematics is becoming more like the natural sciences, but it is a science that Devlin believes will remain "the most secure and precise of the sciences" where proofs of truth "remain the final arbiter" providing "a degree of certainty that the natural sciences rarely come close to" (p. 36).

Thinking Imaginatively. Thinking logically does not rule out mathematicians also thinking imaginatively. Imagination is "seeing" something that is not already present (Ricoeur, 1991). In fact, imagination plays a huge role in mathematicians' thinking when they encounter new problems, old paradoxes, or limits to current thinking in accounting for phenomena that cannot be explained by current theories. Hersh and John-Steiner (2011) see intuition as a form of imagination and consider it a plausible or convincing perception in the absence of proof. They call intuitive perception "essential in discovery" and contrast it with "the more rigorous deductive methods needed for justification" (p. 50) of theory.

When mathematicians make imaginative leaps in logic, they are "shifting paradigms." A paradigm is a global perspective on a topic or a model that governs how a topic is regarded (Kuhn, 1962/1970). A shift in paradigms, therefore, calls for a change of perspective or an acceptance of a new way of thinking and doing things. This involves "seeing" what is not already there. The acceptance of non-Euclidean geometry as equally valid as Euclidean geometry is an example of a shift in mathematical paradigms. In Euclidean geometry, in two dimensions, only one line can go through a point outside another line and not intersect that other line. In other words, these two lines are parallel. In non-Euclidean hyperbolic geometry where two lines curve away from each other, any number of lines can go through a point outside the original line and not intersect the original. In elliptical geometry, all lines through the point will intersect the original line. This paradigm shift was an important challenge of something considered "true" in mathematics, a discipline, which unlike others, still holds on to the possibility of establishing universal truths.

Thinking Flexibly. The reputation for logic in mathematics can also belie the need for occasionally breaking rules. Mahajan (2010), a mathematician at MIT, argues that "too much mathematical rigor teaches *rigor mortis*: the fear of making an unjustified leap even when it lands on a correct result" (p. xiii). In his book *Street-Fighting Mathematics*, Mahajan makes the case that, unlike traditional mathematics classes where students solve "exactly stated problems exactly," mathematical problems in real life are never so exact and usually only require a moderately accurate conclusion. What he calls "educated guessing" and "opportunistic problem-solving" can provide conclusions that may not be precise but are good enough to know that a bridge plan will fail or a circuit design will not work. Mahajan reminds us that mathematicians, especially applied mathematicians, think with a degree of flexibility that is not as evident in math classrooms, flexibility that makes mathematics a useful tool for solving real problems.

UNDERSTANDING MATHEMATICS

The process of developing understanding about mathematics can be considered a two-part process. One part of the process relates to some logical mathematical knowledge that cannot be taught and that has to be developed or constructed. The other part of the process relates to mathematics knowledge and is a matter of social convention. For example, a child does not discover the abstract concept of "chair." Instead, it has to be labeled by someone's saying, "That's a chair." Labeling a chair "chair" is an example of social convention. Given this social convention, children construct a general theory of what a "chair" is by noticing patterns among desk chairs, rocking chairs, and recliners. From that point on, a child knows what a chair is. Developing this general sense of "chair" comes from logical understanding. The equivalent in mathematics is moving from the social convention of knowing that a fraction is "one number on top of another" to understanding that it represents a logical relationship between the two numbers. At that point, a student can understand the abstract concept of $1/x$ as well as the more concrete example of $1/4$.

Many students have a limited understanding of mathematics because too much of it is taught today in the United States only as remembering social convention when, in fact, it should also be taught as promoting logical development. Students learn to say things about mathematics because they learned to say them, but they have not had a chance to understand them because they have not been able to construct the logic behind them. Consequently, learners think of math as a subject where they have to memorize innumerable facts. If you memorized the quadratic equation in a high school math class, but never understood it, or never even considered that it is something that could be understood, you are familiar with this consequence.

The notion that mathematics is about memorizing things becomes particularly untenable around 5th or 6th grade for students who have only memorized things. Even if students are very good at memorizing, there is only so much they can remember when they begin to hit an overload. On the other hand, if students develop a logical understanding of a set of principles, they can do much mathematical thinking based on those principles.

What students know completely controls what they get to know. What they know, however, can be misunderstood by teachers. Around 6th grade, few students have a very solid logical foundation, but there are huge discrepancies in the amount of social conventions about math that some students have memorized, even though they do not understand anything beyond memorization. What that means is that the gap in students' understanding that some teachers see may not be very large at all. The only gap may be in the speed with which some students can retrieve information based on social convention or answer a computational question. The gap is not in mathematical understanding, which might be fairly shallow for almost all students.

Finally, paying attention to the different ways that various cultures have constructed mathematics, a branch of mathematics called *ethnomathematics* can give teachers insight into how different communities within the United States think mathematically. This is not to say that mathematics is different for Latino students, compared to African American students, compared to other students, and so on because of "cultural learning styles." Rather, it is to say that ethnomathematics can expand our views, representations, and presentations of mathematics. It can help us think about how mathematical learning processes, or even the language of numbers, can vary for children based on how math is used or framed at home. For example, "In French, 90 is quatre-vingt-dix (four twenties and ten); its name uses both multiplication and addition. In the West African language Yoruba, 35 is named as 'five from two twenties,' using multiplication and subtraction" (Hersh & John-Steiner, 2011, pp. 307–308).

TEACHING MATHEMATICS

Recently, educators and policymakers have developed a set of new Common Core State Standards (CCSS) in mathematics, which have been adopted by 45 states. The CCSS, also known as the "standards for mathematical practice" emphasize *what* young people should be able to do and *how* young people should be able to think about the world mathematically. The CCSS emphasize that students should not merely memorize information or social convention. Instead they should use mathematics in ways that make sense to them, as a result of logical understanding, to solve problems. This is the difference between knowing that dividing a fraction by a fraction means turning the second fraction "upside down" and multiplying it by the first fraction to get the answer, and understanding why one does that. Most students in U.S. schools have memorized the first operation. Few have developed understanding of why one uses that operation or why it works.

The CCSS include the following:

1. Make sense of problems and persevere in solving them . . .
2. Reason abstractly and quantitatively . . .
3. Construct viable arguments and critique the reasoning of others . . .
4. Model with mathematics . . .

5. Use appropriate tools strategically . . .
6. Attend to precision . . .
7. Look for and make use of structure . . .
8. Look for and express regularity in repeated reasoning . . .
   (Common Core State Standards Initiative, 2010, pp. 6–8)

In these standards, one can see connections to the purposes, knowledge, forms, and methods of the discipline. Looking for regularity and attending to structure are about seeing patterns. Modeling with mathematics is about thinking abstractly. Constructing arguments and critiquing reasoning is about thinking logically.

FUNDAMENTALS OF MATHEMATICS AND POINTS OF INTEGRATION WITH ART

As you think about substantive multidimensional integration of art with mathematics, consider these fundamental ideas about the purposes, knowledge, forms, and methods in mathematics:

1. Finding patterns
2. Solving problems
3. Thinking abstractly
4. Thinking symbolically
5. Recognizing aesthetics of balance, harmony, and simplicity
6. Appreciating aesthetics of conceptual beauty or fit
7. Thinking logically and with certainty
8. Thinking imaginatively
9. Thinking flexibly

Each of these represents a big idea or an important way of thinking in mathematics. Each represents a possible integration point between mathematics and contemporary visual art. In some cases, those integration points represent similar concepts or common ways of thinking between mathematicians and artists; for example, looking for patterns, solving problems, developing abstractions, and attending to the aesthetics of conceptual beauty or fit, meaning the fit between what one wants to express, how one expresses it, and how the idea is received. In other cases, the integration points might come from disjunctions between the two disciplines, where one discipline, art, "troubles" or questions thinking in the other, for example, the certainty of mathematical thinking compared to the ambiguous, contingent thinking of artists; the linear logic of mathematics compared to the nonlinear thinking of artists; or the different regard for concepts like balance and harmony.

CONTEMPORARY ART THAT CONNECTS TO MATHEMATICS

Accumulation, Abstraction, and Meaning

When Georgina Valverde stacks hair curlers in a pile (see Figure 8.3, *Stack 1*, and Figure 8.4, *Stack 2*) something magical—and mathematical—happens. An accumulation of forms becomes a number of forms, and a number of forms become beautiful. This is the beauty of pattern. This is also the beauty of distillation. These are simple household objects that pack a lot of meaning, but when they are assembled into stacks, they become elegant abstract forms. That is to say, they are subsumed by the beauty of abstraction and the math inherent in accumulation.

Figure 8.3. Georgina Valverde, *Stack 1*, 2002.

Image courtesy of the artist.

Figure 8.4. Georgina Valverde, *Stack 2*, 2004.

Image courtesy of the artist.

Making beautiful mathematical piles, Valverde appears to be going against the grain of contemporary art. Much contemporary art is known for its "messiness," its disdain for Modernist formalism and the qualities associated with it, such as balance, harmony, and beauty (Ede, 2005)—qualities valued in mathematics. As we noted above, Parsons and Blocker (1993) find aesthetics to also include pleasure, interest, and fit—not just beauty or form. Fit is the characteristic that is most apt here; Valverde and many other artists today find distillation, abstraction, and beautiful form to *fit* their concept. In Valverde's case, the concept is complex (experience of everyday life), and a simple abstract form, with its allusions to mathematics, provides a subtle yet powerful way to spur thinking about how we think about it.

To her credit, Valverde deftly bridges the gap between Modernist abstraction and distillation (and the formalism inherent in them) and the contemporary penchant to make form a secondary concern and to ground art in the concrete details of real life. The power of her work lies in that tension. Below we discuss the works of Chris Jordan and Jer Thorp, two examples of current art that also engage that tension. Their intention, however, is different from Valverde's. Their artworks do not distill things down to abstract forms and numbers, but *make meaning* of numbers.

Integration (Purpose, Knowledge, Methods, and Forms). It appears that Valverde's *purpose* is to reveal the inherent beauty in everyday objects and to elevate or aestheticize them. On the other hand, she may have another *purpose*: to amplify the ordinariness of her objects. To do this, she taps into our shared *knowledge* of the graphic tropes or *forms* of statistics, in particular the bell curve. Her *methods* also echo those that statisticians use: accumulating, categorizing, grouping, and arranging.

Creative Strategies. In both *Stack 1* and *Stack 2*, Valverde *accumulates, isolates,* and *arranges* objects to show their inherent beauty. She *recontextualizes* these objects to elevate them to the status of art. To allude to the mundane character of everyday life, Valverde uses more associative creative strategies. For instance, in *Stack 1*, she *amplifies* the notion of ordinariness by referencing the bell curve, the shape objects and phenomena naturally fall into when randomly distributed. In referencing this form from statistics, Valverde connects to how statistics ignores the "noise" of a complex phenomenon and boils it down to norms. In this way, a simple evocative shape becomes a *metaphor* for the mundane nature of everyday life.

Meanings Behind Numbers

Chris Jordan is a photographer with a critical message: Wake up! The world is filling up with garbage. Jordan believes that while statistics may tell the story of this cataclysm, it doesn't sink in. It is time we understand the enormity of those numbers. With great urgency, Jordan has been creating gigantic digital photographs composed of hundreds of thousands of minute photographs that represent the things we in the United States discard every day. His latest series *Running the Numbers 11* (2009–present) goes global with large-scale re-creations of famous paintings—*Caps Seurat* (2011) and *Gyre* (2011). This is a clever strategy; in shaping his unpleasant message in the form of works of art, Jordan pulls the audience in with their familiarity and the aesthetic pleasure they afford. Furthermore, Jordan's choice of art to replicate conveys meaning; each of these works is connected to nature and indicative of a time when nature was relatively unsullied. In the case of Jordan's *Caps Seurat* (2011) (see Figures 8.5 and 8.6), Jordan mimics Georges Seurat's *Sunday Afternoon on the Island of La Grande Jatte* (1884). The subject of Seurat's piece is recreation and pleasure in a pristine natural environment. That environment is disappearing, and Jordan makes the point by replacing the paint dots of Seurat with bottle cap "pixels"—the detritus of today's picnics.

Figure 8.5. Chris Jordan, *Caps Seurat,* **2011.**

Photo by Chris Jordan.

Figure 8.6. Chris Jordan, *Caps Seurat,* **Detail, 2011.**

Photo by Chris Jordan.

In the case of *Gyre* (2009), Jordan re-creates Hokusai's *The Great Wave off Kanagawa* (1830) in plastic shards. The theme of Hokusai's *Wave* is the power of nature and the powerlessness of humanity in relationship to it (see Figures 8.7 and 8.8). Jordan turns this notion on its head by alluding to how humans today have conquered the seas with their garbage, in particular the continent-sized gyres of plastic junk that churn in massive circles in the Pacific Ocean. There is another message here: Just as nature in *The Great Wave* is powerful and uncontrollable, so too is the toxic accumulation of detritus that threatens to engulf the oceans today.

Integration (Purpose, Knowledge, Methods, and Forms). Jordan connects art and mathematics on all levels. To address the *purpose* of statistics, which is to inform, Jordan questions whether statistics alone can convey meaning or have an impact. Jordan also crosses over into ecology and the natural sciences, tackling a critical environmental issue, while compelling the viewer to think

Figure 8.7. Chris Jordan, *Gyre, 2009.*

Photo by Chris Jordan.

Figure 8.8. Chris Jordan, *Gyre,* Detail, 2009.

Photo by Chris Jordan.

numerically and to see patterns that underlie numbers. Here he is working with *knowledge* (information and concepts) of math and science. In making the enormity of the numbers visible and, therefore, meaningful, Jordan relates this knowledge directly to us: He forces us to think about our behavior patterns and how many little objects or actions add up to big things and big problems. In doing so, he draws our attention to the fact that statistics mean something; they count. In the dimension of *methods*, Jordan does research in a scientific mode, and he uses the outcomes of his investigation, statistics, as the basis of his interpretations. He also partakes in the numerical thinking, pattern recognition, and relational thinking that characterize the thinking of mathematicians. Regarding the dimension of *forms*, Jordan sticks to the forms of art: painting and photomontage.

Creative Strategies. The creative strategies Jordan uses are *reformatting*; he puts numerical information into the format of a painting; his works are photographic mosaics, massive accumulations of digital images that add up to one coherent picture. He also employs *juxtaposition*; Jordan juxtaposes the concept of environmental degradation with familiar images of pristine, powerful, and aesthetically pleasing natural environments.

Humanizing Data

The lyrical waving lines and circles we see in Figure 8.9, *New York Times 365/360* (2009), represent numbers: the number of times certain topics were covered in the year 2011 by *The New York Times*. The creator of this image, Jer Thorp, is one of many artists working today who transform statistical data into elegant visual diagrams (see visualcomplexity.com). While Thorp straddles the borders of design, art, and digital technology by creating graphs, maps, and animations of data, he also develops the computer software that makes these visualizations possible. From 2010 to 2012, he worked at *The New York Times* as a data artist in residence, chronicling the *Times*'s coverage of events and information. Thorp is both a journalist and a cultural historian. However, Thorp sees himself more as a sociologist in his analysis of data and as an anthropologist in his interest in current culture. His primary interest is in examining and revealing the human systems behind the data we encounter every day, and much of his work is about exploring those systems to underscore the human basis of data. As he states in his TED talk (Thorp, 2011), Thorp's aim is to connect abstract, disembodied numbers to human life—to make data human. He believes that humanizing data will help us to build empathy for each other and respect personal privacy while understanding ourselves as participants in a collective system.

Figure 8.9. Jer Thorp, *New York Times*
365/360, 2009.

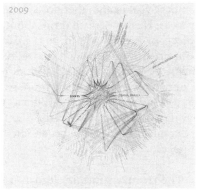

Image courtesy of the artist.

Figure 8.10. The 9/11 Memorial, Ground Zero, New York City, 2011.

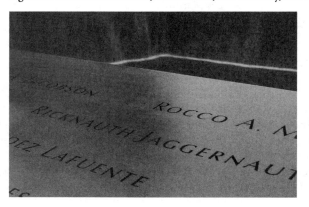

   In many of his animated data-flow pieces (Thorp, 2011), Thorp pictures today's high-tech, information-based society by mapping the passage of information from one person to another and visualizing what Thorp calls "sharing structures." These works came out of Thorp's interest in the ways human beings connect to each other. His attention to human relationships is particularly apparent in his work on the 9/11 Memorial at Ground Zero (see Figure 8.10). Inscribed here are the names of the 2,983 people who died in the attack. Thorp developed the algorithmic software that allowed the victims' names to be arranged according to their relationships with other victims. Arranged in this way, the names tell us how the people who lost their lives that day fit together as bosses, employees, coworkers, colleagues, and friends. This deepens our understanding of the human loss this memorial represents.

Integration (Purpose, Knowledge, Methods, and Forms). For Jer Thorp, numerical data are both the medium of his work and the subject of his critique. While he addresses and works with the *knowledge* that statistics represents, he also critiques the ability of data to make that knowledge meaningful to those who encounter the data. Like Chris Jordan, he finds the knowledge embedded in data of great significance but the numerical presentation of the data woefully ineffective in conveying the meaning behind it. This is where art and visual imagery can make numbers meaningful, fulfilling the *purpose* of statistics. As for *methods*, Thorp uses the methods of mathematicians, historians, and sociologists; he researches and monitors human behavior in collecting his data. He also analyzes data like a statistician in the social sciences, looking for patterns of relationships and behavior. As for forms, Thorp employs the graphics and timeline animation that social scientists and historians use as tools for locating trends and recording them.

Creative Strategies. Thorp partakes in two creative strategies: *reformatting* and *mimicry*. Since his visualizations of data are timelines and maps (information graphics), he uses the formats of science and mathematics to tell his story. Thorp *mimics* journalists and historians, using their methods to examine and represent current events and information.

REFERENCES

Common Core State Standards Initiative. (2010). *Common Core State Standards for Mathematics.* Retrieved from www.corestandards.org/assets/CCSSI_Math%20 Standards.pdf

Courant, R., & Robbins, H. (revised by Stewart, I.). (1996). *What is mathematics? An elementary approach to ideas and methods.* New York, NY: Oxford University Press.

Davis, P., & Hersh, R. (1998). *The mathematical experience.* Boston, MA: Houghton Mifflin.

Devlin, K. (1994). *Mathematics: The science of patterns.* New York, NY: Scientific American.

Devlin, K. (2000). *The math gene: How mathematical thinking evolved and why numbers are like gossip.* New York, NY: Basic Books.

Devlin, K. (2011). What is experimental mathematics? In M. Pitici (Ed.), *The best writing on mathematics 2010* (pp. 32–36). Princeton, NJ: Princeton University Press.

Ede, S. (2005). *Art and science.* London, England: Tauris.

Gowers, T. (2002). *Mathematics: A very short introduction.* New York, NY: Oxford University Press.

Hardy, G. H. (1940/1992). *A mathematician's apology.* Cambridge, England: Cambridge University Press.

Hersh, R., & John-Steiner, V. (2011). *Loving + hating mathematics: Challenging the myths of mathematical life.* Princeton, NJ: Princeton University Press.

Iga, K. (n.d.). *What is topology?* Retrieved from math.pepperdine.edu/kiga/topology.html

Kuhn, T. S. (1962/1970). *The structure of scientific revolutions.* Chicago, IL: University of Chicago Press.

Mahajan, S. (2010). *Street-fighting mathematics: The art of educated guessing and opportunistic problem solving.* Cambridge, MA: MIT Press.

National Science Foundation. (2013). *Mathematics discoveries.* Retrieved from www.nsf.gov/discoveries/index.jsp?prio_area=9

Parsons, M., & Blocker, H. (1993). *Aesthetics and education.* Chicago: University of Illinois.

Ricoeur, P. (1991). The function of fiction in shaping reality. In M. Valdes (Ed.), *A Ricoeur reader: Reflection and imagination* (pp. 117–136). Toronto, Ontario, Canada: University of Toronto Press.

Russell, B. (1919). *Mysticism and logic: And other essays.* London, England: Longmans, Green.

Sullivan, G. (2010). *Art practice as research: Inquiry in the visual arts.* (2nd ed.). Los Angeles, CA: Sage.

Thorp, J. (2011). Make data more human. Retrieved from www.ted.com/talks/jer_thorp_make_data_more_human.html

Thurston, W.P. (2011). Foreword. In M. Pitici (Ed.), *The best writing on mathematics 2010* (pp. xi–xiii). Princeton, NJ: Princeton University Press.

Whitehead, A. N. (1958). *An introduction to mathematics.* New York, NY: Oxford University Press.

9

Curriculum for Art-Centered Integrated Learning

Anne Thulson and Julia Marshall

Contemporary art, with all its challenging imagery and forms, innovative ways of thinking and doing, and myriad methods and materials (including new technologies), presents new, exciting opportunities to teachers who would like to promote integrated learning through contemporary art. In Chapter 1, we present contemporary art as an entry point—a springboard for asking big questions and pondering the puzzles that all the disciplines address and that we deal with in real life. In Chapter 2, we provide a model for following those critical questions and for using art inquiry as a vehicle for integrated learning. Art in this model takes the form of a research trail that follows a question or significant concepts and visits different disciplinary "places" along the way.

The core principle that threads through both chapters is art as inquiry. In Chapter 1, observing, interpreting, and making meaning of an existing artwork spark inquiry, thinking, and conversation that generate understanding. This is building understanding through interpreting art. In Chapter 2, we show how understanding develops over a long process of researching, creating, and reflecting. This is developing understanding through making one's own art. Both viewing/interpreting and creating/making generate similar inquiry processes that lead to understanding. Furthermore, they are not mutually exclusive. When you mix them up, you have the best of both worlds; they build on each other. Indeed, learners need them both.

ART-CENTERED INTEGRATED CURRICULUM

Our primary purpose in this book is to help teachers make the curriculum they develop substantive—deep and meaningful—and multidimensional—touching on a number, if not all, of the four dimensions of art and the academic disciplines. How do we construct a curriculum that does this? Where do we start? In this chapter, we provide a framework and set of guidelines for developing curriculum. We also provide example projects that explore and integrate art across disciplines. We offer these not as recipes to follow but as examples that can be adapted and applied to fit your needs.

In Chapter 2, we propose engaging in integrated learning via an independent research process. What kind of curriculum do we devise for that? Independent art research comes under the rubric of emergent curriculum. That means it starts in one place and then develops as it goes along. This is similar to the conversations that arise when learners view and interpret "difficult" contemporary art. Just as in guiding conversations, "doing" emergent curriculum requires teachers to plan but also be flexible. While they must have a set of understanding goals and an inkling of what might happen, it is critical to encourage learner autonomy within those parameters.

Curriculum, in this instance, is about parameters, protocols, and springboards. It begins with a springboard for learner inquiry—something to start the journey off in a meaningful and rewarding direction. That springboard could be a group project that familiarizes students with the ways contemporary artists approach inquiry and art making. Exploring the artwork presented in this book might be useful in that regard. Also, the project examples at the end of this chapter could act as springboard activities that give learners hands-on, minds-on experience with art research before they launch into their own inquiry. From there, locating a providential topic of interest for each learner is Step 1, and developing a research question to guide the inquiry is Step 2. Step 3 entails following the trail with the help of generative questions, reflective questions, and scaffolding protocols provided by the teacher. "Booster projects" also help to enrich and facilitate independent research. The projects and artwork discussed in this book can be useful for that.

Although we encourage independent art research, we understand that doing it takes skills and dispositions that are acquired through practice and experience. The Harvard Teaching for Understanding Framework (Wiske, 1998) delineates three stages of development toward understanding and mastery: free play, guided instruction, and independent work. Independent art research, of course, suits the advanced stage. Not many learners, however, are ready for that. To meet their needs, the projects and guidelines we introduce in this chapter are designed to work on the middle level. We believe however, that a good project should bring together all three levels or ways of working. That is, they should encourage play and independence within a supportive structure. These projects, therefore, allow for them.

We provide a format and guidelines for projects because we believe art lessons should land somewhere between highly structured curriculum and open-ended, choice-based opportunities. For this reason, we advocate for guided projects that combine structure with open-endedness and teacher-identified goals with learner interest. We liken the ideal curriculum structure to a jungle gym—a flexible, yet strong piece of architecture to grab onto and spring off of, with beams to hang from, swing and play on, room to somersault around in, and boundaries to bounce up against.

GENERAL THOUGHTS ABOUT CURRICULUM

The goals of an integrated art project are to expand out (to make connections or associations), to go deep (to mine deeply into ideas, concepts, and imagery to glean their meaning), and to extend onward (to construct new knowledge within a project and to follow the trail a project leads to). Another goal is to disrupt habitual ways of seeing and provoke learners to think differently. In this chapter, we suggest some basic strategies for meeting these goals. These strategies can be employed by teachers as they develop the curriculum and by students as they follow the curriculum.

To *expand out*, we suggest making a cluster map (also called a mind map, graphic organizer, and concept map) of ideas when you develop curriculum. This opens up your thinking and gives you material for your lessons, the generative questions you ask, and the conversations you have with students.

To *go deep*, we also suggest cluster mapping. Cluster mapping is a great tool for "mining" for meaning because meaning accrues when a web or cluster of associations emerges. Cluster mapping also makes thinking about meaning visible. As you implement your curriculum, continue to cluster map associations and possibilities when ideas pop up or change. Also, do research before you start. If you are an art teacher, use the resources in this book and talk to teachers of the academic subjects you want to explore through art. Ask for their textbooks. If you are a generalist or a teacher of an academic discipline, speak to the art teacher at your school and also use this book.

To *extend*, string projects together. Introduce concepts in the first learning segment and then, in subsequent projects, build on them in different ways by reinterpreting concepts through different methods, creative strategies, or different disciplinary lenses.

To *challenge* learners to see a concept differently—to play with and twist a concept—take inspiration from the thinking and methods of contemporary art. While art today is about ideas, art curriculum should also be about learners' ideas and about their exploring the ideas inherent in the academic disciplines and the world outside of school. Artists' ideas are intriguing and worthy of lengthy discussion, but art is also about individual ways of thinking and seeing the world. We recommend, therefore, that students not appropriate artists' ideas as much as adopt artists' methods and thinking to generate their own ideas. When learners try on artists' ways of thinking and doing, they exercise and stretch their conceptual and procedural muscles. Furthermore, when they see how artists pioneer new ways of thinking and doing, they may be emboldened to invent their own.

In their practice, artists use creative strategies such as metaphor, juxtaposition, reformatting, and projection. A more complete list of strategies is provided in Chapter 2. These strategies are simple ways of making complex meaning. Although they may be couched as art-making strategies, they are also strategies applicable to any creative endeavor, including curriculum development. We suggest you use multiple creative strategies in developing your curriculum, perhaps highlighting a different one in each learning segment.

Figure 9.1. Julia Marshall, *Map for*
Entering Curriculum Through
Academic Content, 2014.

Figure 9.2. Julia Marshall, *Map for*
Entering Curriculum Through Art,
2014.

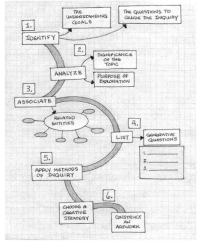

Image courtesy of the artist.

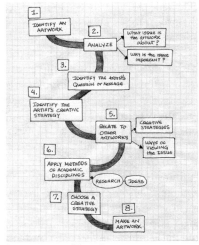

Image courtesy of the artist.

Figures 9.1 and 9.2 illustrate two routes in curriculum development, each with its own entry point. The specific steps and strategies involved in these two routes are described below.

Guidelines for Curriculum Development: Entry Through Academic Content

Step 1: Identify the Topic. Look closely at the academic subject or concept you wish to research with your students and what you want them to understand about it. For example, the discipline you teach is social studies, and as part of a unit on culture and identity, your goal is for students to understand how we all have multiple intersecting identities. In other words, you want them to comprehend how people identify by various aspects of themselves, such as gender, race, nationality, age group, interest group, or class. Social scientists call the confluence of these various identities "intersectionality" of identity.

Step 2: Analyze the Significance of the Topic. Consider why knowledge about your topic is significant: what that knowledge means to the discipline of social studies, why it is important outside the discipline, why it is important to learners, and what the purpose is in exploring and understanding it. These points should be the basis of your understanding goals for the lesson. For example, students (adolescents and teenagers, in particular) are interested in personal identity and are often grappling with how the multiple factors in their lives shape their sense of self. Moreover, intersectionality is an important concept for many social scientists trying to understand human experience without oversimplifying or reducing people's experience to one category of their identity.

Step 3: Develop a Research Question. This question should encapsulate the project's definitive understanding goal. A research question for an inquiry into intersectionality of identities could be this: How is an individual's identity a hybrid of intersecting identities, and what does that mean to each of us and to the society in which we live?

Step 4: Connect the Topic. Connect the concept/subject matter to all the things you associate with it: objects, images, events, eras, cultures, societies, people, and places. For this, you can make a cluster map for free-associating ideas. This will prepare a foundation for exploring multiple associated ideas and lesson possibilities. This is also where you can see how the project can slip across many disciplinary boundaries.

Step 5: Develop Questions. Make an inventory of questions to ask that will jumpstart the inquiry and get your students thinking. In the *Teaching for Understanding* approach (Wiske, 1998), these questions are called *generative questions*. In *Understanding by Design* (Wiggins & McTighe, 2005), they are *essential questions*. Whatever you call them, such questions are specific enough to invite investigation and open-ended enough to have multiple answers. They are also meaningful and engaging for both learners and teacher (Wiske, 1998).

In regard to intersecting identities, generative questions should begin with concrete questions such as these: What are the facets—my gender, ethnicity, age, religion, family situation, economic circumstances, and various roles in life—that make me who I am? How do my family, my friends, my classmates, my teachers, and all the people I know influence me? How does my cultural background, socioeconomic status, and family shape my sense of self? How do the things I like to do or am interested in make me the person I am? Questions such as these can then be followed by more general or conceptual questions—questions sociologists grapple with—such as these: Are categories of identity inherent and "natural" or constructed and socially determined? What are the issues and problems of focusing only on one aspect of a person's or a group of people's identity? Are some aspects of identity more important than others in shaping people's experiences, values, and beliefs? How are different people's identities portrayed in literature, the media, and popular culture? How do we find out about our own intersecting identities and those of others?

Step 6: Identify Disciplinary Methods. Go back to your original concept or subject. Identify the *methods* professional scholars in the various disciplines apply to study that concept and gather knowledge. These methods can be used to explore the concept and answer the questions posed. They can involve activities such as mapping, interviewing fellow learners, analyzing statistical data, and writing literary or media criticism.

Step 7: Identify a Creative Strategy or Strategies for Making Art. Choose a creative strategy. You can do this by following a model from contemporary art, or you can identify one in the list in Chapter 2 of this book. When you do this, think about how artists take ideas and concepts and transform them by putting a little twist on them to add meaning, change meaning, or reveal hidden meanings.

For example, use metaphor. Prompt students to explore the multiple components of their identities and choose a metaphor from the natural sciences to represent how these factors shape their identities. Perhaps one's identity is like a living system with many interacting components and feedback loops; to understand it, one must see how the system is created by the dynamics (among the intersecting identities) within it. Or perhaps one's identity is like a geological formation with multiple overlapping layers. To fully understand the layers and see how they add up, one must take a core sample.

Step 8: Map out the Project. Outline your lesson or project according to the format presented later in this chapter.

Guidelines for Curriculum Development: Entry Through Art

For teachers who want to enter through art, here are guidelines for that approach. For teachers who begin with academic subject matter, these guidelines can be used to develop an extension of their initial curriculum. For that reason, we continue to follow the theme of intersectionality of identity.

Step 1: Identify an Artwork. Choose an artist's work that you find to be compelling that also addresses the *knowledge* (topic, concepts, problem, or issue) you want to explore in your curriculum. Let's say you want to enter through and explore the work of Awol Erizku. Erizku is a New York–based photographer of Ethiopian descent who portrays young African American women in the manner of European art history classics. In his sumptuous photographs, Vermeer's *Girl with a Pearl Earring* (1665) becomes *Girl with a Bamboo Earring* (2009), and Leonardo's *Lady with an Ermine* (1489) morphs into *Lady with a Pitbull* (2009) (see Figures 9.3 and 9.4).

Step 2: Analyze the Artwork for Concepts. Look closely at what the artwork reveals about how identity is constructed, understood, and represented over time. Record the artist's points and perspective as you see them. In Erizku's work, the artist explores African American female identity and notions of feminine beauty. He raises questions about how these concepts are expressed and understood today given canonical notions of beauty throughout Western history. Identify what discipline or disciplines this topic relates to. Think about why this knowledge is important to the discipline(s), to the world in general, and to learners.

Step 3: Identify Creative Strategies the Artist Uses. What *creative strategy* or strategies does the artist use to add to our understandings of the concept or to transform our thinking about it? In Erizku's example, he juxtaposes contemporary faces with familiar Western art historical imagery—in this case, iconic images of serene anonymous women who have come to symbolize youthful beauty.

Figure 9.3. Awol Erizku, *Girl With a*
Bamboo Earring, 2009.

Figure 9.4. Awol Erizku, *Lady With a*
Pitbull, 2009.

Image courtesy of the artist and Hasted
Kraeutler, New York City.

Image courtesy of the artist and Hasted
Kraeutler, New York City.

Step 4: Relate to Concepts and Strategies in Other Artwork. Look at *creative strategies* other artists use to explore similar questions or topics. Students could link Erizku's imagery to artworks that also reference European art icons to explore the intersection of diverse notions of identity, beauty, femininity, masculinity, ethnicity, and power in American society and in global culture. Two examples are Kehinde Wiley's portraits of young Black men done in a grand Baroque style (see Figure 9.5) and Dedron's reinterpretation of the Mona Lisa with Tibetan imagery (see Figure 9.6).

Students could also examine works that approach identity through history and culture in a somewhat different way. An example of this is the work of Paul Anthony Smith, who superimposes traditional Haitian beaded masks onto photographs of modern-day people (see Figures 9.7 and 9.8). This strategy stands in contrast to Erizku's. Here we see an artist obscuring the features of his subjects to speak about how identity is an amalgam of one's present life and one's cultural, historical roots. The roots, in this case, are in the African Diaspora.

Step 5: Identify Disciplinary Methods for Art Inquiry. Choose one or two *methods* disciplinary practitioners (mathematicians, natural scientists, social scientists, historians, geographers, and writers) use in their research to explore and interpret the topic. For instance, learners could mimic anthropologists and interview their peers about social and ethnic groups in their school and how they represent themselves. They could study how Black writers, musicians, and social critics, including comedians, portray African Americans. They could do a similar inquiry into how other groups present themselves.

Figure 9.5. Kehinde Wiley, *Count Potocki*, 2008.

Oil and enamel on canvas, 108 x 108 inches. Image courtesy of the artist and Roberts & Tilton, Culver City, California.

Figure 9.6. Dedron, *Mona Lisa*, 2012.

Mineral pigment on canvas, 39 1/4 x 31 inches (99.7 x 78.7 cm.). Image courtesy of Shelly and Donald Rubin Private Collection.

Figure 9.7. Paul Anthony Smith, *Woman #3*, 2013.

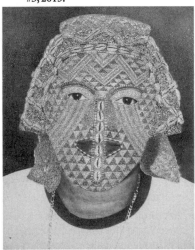

Unique picotage on pigment print, 29 x 24 inches. Image courtesy of the artist and ZieherSmith, New York.

Figure 9.8. Paul Anthony Smith, *Woman #5*, 2013.

Unique picotage on pigment print. 29 x 24 inches. Image courtesy of the artist and ZieherSmith, New York.

Step 6: Develop Guidelines for Inquiry That Combines Methods and Strategies.
This entails developing generative questions, supplying tools for inquiry, prompting learners to explore a topic and choose a *creative strategy* to illuminate or put a twist on what has been learned about the topic. Inspired by Awol Erizku's or Kehinde Wiley's work, students could make images of prominent people (e.g., figures from politics, the media, and popular culture) in the manner of classical Renaissance or Baroque art to explore how picturing a contemporary celebrity in this way places him or her within a Western cultural history of fame and fortune. This could reveal how status, celebrity, and power are timeless themes in art, and how art was (and still is) a vehicle for identity-construction and propaganda. To address the intersectionality of identity, many facets of a celebrity's life could be represented in images and symbols in the portrait. Art, of course, can have multiple messages; a depiction such as this could also expose the chasm between traditional Western culture and the diverse, multifaceted, fast-moving, and media-driven culture of today.

Students could also explore identity in other ways. Inspired by Paul Anthony Smith, they could depict contemporary celebrities in the mode of traditional folk art—particularly the folk art of a famous figure's ancestral culture. Here a learner would convey the intersectionality of his or her subject's identity by superimposing images from his or her historic and cultural background onto the "self" the celebrity currently presents to the public.

The following is a project or curriculum form that can help you think through and plan a lesson or project. The plan is organized according to the four dimensions of understanding that Mansilla and Gardner (1998) maintain are the bedrock of understanding. You will also recognize them as the components of the disciplines.

Project or Curriculum Plan

Overview. Describe what learners will do and make in this project. This should be brief—a couple of sentences.

Purpose. Here you designate why doing this project is important. This can include how it does the following: expands learners' knowledge of the academic subject and art; builds understanding of important concepts; challenges and enables learners to look at a problem, issue, or concept differently; fosters understanding of the academic discipline(s) and art; enables students to learn techniques, ways of thinking, and creative strategies through active participation and creation; and generates integrative thinking and an understanding of how the disciplines fit together as a system.

Knowledge. Knowledge includes the big ideas or overarching concepts learners will come to understand and the specific knowledge learners will acquire, including knowledge about the discipline, its relationship to other disciplines and to art research and research in general, and the kind of thinking that takes place in the discipline and in art.

Questions. In this section, you list generative questions that will jumpstart and guide the exploration of the knowledge to be explored.

Methods and Forms. Here you outline, in order of occurrence, what students will do in the project, including research methods and creative strategies, and what forms will be used.

Reflection. Reflection can entail writing, talking, or making visual imagery. It can be serious and playful. We suggest folding reflection into the inquiry process— asking questions along the way. Questions for reflection might include these: What concepts does my artwork address? How does it convey these concepts? How does it bring a new perspective to the concepts? How is my understanding of the concept deepened and broadened through making art about it? What did I learn from this process—about the concept, about art making and art, and about my creative process? How can I take this further? What more do I want to explore and express?

We also recommend making reflection a creative activity, as part of a creative elaboration. Perhaps learners could literally frame their two-dimensional images with their reflections, writing them on a margin around the central image. Perhaps they could make a container, a box or a bag for a three-dimensional artwork with their reflections written on it. Individual reflections could also take the form of artist or curator statements in a class exhibition catalogue.

Extension. No real inquiry ever ends; it always leads to new questions, new problems, and new ideas. In this section, you list what you think the next steps might be. These could be reflecting in a creative manner, such as making more art about what you learned or embarking on a new related project. We also recommend that you ask your students what the next steps could be. Their suggestions will give you clues to the understandings they came to during the project.

Extending a project has other benefits. Learners can demonstrate what they learned in the last project by applying it to a new related inquiry. Furthermore, an extension of a project or a new related project can challenge students to see what they learned in the prior project differently. In this way, extension activities could even challenge learners' newly acquired understandings. Lastly, extending a project shows learners that there is always something more to learn about a topic and there are multiple ways to enter into that learning.

SOME MODEL PROJECTS

Picturing What Matters: Art, Math, and Social Studies

Overview/Process. Learners will create questionnaires and interview their peers about things that concern them: music, fashion, sports, romance, gaming, shopping, food, parents, school culture, body image, relationships, status, and celebrities, to name a few. Students will then collate, analyze, and synthesize the data they collected from these interviews and create graphs, charts, or maps to represent it, incorporating images and objects associated with the data. For instance, a bar graph of fashion preferences could be composed of copied and hand-colored tags from various clothing brands. An enlarged outline of the human body taken from a science textbook could be charted with numbers to mark the location and amount of tattoos on the collective student body.

Purpose. To understand what is significant to teenagers and the symbolic power of objects and graphic forms. Also, to understand the methods social scientists use to create, collect, make sense of, and communicate data.

Knowledge. How statistics represent social data; the many qualities and facets of youth culture.

Methods. Construct interviews and questionnaires, and use them. Collect, summarize, and interpret data, and represent the data visually.

Forms. Maps, graphs, and charts of data and the concepts the data represent.

Creative Strategies. Format (put numerical information into graphic form); translate (transpose graphic forms into mixed-media artworks); use metaphor of materials (use objects and images associated with the concepts represented).

Materials. Mixed media, pens, and large white paper.

Connected Art. Chris Jordan and Jer Thorp.

Small Stories: Art and Storytelling

Overview/Process. Learners will examine the "meta-narrative" or message behind a movie, a TV show, or a news article—narratives such as the importance of community and family ties; the value of standing up for one's beliefs; the centrality of individualism, entrepreneurship, and independence in current American culture; the value of behaving according to rules; or the enduring belief in the American Dream. Students will then create a sequence of photographs to tell a background, tangential, or counterbalancing story to that larger, well-known narrative. For these photographs, learners will arrange small found objects, such as miniature toy figures and objects from model train kits, in existing environments.

Purpose. To understand and critique the meta-narratives that explain our world and influence our perspectives and behavior. To understand the photographic concept of point of view and the role of perspective in storytelling.

Knowledge. Principles and components of storytelling. Overarching narratives that govern our lives.

Methods. Analyze and interpret a text. Use nonverbal cues to describe and express ideas and concepts.

Forms. Storyboard, photography, stagecraft, site-specific installation.

Creative Strategies. Juxtapose (tangential stories with grand narratives); elaborate (on narratives through new stories); change scale (make miniature tableaux).

Materials. Found objects and sites, camera, printer.

Connected Art. Liliana Porter's stories constructed with found iconic imagery, illustrated in Figure 9.9, and Slinkachu's miniature street installations, illustrated in Figure 9.10.

Figure 9.9. Liliana Porter, *Joan of Arc,*
***Elvis, Che,* 2011.**

Digital Duraflex, 35 x 29 inches. Image
courtesy of the artist.

Figure 9.10. Slinkachu, *Local Amenities for Children,* 2008.

Image courtesy of Slinkachu / Andipa Gallery.

Walk in My Shoes: Art, Social Studies, and Geography

Overview/Process. Learners will create individual video tours of their school's hallways and public spaces that, through the selection and mapping of sites and routes through the school, will reflect the artist–learner's personal experience of school. Initially recording without sound, the learner will later add his or her voice-over commentary to the video, which will explain the significance of the sites on the tour. In an art event, viewers will watch the videos on handheld video devices and listen to the commentary as they follow their tour through the school hallways.

Purpose. Understand and ask questions about the ways we navigate, work in, and live in different environments, how those spaces shape our experiences, and how we attach meaning to places.

Knowledge. Knowledge of how places have meaning and this meaning often is collectively constructed over time but can also be different for each individual.

Methods. Mapping sites and routes through the school; guiding a tour according to those maps; writing a script of the tour.

Forms. Digital video and audio tracks. Maps of the school.

Creative Strategies. Layer (superimpose a scripted experience onto a "lived" experience); format (map sites and routes in the school); mimic (use the methods of geographers and documentary video makers).

Materials. Smartphones, iPads, iPods, and/or video cameras, computers, and editing software.

Connected Art. Janet Cardiff and George Bures Miller's *Alter Bahnhof Video Walk.*

Visual Cousins: Art and Science

Overview/Process. Students will create curious new drawings through reworking scientific illustrations. They will trace on a piece of clear acetate an illustration from a science textbook. This could be a map of a natural process, such as the nitrogen cycle; the relationships between parts of an ecosystem; or the cross-section of an organism, and so on. Each learner will search for a two-dimensional art image that physically resembles the illustration or relates to its meaning, print it out, and place it under the tracing of the scientific illustration. She or he will then combine the two images in a third drawing, painting, or mixed-media sculpture.

Purpose. To understand how meaning can be constructed through the synthesis of two related images from different disciplinary "worlds."

Knowledge. Knowledge of the symbols and conventions of scientific illustration and the differences in style and meaning-making between art and scientific illustration.

Methods. Visual and conceptual analysis of scientific and art imagery.

Forms. Scientific illustration, drawing, painting, collage, and sculpture.

Creative Strategies. Layer (a scientific image onto an art image); analogy (point out visual and conceptual likenesses between a scientific image and an art image); juxtapose (contrast the scientific image with the art image); elaborate (take the ideas embedded in the imagery further); synthesize (blend scientific and art imagery and ideas).

Materials. Permanent pens, acetate, drawing paper, mixed media, a reproduction of a painting.

Connected Art. Nathalie Miebach's diagrams and sculptures of storms; Nene Humphreys's drawings of the brain and braided sculptures resembling nerve ganglia.

Systems Fun House: Art and Science

Overview/Process. Working together, students will create a walk-through installation that represents a natural system. They will study an illustration of a system from the life sciences, build forms for their "system environment," and create fanciful objects and imagery that metaphorically represent the components and dynamics of their system. For example, learners could construct a whimsical version of the human digestive system in which viewers could become "food" and follow the path from eating, to absorption, to elimination. Along the way, they could encounter objects and imagery that represent various parts of the alimentary canal. Viewers could also experience the human visual system by acting like light and "beaming" through the eye and along the optic nerve to the visual cortex, or they could become nutrients being processed in a cell. Students could also create for viewers a map of the trail through the system that guides them through it and explains the installation and how each object and image adds to its meaning. Models for maps are illustrated in Figures 9.11 and 9.12, scientific illustrations by pioneering neuroscientist Santiago Ramón y Cajal (1852–1934).

Purpose. To understand how visual objects and images can be metaphorical, and how, as metaphors, they connote the function and meaning of a natural system. Understand how reenacting the processes of a system can build understanding of that system—what it does and how it does it.

Knowledge. Natural systems, their dynamics, and related concepts: cause and effect, feedback loops, change and stability.

Methods. Observational drawing (of parts of the system); sculpture (found objects and created objects to represent parts of a system); installation (of sculpture, drawings, and paintings); formatting (mapping the system and the route through the installation).

Figure 9.11. Santiago Ramón y Cajal,
Drawing (Inventory 11324), **undated.**

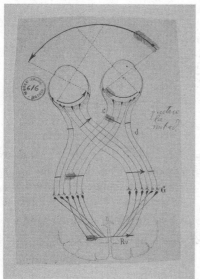

Image courtesy of Santiago Ramón y Cajal.
Legado Cajal. Instituto Cajal (CSIC)
Madrid, Spain.

Figure 9.12. Santiago Ramón y Cajal,
Drawing (Inventory 3836), **undated.**

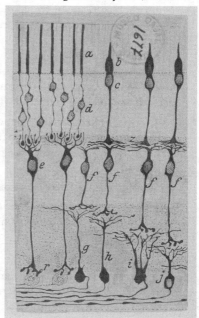

Image courtesy of Santiago Ramón y Cajal.
Legado Cajal. Instituto Cajal (CSIC)
Madrid, Spain.

Forms. Drawing, sculpture, maps, mixed-media installation.

Creative Strategies. Render (illustrate of parts of a system); use metaphor (cast various system parts and processes in terms of something else); translate (transform scientific concepts and images into an artwork or art experience); change scale (make the system large enough to walk around in and to experience).

Materials. Tempera paint, pens, drawing paper, wire, large paper, fabric, string, lightweight objects, video, or slide projection.

Connected Art. Nathalie Miebach's sculptural maps of storms; Nene Humphreys's braided sculptures.

Sci-Fi Pet: Art and Science

Overview/Process. Students will create a startling image of a mysterious creature and then project it in a school hallway. This creature will actually be a live "class pet," such as a guinea pig or a salamander, housed in a cooperating classroom. Learners will create this image by filming or photographing part of the critter, like the leg of a spider or the tail of a reptile. Through Photoshop software or by hand, learners will transform the image by manipulating scale, color, texture, or value. The projected video or still images could be accompanied by audio recordings of related sounds like the bubbling of an aquarium, the scratching of claws, or the spinning of a hamster wheel. After viewers observe the mysterious image and ponder about what it is, they will write about the associations the image and sound recording evoke for them and what they infer the image and sounds to be.

Purpose. To promote collective participation in observation and analysis of a something puzzling from the natural world. To engage the imagination of viewers; to present them with a mystery.

Knowledge. Knowledge of animals and their parts; knowledge of metonymy as a creative device that may come out of poetry but is also applied in the visual arts.

Methods. Observation and analysis of a natural organism to figure out what it is.

Forms. Photography, film, sound recording; close-ups of body parts.

Creative Strategies. Edit (leave out extraneous parts); change scale (make an image, a body part, or visual element big); use metonymy (show a part of the animal to allude to the whole); reinterpret (change colors, proportions, and textures); amplify/magnify (exaggerate parts; make them larger than life).

Materials. Cameras, printers, photo-frame video players, speakers.

Connected Art. Amy Youngs's *Intraterrestrial Soundings.*

The Person Most Likely to . . . : Art, History, and Creative Writing

Overview/Process. Students will create imaginary people who have their own history by cutting and collaging photos and texts from old school yearbooks. They will illustrate the lives of these hybridized persons through a zine created from the images and words from the yearbook and other sources from the same era. This zine may take the form of a short story, a personal diary/scrapbook, a school yearbook, or any other literary form. Learners could also use the stories they create to critique and reimagine outdated notions of class, gender, race, and other stereotypes common in old school yearbooks.

Purpose. To create historical stories and think imaginatively and critically about the formats of reporting and recounting facts and history.

Knowledge. Concepts of pastness (understanding the past on its own terms) and presentism (judging the past on present values). Storytelling through visual imagery and writing.

Methods. Historical research through yearbooks and through other historical documents; storytelling.

Forms. School yearbooks, zines, small books, and short stories.

Creative Strategies. Hybridize (mix and match parts of yearbook portraits); appropriate (use yearbook pictures to tell a new story); format (present a story in a zine); project (speculate about the life and times of an imaginary historical person); elaborate (create a character and generate many facets of his or her personality and life; write a story about this person).

Materials. Photocopy machine, scissors, glue or scanner, Photoshop technology and printer.

Connected Art. Wang Du's critique of the media; Do Ho Suh's exploration of yearbook imagery: *Who Am We?* (1997).

Collections from Today's Nacirema Youth: Art and Anthropology

Overview/Process. Learners will interview each other about their current social life and culture. They will create a museum of plaster forms cast from items they believe represent their world and the general material culture of American adolescents and teens. From there, they will create a display of these forms in which the artifacts are categorized, labeled, described, and explained. This display will be augmented with a museum guide to the lives of American youth presented in a detached, scientific/anthropological format and written in the language of museums. The guide will include a map of the display and a description of the artifacts and the "civilization" from which they come. This could be in the form of a brief ethnography.

Purpose. To understand students' social life and culture through the disciplinary (anthropological/sociological) constructions we use to make sense of material culture. To critique the formats and dispositions of the social sciences that collect "facts" and shape them into social theories.

Knowledge. Youth culture and the artifacts that embody it. The ways anthropology collects, understands, and represents cultural information.

Methods. Cultural analysis, plaster casting, museum display practices, mapping, and academic (anthropological/ethnographic) writing.

Forms. Sculpture and display installation formats, written guide, and ethnography.

Creative Strategies. Translate (transform common objects into plaster reproductions); recontextualize (place ordinary objects in a scientific environment—a museum display); reformat (arrange objects in a form from anthropology); mimic (use the methods of anthropology: interviews and collecting and categorizing artifacts).

Materials. Plaster, clay, found artifacts, labels, tags, paper, makeshift pedestals.

Connected Art. Michael Arcega's *Baby and the Nacirema.*

SOME FINAL THOUGHTS

As we conclude, we return to the wisdom of Jerome Bruner. Bruner is one of the great sages of education, contributing considerable insight into how we learn and how to construct curriculum to foster that learning. One of his many gifts to education is to remind us of what is truly important. Bruner argues that "a curriculum ought to be built around the great ideas, principles, and values that a society deems worthy of the continual concern of its members" (2006, p. 56). If our curriculum is to meet Bruner's challenge, it must focus like a laser on those ideas, principles, and values of which he speaks. We believe that integrated learning—learning that is meaningful, purposeful, and connected—is the key.

Our goal in this book has been to demonstrate how contemporary art can activate and facilitate integrated learning. Indeed, we see contemporary art as one of the most powerful learning tools available to us—a natural and effective partner of integrated learning. The intention of this book is also to supply some substance on which new, inventive, and meaningful pedagogy and practice can be created.

Although this book provides up-to-date examples of work from diverse artists, we must remember that contemporary art is always changing, ever evolving. This book, therefore, is just the beginning—a primer and a hook. We hope the artwork presented here serves as a primer by providing a foundation on which to build your practice. We also hope it has hooked you by whetting your appetite for contemporary art and sparking a commitment to follow it wherever it goes, however it changes.

We also hope the connections made here between art and the academic disciplines have generated for you new ways of thinking about the academic disciplines as well as about art's place in education and in your teaching practice. This includes an understanding that practice is always under construction. Like contemporary art, curriculum changes and progresses over time. To keep up with our students and the important ideas, principles, and values that Bruner reminds us are core to education, teaching and learning must evolve. Contemporary art can help to keep up the momentum because art never stops inventing, provoking, and surprising. Furthermore, art often focuses on things we have yet to consider—things of importance. Art keeps us on our toes and moving ahead. With that in mind, we wish you all—teachers and learners alike—a joyful, meaningful, ever-changing integrated learning adventure through contemporary art. We do this in the spirit of a found poem from the artist who opened our book, Nina Katchadourian (see Figure 9.13).

REFERENCES

Bruner, J. (2006). Readiness for learning. In *In search of pedagogy: Vol. 1. The selected works of Jerome Bruner* (pp. 47–56). New York, NY: Routledge.

Mansilla, V., & Gardner, H. (1998). What are the qualities of understanding? In M. S. Wiske (Ed.), *Teaching for understanding: Linking research with practice* (pp. 161–183). San Francisco, CA: Jossey-Bass.

Wiggins, G., & McTighe, J. (2005). *Understanding by design.* Alexandria, VA: Association for Supervision and Curriculum Development.

Wiske, M. S. (1998). *Teaching for understanding: Linking research with practice.* San Francisco, CA: Jossey-Bass.

Figure 9.13. Nina Katchadourian, *Hope and Have/ The Life That Counts* **from** *Sorted Books,* **1993–present.**

Image courtesy of the artist and Catharine Clark Gallery, San Francisco.

Index

About the Authors

Julia Marshall is a professor of art education at San Francisco State University where she oversees the art education program and teaches undergraduate and graduate courses. She holds a BA in art from George Washington University; an MFA from the University of Wisconsin, Madison; and an EdD in International and Multicultural Education from the University of San Francisco. Her scholarship lies in art-centered, inquiry-based integrated learning, the uses of contemporary art and visual culture in art education, and the intersection between creativity and learning. Julia has written extensively on these topics with articles in *Studies in Art Education, Art Education Journal, International Journal of Art Education,* and chapters in national art education anthologies.

David M. Donahue is professor of education and associate provost, Mills College, Oakland, California, where he has worked with teacher credential students preparing to teach art, English, history, and world languages in secondary schools and with graduate students investigating teaching and learning with a focus on equity in urban contexts. He received a BA in history and MAT in social studies from Brown University and an MA in history and PhD in education from Stanford University. He is coeditor with Jennifer Stuart of the book *Artful Teaching: Integrating the Arts for Understanding Across the Curriculum,* published in 2010 by Teachers College Press, and with Christine Cress of *Democratic Dilemmas of Teaching Service Learning: Curricular Strategies for Success,* published in 2011.

Rick Ayers founded the Communication Arts and Sciences small school at Berkeley High School, known for innovative strategies for academic and social success for a diverse range of students. He is a professor of education at the University of San Francisco in the Urban Education and Social Justice cohort. He is the coauthor, with his brother William Ayers, of *Teaching the Taboo: Courage and Imagination in the Classroom* and is also author of *Great Books for High School Kids* and *A Teacher's Guide to Studs Terkel's Working.* He is a regular blogger on education for the *Huffington Post.*

Ruth Cossey is professor of education and director of the Mid Career Math and Science Teacher Education Program at Mills College. She serves as co–principal investigator on a grant from National Science Foundation's Robert Noyce Teacher Scholarship Program to improve student learning opportunities and increase the number of STEM secondary teachers in the Oakland Unified School District. Her research interests include preservice and inservice mathematics and science education, sociology of education in urban environments, and mathematics reform in elementary and secondary schools.

Steven D. Drouin, EdD, teacher, Tracy High School, Tracy, California, teaches social studies courses to diverse groups of high school students. His research interests include heterogeneous/democratic instruction, detracking, and narrative inquiry. In 2013, he was voted Outstanding Teacher of the Year for Tracy High School.

Lawrence Horvath completed his PhD in science education at the University of California, Davis (2008). He also holds degrees in curriculum and instruction and zoology. Dr. Horvath is currently an assistant professor of secondary education at San Francisco State University (SFSU). At SFSU he is the lead science faculty in residence for the Center for Science and Math Education and the principal investigator for the National Science Foundation Robert Noyce Teacher Scholarship Program. Previously, Dr. Horvath taught middle and high school science for 13 years—7 years in California, 3 years in Rome, and 3 years in Istanbul.

Anne Thulson is an assistant professor in art education at the Metropolitan State University of Denver. She directs the School of the Poetic City, a contemporary art camp for children in Denver. She has an MFA in painting from Cranbrook Academy of Art and practices socially engaged art.